PEYTON MANNING

PEYTON MANNING

The Last Rodeo

Mark Kiszla

TAYLOR TRADE PUBLISHING
Lanham • Boulder • New York • London

Published by Taylor Trade Publishing
An imprint of The Rowman & Littlefield Publishing Group, Inc.
4501 Forbes Boulevard, Suite 200, Lanham, Maryland 20706
www.rowman.com

Unit A, Whitacre Mews, 26-34 Stannary Street, London SE11 4AB, United
Kingdom

Distributed by NATIONAL BOOK NETWORK

British Library Cataloguing in Publication Information Available

Library of Congress Cataloging-in-Publication Available

ISBN 978-1-63076-284-1 (pbk. : alk. paper)
ISBN 978-1-63076-285-8 (electronic)

LCCN 2016033160 (print) | LCCN 2016033652 (ebook)

♾ ™ The paper used in this publication meets the minimum requirements of
American National Standard for Information Sciences Permanence of Paper
for Printed Library Materials, ANSI/NISO Z39.48-1992.

Printed in the United States of America

CONTENTS

PREFACE

The high-pitched screech of a circular saw startled Peyton Manning. The awful noise shot straight through him, causing his broad shoulders to flinch. We stood backstage at Manning's final act as quarterback of the Denver Broncos. And no different from the 293 game days he had worked as a quarterback in the NFL, Manning was still wound tightly after his work was done, as the adrenaline began to dissipate slowly from his body upon the conclusion of a retirement ceremony he had carefully pondered and meticulously planned for weeks, ever since the 39-year-old quarterback cradled the Lombardi Trophy, his reward for Denver beating Carolina in Super Bowl 50.

Only 45 minutes earlier, Manning had stared intently at his script, trying very hard not to get all weepy in an auditorium filled to capacity, as No. 18 announced his retirement after 18 record-breaking professional seasons to a crowd that spanned in age from his 66-year-old father to his 4-year-old twin children, and everybody in between from the quarterback's large NFL family.

Think of how hard it must have been. For 293 days—nearly a full year of Manning's life—he had buckled his chinstrap and gone out to play quarterback in the NFL. And now it was over.

Jeff Saturday, the Colts center who snapped Manning the ball more than 10,000 times during the dozen years they played together in Indianapolis, couldn't stop grinning. He had bet former teammate Brandon Stokley that Manning would not cry, and Saturday was winning.

Broncos president Joe Ellis, the man who first proposed this bold idea of bringing Manning to Colorado, had no such luck controlling his own emotions, though. Sitting off to the side of the podium where Manning spoke, Ellis dabbed at the tears making a puddle of his eyes.

Demaryius Thomas, the receiver who told Manning he loved him after each of 40 touchdown passes caught in Denver, gave gentle hugs to young Mosley and Marshall Manning, while their Daddy talked about his greatest gift from playing in the NFL: the people sitting in front of him.

With an early March storm roaring like a lion outside the team's Dove Valley headquarters, friends, relatives, teammates and too many reporters to count had taken assigned seats in the theater. All gathered to hear Manning utter the one word that nobody who loved the sound of him shouting "Omaha!" at the line of scrimmage ever wanted to hear.

Goodbye.

"I revere football. I love the game," said Manning, his voice choking on all the memories the retirement speech stirred in his heart. "So you don't have to wonder if I will miss it. Absolutely. Absolutely I will."

After the television cameras from the NFL Network and ESPN stopped rolling, Manning drifted off to a hallway outside the Broncos locker room, where the ear-piercing sounds of construction work— from the whirring of an electric saw to the sledgehammer's heavy thump—made it clear the team was already getting on with life without him. Yes, during four seasons in Denver, Manning had completed passes that traveled nearly 10 miles, rewritten the NFL record book on what seemed like a daily basis, been named the league's most valuable player for a fifth time and won the 200th game of his brilliant pro career with a stunning 24–10 upset of Carolina in the Super Bowl, which the Panthers had entered as 5½-point favorites.

But nothing is forever in sports. And now a pain-in-the-butt perfectionist had no game plan to master and no practice to attend for the first time since Manning joined the NFL as a rookie from the University of

Tennessee in 1998. With his 40th birthday lurking, it was time for the legend to go home.

Outside, as the rain turned to snow, Manning peered down the hallway through the glass panes of double doors, looking one more time at the practice field where he taught the Broncos how to be an elite franchise again. Big, wet flakes splattered on the sidewalk, and Manning dreamed of getting away to play golf at a famous course way down south in Dixie with his brothers, Cooper and Eli.

Standing five feet from him, however, I could distinctly sense the gears grinding Manning's brain, still crammed with a humming energy that radiated heat. "I'm totally convinced that the end of my football career is just the beginning of something I haven't even discovered yet," Manning had vowed during his 11-minute, 45-second retirement speech. "Life is not shrinking for me, it's morphing into the a whole new world of possibilities."

So I wanted to know: What was next for Manning? Football behind him, how would he fill the void during the next 40 years of his life? The possibilities are endless. Could his competitive juices be stoked by buying a stake in an NFL franchise, maybe as an owner-operator of the Tennessee Titans? Does he harbor political aspirations? Or did his *Saturday Night Live* appearances foreshadow a future in front of the television camera?

"I don't know," replied Manning, setting up a punch line with the aw-shucks humor that made him America's favorite quarterback. "I might put an ad in the newspaper."

Let the record show Manning retired on March 7, 2016, exactly one month after earning a championship ring with Denver in what proved to be his final game. His long goodbye had caused consternation in Broncos Country and speculation to run rampant throughout the Twitterverse that Manning might not be done playing, and maybe he would take a job with the Rams, newly relocated to Los Angeles and in need of a marketable star, or another franchise desperate for a quarterback.

The grand farewell was staged only hours before Elway, who had zero intention of honoring the $19 million due Manning in the final year of his original five-year contract with the Broncos, would have been forced to cut a distinguished quarterback with 539 career touchdown passes on his resume. We all understand it's never easy to hang up your cleats, but why had Manning waited until the last minute to retire?

"I wanted to be an NFL quarterback as long as I possibly could," Manning joked.

Understand this: Manning does nothing by accident. As a quarterback, no detail was too small for him to memorize with an obsessive need to ace every test. So believe this: It was not by happenstance that the tie Manning wore to his retirement ceremony was Colts blue. He cherished every day of his 14 seasons in Indianapolis until the bitter end, when a team Manning put on the NFL map fired him.

That's why when Manning saw March 7 on the calendar, he instantly recognized the poetry in the timing of his goodbye. It was the fourth anniversary of the exact date in 2012 when the Colts cut him. Now, four years later, Manning could retire as a champion in Denver, and the redemption in his departure was as perfect as the spin on his most gorgeous spiral. "Grateful is the word that comes to my mind when thinking of the Denver Broncos," he said. "Thank you for what you've done for this old quarterback."

His appreciation, and the story in this book, began with one little phone call Manning received from Colorado on the worst day of his football life. Let's take you back to March 2012. Recovering from four neck surgeries and with a $28 million roster bonus coming due, Manning was cast aside by the Colts for a hot prospect named Andrew Luck.

The move made dollars and football sense for Indianapolis. It also left a hole in Manning's heart. He went home and sat on the sofa like a zombie.

Then, in his darkest hour as an athlete, the phone rang.

"It was John Fox," Manning recalled on the day he retired from the Broncos. "With Fox, of course it's a fun conversation. It's upbeat. It kind of got me in a good mood again. Then, John [Elway] got on and just said: 'Hey, when you're ready, we'd love you to come out.'"

Denver was the first team to reach out and contact a suddenly un-employed quarterback. There was no hard sell. The Broncos merely wanted Manning to know they felt his pain and were there to help make it go away.

"Four years ago, when the unimaginable happened—and that Peyton Manning was going to be a free agent—at first, did we actually think we had a shot? You know what, I didn't think we had a shot," Elway said. "But, fortunately, we got the first call in and we got the first [recruiting] trip."

There was No Plan B.

"When I visited Denver four years ago, if John Elway had sat me down and said: 'Peyton, here's what we're going to do. We're going to win over 50 games, win four straight division championships, lose only three division games in four years and none will be on the road, we'll beat the Patriots in two championship games and you're going to win NFL comeback player of the year, another MVP, your offense will set a single-season passing records, you'll break a couple more all-time records, and we'll go to a couple of Super Bowls,' I think I would have taken that deal," Manning said, before adding a friendly little dig, just to remind how much he helped the Broncos achieve.

"John, you did tell me that, didn't you?"

The four years in Colorado weren't always perfect. There were em-barrassing losses in the playoffs. There was a time during his 18th pro season, with Manning stuck on the Denver bench with an aching foot, when everybody who really cared about him was uncertain if he would ever play another snap for the Broncos.

We always remember the fairy-tale ending. We forget the muck on the boots during the journey. The last rodeo of Manning was one bumpy ride. In the end, with his talent diminished by age, he held on with little more than a stubborn refusal to quit. The one rap against Manning was always that his game was too pretty, too technical . . . too soft. But almost nothing went according to the script in Manning's last game, when he struggled to complete 13 passes for a meager 141 yards against Carolina in the Super Bowl. The grit and the resolve of Manning is what made his last rodeo so beautiful.

This time, on March 7, Manning got to say goodbye from an NFL team on his terms. His validation was complete. And the irony was not lost on him, because committing every little detail to memory is what made Manning great. "It was a difficult day going through that press conference in Indianapolis," he said with a knowing grin, "which I think was four years ago today."

The NFL Nation stood and applauded Manning on March 7, 2016, precisely four years to the date when a broken quarterback's career was left for dead in Indianapolis.

The Last Rodeo ended in an orange sunset.

"Pundits will speculate that my effort and drive over the past 18 years were about mastery and working to master every aspect of the NFL game. Well, don't believe them. Because every moment, every drop of sweat, every bleary-eyed night of preparation, every note I took and every frame of film I watched was about one thing, reverence for the game," Manning said. "When I look back on my NFL career, I'll know without a doubt that I gave everything I had to help my teams walk away with a win. There were other players who were more talented, but there was no one who could out-prepare me and because of that I have no regrets."

Where did the time go? And how did we get here, in a room at Broncos headquarters, with everyone standing and clapping and dabbing tears of joy as Manning said goodbye to the game he loves?

It all started with one phone call on a dark winter day, when what a Hall of Fame quarterback needed most was a friend.

I

GET LOST

If Peyton Manning can get fired, then it is damn certain the rest of us can be dumbsized, pink-slipped, or kicked to the curb.

For a National Football League quarterback with 150 regular-season and playoff victories on his resume, the last words Manning thought he would ever hear from the team he loved: Get lost. Players kid that NFL means Not For Long. But, during uncertain economic times, loyalty has become as big a joke in this $9.5 billion annual sports industry as in the rest of corporate America.

In March of 2012, on the verge of his 36th birthday, Manning joined more than 12 million Americans in the ranks of the unemployed. The Indianapolis Colts fired Peyton Freaking Manning? Are you kidding? The inconceivable became harsh reality.

Oh, the Colts were polite when they told Manning his services were no longer required. Like being told politely your broken-down old bones have no future in the organization is supposed to make a guy feel better. Yeah, right. Helmet in hand, Manning was forced to pull up stakes and go looking for work. For any man who takes pride in his job, it stinks.

If the shock and insult of being fired was only about the money, Manning could have gone home and slept easy on a bed of gold. But nobody in the NFL takes his job more seriously than Manning, for whom football is a 10,000-piece puzzle obsessively studied, until every last piece fits.

Weary from the Great Recession, maybe we were ready for a broken football hero who could show us how to put a career back together again. Enter Manning.

"You always wish you could be 25 years old and playing football. That's what you always wish. You wish you never had to stop playing," said Hall of Fame quarterback John Elway, talking from the chair that chains the 52-year-old Broncos legend to an office at the team's Dove Valley headquarters. Elway now performs his magic as the executive vice president of football operations.

If not for Elway, there would be no Super Bowl trophies in Denver. If not for Elway, there would be no Peyton Manning in Colorado.

"Peyton was a friend before he came to work here for the Broncos. And I still look at him as a friend. But I respect the hell out him as a player," said Elway, who brought the four-time MVP to town on the strength of the bond shared by two of the greatest quarterbacks ever to play the game. The Broncos landed the most famous free agent in NFL history, 13 short days after the Colts dumped Manning.

"I cannot imagine what it's like to get cut," Elway said. From the time he picked up a football as a boy in Montana to the last snap he took with the Broncos, Elway was the most revered player on the field.

"Peyton told me he planned on ending his career in Indianapolis, no doubt about it. And then to get kicked to the curb like that? He couldn't believe it happened. So you know he had a chip on his shoulder when he came to Denver. I mean, he's always had a passion that burned. But when the Colts told him they no longer needed him? That's when the chimney fire became a forest fire."

The football gods must have a wicked sense of humor. On the road to the Super Bowl with the Broncos, riding high with the number one seed in the American Football Conference entering the playoffs, Denver was stunned by a 38–35 overtime loss at home against Baltimore on January 12, 2013. As a consolation prize, Manning was sent off to the

Pro Bowl in Hawaii. It might be a dream vacation spot, but definitely not where Manning wanted to be at the time.

During a week of practice for an all-star game where the final score counts for nothing, Manning was stuck on the island in the middle of the Pacific Ocean with a rookie named Andrew Luck. Yes, the same hot, young quarterback who made Manning expendable in Indianapolis. Welcome to paradise, big guy. Grab some SPF 50 from the beach bag. The sun is not the only thing that can make a man do a slow burn.

It had to be surreal, watching Luck wear the Indianapolis blue and the horseshoe of the Colts that Manning represented so well, for so many years, since he joined the NFL out of the University of Tennessee as the number one overall selection in the 1998 draft.

Irreverent curiosity is sometimes poured with a side of sarcasm. With apologies for my lack of respect for a potentially touchy subject, I had to ask Manning: "Do you ever look at Luck and think: 'What the heck? Who does this guy think he is, anyway? That's my Indianapolis Colts helmet that this dude Luck is wearing'?"

Without a second of hesitation, Manning sternly replied: "No."

The answer, however, hurt Manning more than it did me. He showed unmistakable displeasure at the question, and did it without adding a single word. How? Manning shot me the most famous frown in professional football.

Any NFL official who has blown a call and receivers who have run the wrong pass route know the look. The angry red blotch on his forehead where the helmet rubs Manning the wrong way can sear a hole in a man's soul. It can be such an intimidating yippee-ki-yay glare that it could make NYPD cop John McClane think maybe this would be a good day to die hard, rather than risk the wrath of Manning. The quarterback's nose crinkles into a snarl that could scare a whole pack of wolves. Actress Bette Davis was known for her eyes. Jennifer Lopez danced her way to fame backed by the most famous booty in the world. Without a doubt, one of the greatest motivating forces in the sports universe is Peyton frowning Manning.

On any given Sunday, or the other six days of the week, for that matter, you can get hit with a bad case of perturbed Manning face with the mere mention of two words: Indianapolis Colts.

The obvious pain of the memory of how it all ended in Indy is what reveals the vulnerable heart of Manning. Sure, he might be called "MacBook" by Baltimore Ravens safety Bernard Pollard, because here is a quarterback who processes and analyzes every detail on the football field like a freaking computer. But, contrary to myth, Manning is not a cyborg under center. He can be hurt. And getting cut hurts to the bone. Not making the team hurts just the same, whether you are a veteran quarterback turning in your playbook to an NFL team or a disappointed teenager checking in your shoulder pads to the equipment manager of a local high school.

The scars will never heal. Four medical procedures on Manning's injured neck have left a jagged, ugly mark that is impossible to miss even now, when he bends over center at the line of scrimmage as quarterback of the Broncos, shouting "Hurry! Hurry!" in anticipation of the football being snapped.

The scar emerges from under his helmet and darts toward his shoulder pads beneath the number 18 jersey. Those surgeries turned a quarterback known as P-Money in Indianapolis into a health gamble the Colts were unwilling to back with a $28 million roster bonus due Manning early in 2012. Nerve damage had robbed Manning's famous right arm of the most amazing, on-the-button passing touch the NFL has ever seen. Imagine, at the height of his powers, legendary pianist Sergey Rachmaninoff losing all feel in his fingertips for the ivories. A stretch? Not by much.

After turning Indianapolis into an elite city on the NFL map and then leading the Colts to victory at Super Bowl XLI, Manning was reduced to a helpless bystander on the NFL sidelines in 2011, when chronic arm weakness required a father-and-son surgical team led by Dr. Robert Watkins Sr. to perform a single-level fusion of the veteran quarterback's spine in September. Tissue as soft as crabmeat between two vertebrae was removed, so the spine could be fused, with a chunk of Manning's hip bone used as mortar and a piece of titanium added for support.

But just as the quarterback's body was finally starting to heal, a beautiful business relationship between Manning and Colts owner Jim Irsay began to fall apart. As Indianapolis plummeted toward the bottom of the league standings, the possibility of drafting Luck out of Stanford with the number one pick moved closer to reality for the Colts. An end game that Manning long had regarded as unthinkable quickly became unavoidable: A four-time winner of the Most Valuable Player Award would be shoved out the door.

Once upon a time in America, maybe loyalty in the workplace really did matter. But in a sport ruled by the harsh economics of a salary cap, football teams profess to be family only until business intrudes on the charade, and then money counts for more than love. The Colts did the right thing from a football and financial standpoint. Certainly, Manning saw the breakup coming. But he covered his eyes.

"Nobody loves their job more than I do. Nobody loves playing quarterback more than I do. I still want to play. But there is no other team I wanted to play for," confessed Manning, who stubbornly—and perhaps naively—believed the Colts would find a way to keep him until 24 hours before fighting back tears as his release was announced with Irsay at his side. "I guess, in life and in sports, we all know nothing lasts forever. Times change, circumstances change, and that's the reality of playing in the NFL."

And the reality is: The hurt might turn into a dull ache, but in a country where a man's self-worth is often defined by day after day of the blood, sweat, and tears he puts into a job, a termination notice is as permanent as a tattoo.

Slowly unwinding after his final game of his first season as Broncos quarterback, Manning pulled off his dirty socks in the sparse locker room of Aloha Stadium and sat alongside Luck, cracking wise about the questionable music tastes of teammates on the AFC all-star roster, as if the rookie quarterback and the man he pushed out of Indianapolis had been friends for years. Harbor bitterness for Luck? No way. Resenting Luck would be a sloppy manifestation of Manning's pain.

Manning is the son of Archie, the brother of Eli. Dad suffered as the QB of hapless New Orleans, where he went 1-15 with the Saints in 1980. Baby brother takes the heat of playing for the Giants in New York. Having grown up in the America's first family of quarterbacks, Manning has too much respect for the job to hate anybody who does it.

"I've always believed NFL quarterbacks were an elite fraternity. Unless you are an NFL quarterback, you really don't know what it's like," he said.

As he stood up to say good-bye to Luck and head to the shower, however, Manning took a slight detour. He stopped with a purpose in the middle of the locker room, grabbing my attention with the quiet urgency of words too important to be left unsaid. Something about his comments on the field 20 minutes earlier didn't sit right with Manning. Polite to a fault, Manning did not want to sound brusque in the dismissal of seeing Luck in a Colts helmet. But, far more revealing, Manning did not want his curt answer to be misinterpreted. Anyone who deals with Manning quickly learns he is more fastidiously precise than a Swiss watch, and the wheel whirring inside his brain never sleeps.

"Hey, I wanted to explain something to you," said Manning, his voice as light and friendly as the touch of his hand above my right elbow. "All my great memories of Indianapolis will be forever. But I've stored them all away. Like in a time capsule. You know what I mean?"

The admission was startling. Every smile Manning ever made in Indianapolis is sealed in bubble wrap, not to be touched: His first NFL touchdown pass to Marvin Harrison as a rookie in 1998; the playoff perfection on an otherworldly quarterback rating of 158.3 in the 41–10 dismantling of the Broncos in January 2004; beating the Chicago Bears in the rain to win Super Bowl XLI.

When Manning was released by the franchise he defined, the headlines and television scrolls were unavoidable. He was standing right there, three feet from the spot where Irsay approached a microphone and emotionally told a press conference in Indianapolis: "It's a difficult day here of shared pain between Peyton, myself, the fans, everyone. In that vein, the 18 jersey will never be worn again by a Colt on the field." Seeking closure, Manning put aside an hour for 30 Indy staffers, from secretaries to equipment guys, so there was time for proper good-byes. The quarterback went home and talked with Ashley, his wife, about the strange turns life can take.

But, after all that, Manning was as numb as a zombie, unable to fully comprehend what had happened. Legends don't get cut. So Manning locked it all away, all the happy memories in safekeeping for another day far down the road.

"I had 14 terrific years in Indianapolis. Nothing ever can or ever will change that," Manning said. "But every memory I have from there is locked in a time capsule. It's locked in. I don't take those memories out."

Manning still loves the Colts. How could he not? He will always love the Colts. "He's always part of the horseshoe," Irsay insisted.

But have you ever been dumped by the love of your life? You hide the photographs. The heartache is too raw. You put the pictures away in the closet, because it is impossible to get anywhere in the future when you're lost in the past. Bitterness is a disease of regret. Refusing to look back, Manning chased a breath of fresh air.

"This is the next chapter of my football career, here in Denver. That's what and how I live day to day," Manning said. "Once I stop playing, I'll finally go back and combine both chapters in my head. But when you're living your next chapter, it's hard to look back. That's the way I've got to look it at. That's what works best for me."

Across the country, the Manning who is welcomed into our homes comes knocking with an easy charm and down-home humor. In commercials, Manning is the guy who drives a Buick to a barbecue at his father's house or roots for the neighborhood butcher with the chant: "Cut that meat!"

Here is the beautiful disguise: With his southern drawl and slouched shoulders, Manning is to be the quarterback next door. He could be your neighbor, provided your neighbor was a borderline obsessive-compulsive neatnik. Oh, in person, during life's silly moments, Manning can be as genuinely funny as a *Saturday Night Live* skit. But in a Twitterverse where personal communication is often a 140-character snark attack, Manning possesses the white tablecloth manners that would do any mother proud. The first time we formally met at Broncos headquarters, a quarterback with more than 50,000 yards on his NFL resume extended a handshake and said: "Hi, I'm Peyton Manning."

Hey, I knew that. But what it did not take long to discover: There is little about Manning that could be considered remotely spontaneous. He is a perfectionist, working from a script 24/7. In his perfect world, there are zero surprises. Yep, Manning gets lost on a trip to the barber in a new town. And it drives him nuts. But give Manning this: Rather than driving around in circles, he is the rare guy who is not afraid to bury the testosterone, swallow the pride, and call his wife to ask for directions.

Has any quarterback ever controlled the chaos of the game more efficiently than Manning, whether the task is calling an audible at the line of scrimmage or calling the shots while picking a new employer? Manning likes everything in his world to fit as comfortably as a pair of old jeans. He craves familiarity. So, in the end, maybe it is not such a big mystery why Manning picked Denver.

Elway knew what it was like to be a 36-year-old QB who craved another shot at the Super Bowl. Colorado Rockies first baseman Todd Helton, a friend since their college days at Tennessee, had opened the National League baseball team's workout facilities during Manning's rehab. Former Indy teammate Brandon Stokley lived in suburban Denver and gave more convincing reasons for why this was God's country than a $1 million Chamber of Commerce campaign ever could.

Go ahead. Try to name 10 quarterbacks in NFL history with a slicker resume than Manning. While you are stuck on the list somewhere between Joe Montana and Johnny Unitas, we will race back down the timeline to what tennis star Andy Roddick tweeted back on that fateful day when Irsay dumped Manning for a younger, sexier quarterback:

"The Colts cutting Peyton feels like the North Pole kicking out Santa."

Success, of course, is the best revenge.

In his debut season as quarterback in Denver, Manning threw 37 touchdown passes. He made the city forget Tim Tebow, whose controversial mix of football and religion had divided Broncos Country into devout believers and unholy doubters. With a 13-3 record and a first-place finish in the American Football Conference's West Division, Manning led Denver to its most regular-season victories since 2005.

But loyalty is platinum, silver, and gold to Manning. Pulling on a Broncos uniform was much harder than Manning made it look. It was never easy being orange, after 14 years of wearing Indianapolis blue. Pain is what pushed Manning to be an All-Pro quarterback for the Broncos, pain as real as the hurt in his voice when he was forced to say good-bye to Indy: "I will always be a Colt. I always will be. That will never change."

The cut went deep, straight to the core of Manning's very identity as an athlete who was always in control.

Yes, football heroes bleed when cut.

The scars go on forever.

Determined to make the most of what remains of his football life, Manning set aside the pain and turned the page, to chapter 2.

2

NO PLAN B

This was a marriage born of desperation.

In shocked disbelief after the Colts had dumped him, Manning was on the rebound, looking for a new NFL team to love.

Broncos owner Pat Bowlen had endured 13 long years since his last NFL championship, and, at age 67, Bowlen could not count on waiting another 13 years to get back on top as a viable option.

With his folksy humor, coach John Fox does not seem to sweat the small stuff. But every loss leaves a scar for the author of a game plan. When Fox signed a four-year, $13 million contract to become the 14th head coach in Broncos history, it figured to give him enough money to make retirement sound tempting after the deal ran its course.

As executive vice president of football operations, Elway was the leader of Broncos Country, divided by the Tim Tebow dilemma, with the young quarterback's believers and detractors too often arguing about sports and religion rather than wins and losses.

Exhibiting the patience to wait for Tebow to grow up as an NFL quarterback would have been a laudable exercise. But the movers and shakers at Dove Valley were not in the mood to be patient. Bowlen, Fox, and Elway all felt the clock ticking. They wanted a big score. And they wanted it now.

"My goal is to make Peyton Manning the best quarterback to ever play the game," Elway declared as he proudly presented his new quarterback to Denver on March 20, 2012. "And he's got that ability with the football he's got left."

The goal for Manning was audacious: Better than Tom Brady. Better than Joe Montana. Better than Elway himself.

History suggested Elway's goal was crazy impossible. The greatness of a quarterback is always measured in championships. Elway undoubtedly recalled that he never won a championship until age 37, and won the Super Bowl a second time as a grizzled 38-year-old veteran, when the Broncos routed Atlanta 34–19 on the final night of January 1999.

But in all the years since Elway retired, every quarterback who has won a Super Bowl, from Tom Brady to Brett Favre, was younger when lifting the Lombardi Trophy than the 35 years and 361 days that Manning had been on this earth when he officially became a member of the Broncos.

On the Tuesday afternoon Manning was introduced to Denver, after every imaginable question was exhausted by media members who occupied every last seat in a huge theater at the team's headquarters, Elway was asked one more thing, almost as an afterthought in that awkward, out-of-gas moment at every big event when it seems like time to go, but nobody wants to be the first to put on a coat and leave.

Lisa Snyder, host of a weekend show on Mile High Sports Radio, wanted to know if Elway had a fallback position in the event Manning turned down this offer to join the Broncos. The question was beautiful in its simplicity, going directly to the heart of Elway's anxiety as he waited to hear Manning's decision on whether he would continue his football career in Denver . . . or San Francisco . . . or Nashville, Tennessee. Had Elway been spurned, was there a Plan B?

"Plan B?" replied Elway. A look of utter disbelief filled his blue eyes to the brim. He shook his head. His mouth fell open, as if it were impossible for Denver's hero of The Drive and 46 other late-game comebacks to fathom defeat.

"We don't have a Plan B," said Elway. Laughter filled the room, and his trademark toothy grin brightened Elway's face as he thought of the exclamation point to put on the Manning signing: "We're going [with] Plan A!"

The line was so perfect it made even a jaded newspaper hack break into spontaneous applause. And the line was so very Elway, the words so bold they swaggered coming off his lips.

Sure, Manning was the player recovering from physical ailments, a veteran struggling to regain his passing touch. "It's not where I want it to be," Manning admitted. "I want it to be where I was before I was injured. There's a lot of work to do to get where we want to be from a health standpoint."

Make no mistake, though. It was Elway's neck on the line. He was all in, pushing the chips to the center of the table, gambling his reputation and the franchise's future that Manning could play like an MVP again. It was Manning or bust. But what football executive in his right mind would be so crazy optimistic to expect damaged goods to replicate the forty-nine touchdown passes and 4,557 yards that Manning produced back in 2004?

More than 65 percent of respondents to a *Denver Post* poll gave a huge thumbs-up to the Broncos' pursuit of Manning. Outside the walls of Dove Valley, however, there was loud grousing from the other 35 percent, an extremely vocal minority that insisted Elway had thrown away the trust of paying customers who had invested emotionally and financially, to the tune of $79.95 replica jerseys, in Tebow.

After declaring that Tebow had earned the right to be the starting quarterback when the Broncos opened training camp in the summer of 2012, Elway was being called a liar—and worse four-letter words—by fans that felt betrayed. The sense of betrayal among Tebow supporters would not be as easy to erase as removing photographs of the young quarterback from the walls at team headquarters.

"The acquisition of Peyton Manning is the worst day of my life where the Broncos are concerned," said David Burns, a fan from Craig, a beautiful little town in the far northwestern corner of Colorado, where you can awake to the bugle call of elk. "I'm sure Manning's a great guy and a wonderful human being, but I can't forget how he has humiliated the Broncos during his tenure with the Colts. I've referred to him numerous times as the Broncos Killer, and Peyton landing in Denver is just despicable and weird. Some things are unnatural. Peyton in orange and blue is that to me."

Tebow had the uncanny ability to transform even the most cynical spectator in the stadium into a Little League parent. Bless their hearts, but all Little League parents grow very defensive when the criticism strikes too close to home.

That's why Burns spoke for tens of thousands of people who threw their arms around Tebow and adopted him as Colorado's favorite son: "I told my best friend we had waited 14 years for a quarterback to excite the stadium like the old days. We found that quarterback in Tim Tebow. Management has handled Tim with such disrespect, disgrace, and disregard that it feels like a punch to the gut. I know I am not the only fan who recognizes this truth: John Elway said Tebow would be the quarterback going into camp. When that doesn't happen, you know what that makes the Broncos' vice president of football operations?"

How do you tell a nine-year-old boy his football hero has been demoted? In the eyes of a child, a Tebow poster on the bedroom wall is a shrine. That number 15 jersey can't be tossed to the back of the closet, discarded like a broken toy. Football is not business to a kid. It's all heart. And hearts break.

The illusion of sports is never richer than when you are nine years old, as Kyle Nowak was when his father shattered the illusion with the harsh truth. "Kyle, did you hear?" Neil Nowak said. "Eli Manning's older, physically disabled, overpriced and overhyped brother will be taking the fan-favorite, playing-winning Tim Tebow's position on the Broncos. It will be a great two games in the season, and Peyton will be in the hospital, earning his $90 million-plus, while Tebow will be in some other city, taking that team to the playoffs."

When I told Elway that story, the old quarterback cringed, as if preparing his body for a hit that would leave a mark.

"You hate some decisions you have to make in football. But that doesn't prevent you from making them. You do what's best for your team. But that doesn't take away the heartache. You're dealing with human beings. It hurts," Elway told me after the press conference to introduce Manning broke up.

Of all people, Elway understands how a quarterback who wins for the Broncos is embraced like a member of the family in Denver. Elway was throwing Tebow out of the house. We like to paint sports heroes as 10 feet tall and bulletproof. When calling Tebow to tell him of the Broncos' change in direction, the pain in Elway's eyes was genuine.

"I don't want to alienate people to the Denver Broncos," Elway said. "People may disagree with me. But the thing they need to know is it does bother me when I see these people want to run me out of town. Obviously, that bothers me a little bit. You never get used to that."

There is the football fanatic who paints his face orange and blue on NFL Sunday afternoons. But that obsession with the Broncos paled in comparison to the religious zealots who faithfully believed Tebow was God's quarterback. Elway is a football god in Denver. But as big or powerful as John 3:16 to Tebow disciples? Heavens no, and arguing otherwise was decried as blasphemy.

As a quarterback who won two national championships and the Heisman Trophy at the University of Florida, the football field was Tebow's bully pulpit. Tebow reached out and touched the unwashed masses by painting Bible verses on eye black patches he carefully selected and wore on game day. Prior to the Senior Bowl, where professional scouts hotly debated his throwing mechanics, Tebow wrote "James 1:2–4" on his eye black as a message to his doubters: "Consider it pure joy, my brothers, whenever you face trials of many kinds, because you know that the testing of your faith develops perseverance. Perseverance must finish its work so that you may be mature and complete, not lacking anything."

It takes more than faith, however, to throw a tight spiral into zone coverage. Regardless of how hard he tried or how long after practice he stayed, Tebow lacked the skill set to beat NFL teams consistently from the pocket in a pass-happy league.

When Elway stubbornly withheld unconditional praise as the Broncos made an unlikely run to the playoffs, The Tower of Tebow babbled that the aging legend had to be insanely jealous of his Bible-quoting quarterback, who also made miracles happen on the field when all looked lost with Kyle Orton unable to get the offense moving at the outset of the 2011 season.

"Elway doesn't like the fact his star has been eclipsed by this young punk Tebow," theorized Fred Coolidge, a distinguished professor of psychology at the University of Colorado–Colorado Springs and, it should be duly noted, a proud Florida Gators alum. "At some level, he is jealous of Tebow. Elway believes there should be no football gods before him. I think this whole thing is very Freudian. This is called an Oedipal conflict. Freud said all little boys naturally fight with their father. The Oedipal conflict can be exacerbated, especially if the son is bigger than the father."

The theory was balderdash. But it was balderdash eaten up by Tebow disciples.

Oedipal conflict? Nothing could have been further from reality.

It was doubt, rather than envy, that gnawed at Elway every time he watched number 15 play, even as Tebow ended six long years without a Denver playoff victory when his 80-yard touchdown pass to Demaryius Thomas in overtime beat the Pittsburgh Steelers 29–23 on January 8, 2012.

Elway feared being surpassed by Tebow as the greatest player in Broncos history? No way. No how. To blind supporters of Tebow, the real truth was a slap in the face they never saw coming. So long as Tebow was quarterback in Denver, Elway had little faith the Broncos could ever win another NFL championship.

With Tebow, a creative offensive coordinator, and a stout defense, maybe the Broncos could have expected 10-6 records year after year. Elway's aspirations, however, were loftier than operating a B-plus football operation.

As fall turned to winter in 2012, and the legend of Tebow grew. His you-gotta-be-kidding exploits ranged from the absurd, finding a way to win in Kansas City despite completing only two passes, to the sublime, with a 149.3 quarterback rating that allowed him to overcome an eight-point, fourth-quarter deficit in Minnesota, I could never shake one image of Elway. It was a grimace. Elway gave me the look on a 77-degree afternoon in South Florida on the late October day that Tebow celebrated his first start after taking over for Orton, returning to his old stomping grounds to stomp, bully, and will his way past the Miami Dolphins for an 18–15 overtime victory built on true grit.

In the tunnel of Sun Life Stadium after the game, as Elway walked to the team bus, he stopped in his tracks to chew on a question. I asked Old No. 7 if something about Tebow's refusal to lose reminded Elway of himself back in the day. The competitive spirit in Elway rose up and flashed a moment of irritation across his face. It was one breathtaking comeback win by Tebow, to be sure. But it was only one win. Elway said: "Let's not get carried away."

That was the thing. Elway never got carried away on the giddy wave of Tebowmania. The analysis was based on his core principles. When one of the greatest quarterbacks ever to play the game is the architect of your franchise, I will give you one guess what position the Broncos regarded as essential for success.

"The key thing for every NFL team, and I believe this whole-heartedly, is you need a quarterback," said Elway, who knows full well which way the rules are tilted in today's pro game. "A great quarterback makes up for so many other voids on your football team, because you've got that guy who touches the ball on every snap. And, if you don't have that guy, the weaknesses are more exposed."

Elway, however, did not enter this deal blindly, without regard to the wallet of Bowlen. The $96 million in the contract offered Manning made eyes bulge. But only the first season was guaranteed money. And know what? That was the way Manning wanted it.

During the recruitment process, as he crisscrossed the country, Manning made a conscious effort to avoid conversations with his financial advisors. He wanted the decision to be based on football. The final details of the document signed with the Broncos revealed the depths of

Manning's integrity. If betting on his full return to health was a gamble, he wanted to share the risk.

"They've got to be protected. That's why with the whole medical situation I was as open book as I could be. I told them exactly how I feel, what I was working on. They have to know everything to make their decision," said Manning, in a private moment of reflection after the television camera lights were turned off.

When it came time to talk money with the Broncos, Manning actually negotiated against himself.

"Even today, at the last minute, I said: 'John, put it the way you want it in the contract.' He and I talked about that from the get-go, on that first visit. You don't start off on a bad foot," Manning said. "I kind of argued with them a little bit . . . on their side. Nobody believes you when you say that. But it's got to be what they're comfortable with."

Sealed with mutual trust, here was the deal:

In 2012, Manning would be paid $18 million, no matter how many snaps he took.

Before $20 million salaries for both the 2013 and 2014 seasons kicked in, however, Manning would need to show his neck was physically sound.

The final $38 million of the contract, to be paid evenly in 2015 and 2016, came with no guarantees. In other words: Manning had a burning desire to show he was worth every last penny through his very last play for the Broncos.

"I don't consider it much of a risk, knowing Peyton Manning and his willingness to tell us everything," Elway said.

The negotiation really came down to a single question.

Elway: "Can you be the Peyton Manning of old?"

Manning: "There's no doubt in my mind."

Draw up the paperwork. Break out a pen. Where do we sign?

Manning could look Elway in the eye as a peer. Elway was never going to see Tebow as anything more than a project. Football, like the rest of life, is built on relationships.

"This is sort of a historic meeting," said Bowlen, understanding full well that most NFL owners feel blessed by one Elway or one Manning in a football lifetime. "We're glad to have two Hall of Fame quarterbacks. Our goal here has always been to win Super Bowls. Peyton gives us another chance to win a world championship."

And, at age 67, what more can any owner, in any business, want other than to feel he is still a major player in the game?

On the day the Broncos signed a four-time league MVP to be their quarterback, Elway stood in a hallway of the team's Dove Valley headquarters and dug deep, searching for words to express his genuine gratitude for Tebow. But, in the process, Elway also gave the coldest, most direct scouting report ever filed on Tebow as an NFL quarterback:

"Tim Tebow is a great kid," Elway said. "If I want someone to marry my daughter, it would be him."

Elway was not in the market for a son-in-law. That is why Tebow had to go. He was an inspiration, a winner, and a role model beyond reproach. But Tebow was no NFL quarterback.

When looking for a new team, Manning did not join the Broncos over the 49ers or the Titans to finish second. A slow fade to retirement is not his style. Before putting his signature on a five-year contract with few financial guarantees, he set his jaw with rock-hard determination and flat-out told me that his intention was not only to win a Super Bowl in Denver, but to make a habit of collecting championship rings with the Broncos.

"Three or four would be great. I'd like to win as many as we can. That's the goal: to win. There's always that debate every year. If you don't win the Super Bowl, is it a complete failure?" Manning said.

"Knowing I don't have 15 years to play football, there is a sense of urgency to win championships."

There was no time to waste. There would be no excuses for failure. There could be no looking back.

No Plan B.

3

RIDDLE ME THIS

Jabber, jabber, jabber.

This young'un would not shut up. As the car rolled down the highway, across the state of Mississippi, an eight-year-old Peyton Manning clicked off questions as quickly and endlessly as the mile posts whizzing by outside the window.

"From a young age, Peyton was very driven. It was so intense, I don't even know where it came from," said legendary Archie Manning, wrapping his 63-year-old bones in the warm fuzzies of a happy Denver locker room during the Broncos' eleven-game winning streak of 2012.

"I'm telling you, Peyton was never fast. He could not have won a foot race on the grade-school playground. I don't want to say he wasn't athletic, because that sounds bad. But his feet weren't very good. Well, I can say this: He did have size. He was always tall. And had a natural throwing motion. But here is what Peyton understood from the start: It was going to take hard work for him to be any kind of quarterback. And he used to ask a lot of questions. A whole lot of questions."

Archie Manning worked in New Orleans, as quarterback for the Saints. But he grew up in the old plantation country of Sunflower County, Mississippi. Olivia, who gave him three handsome sons, was raised in Philadelphia, another tiny Deep South town that was famous for being a battleground in the civil rights movement long before giving birth to the legend of Marcus Dupree, who scored 87 touchdowns for the local high school. Mr. and Mrs. Manning both attended Ole Miss, in Oxford.

So there was always a Sunday dinner or a speaking engagement or some such waiting for the longtime Saints star in Mississippi. From the time he was knee high to a grasshopper, young Peyton, the middle child of three, loved to tag along on the road trips. He would ride shotgun with his father as they drove three or four hours out of New Orleans. Dad never got a chance to sit back and listen to the radio. Every second of dead air was filled with questions from Peyton. Football questions. As the kid grew older, the car became a mobile course in advanced quarterbacking theory.

"Oh, there were so many questions. So many. Peyton used to ask me, 'OK, now let's go over the two-minute drill. What do I need to remember in the two-minute drill?' And then it was 'How do you check down against the blitz?' And then it was something else. Always something else. It never stopped," recalled Archie Manning with a sigh of bemusement, as if he was still weary from a 30-year-old memory of his eardrums being worn thin by Peyton's curiosity.

"He used to ask so many questions, I started calling him The Riddler."

Batman debuted on the ABC-TV Network in 1966, when Archie Manning was a junior at Drew High School. The first episode was entitled "Hi Diddle Riddle." The television show's first guest villain was Frank Gorshin as The Riddler.

It obviously made an impression on Archie. How could it not? The theme song, the Bam! graphics and the catchphrases from *Batman* became etched in the brain of every child of the '60s.

"Riddle me this!" demanded the Riddler, whose favorite suit was green and adorned with question marks.

The riddles, inspired by a mix of felonious mayhem and criminally bad puns, required the Caped Crusader to retreat to the Batcave for computer analysis.

"When's the time of a clock like a whistle of a train?" Batman would ask pensively, as if the answer might hold the key to the universe.

And with the unbridled enthusiasm of a teacher's pet, Robin would reply: "When it's two to two. Tootootoo!"

Hey, they didn't call him the Boy Wonder for nothing.

Is a boy born to greatness? But being born with a predisposition for throwing a spiral does not ensure you will die with Super Bowl rings and a Hall of Fame plaque to your name.

Peyton and Eli Manning are brothers, the sons of the ultimate Ole Miss Rebel and a homecoming queen. "People always said our boys were born to be NFL quarterbacks," Archie Manning told me. "But, to be honest, that idea always scared me a little. I never wanted to be that Little League Dad who irritated everybody. Raise an NFL quarterback? All my Olivia and I were trying to do as parents were raise good young men."

Being blessed in the deep, rich end of the gene pool did not guarantee the number one spot on an NFL depth chart.

We all fear the unknown. From a young age, Peyton Manning learned to take charge of an uncertain situation by exhausting his anxiety under the weight of relentless questions. If he had not grown up to be a quarterback, Manning would have been a district attorney worthy of a John Grisham novel. The answers provided Manning with the tools to solve any riddle.

"When I first got to know Peyton, he was a tall, thin, pimple-faced college freshman. Little did you think that one day he would be a Super Bowl MVP," Dan Carlson told me after one of Manning's early spring practices with the Broncos.

During the 1990s, Carlson began a long career at the University of Tennessee working as a graduate assistant in the football office. One of his first tasks on the job was organizing a recruiting visit by a promising class of prospects for coach Phil Fulmer. Who stood out in the group of teenage athletes? A string-bean teen from New Orleans with a famous football name.

But it did not take long for Manning to convince Carlson that this quarterback was much more than Archie's kid. If he was born with a silver spoon, Manning was using it to dig in and get ready to win.

"He came in with questions for the football staff. He really grilled them," Carlson recalled, the memory of a young Manning's audacity causing laughter. "He wasn't coming in to Knoxville just to take in the sights. He had a list of things he wanted to know. Imagine that for a high school senior."

To this day, Manning does command the room with a sly know-it-all smirk. But here is the refreshing part. There is a childlike sense of wonder about Manning, a quest for knowledge that never grows old. Facts are like ice cream. He still greedily devours every last spoonful of information.

After nearly 36 years of asking and jabbering and inquiring some more, Archie's kid rolled down the highway from Indianapolis to Denver to become the Broncos' new quarterback. Manning was all grown up, but his infinite curiosity showed zero signs of abating.

Manning immersed himself in the team's offensive terminology. He asked receivers to improve their speed reads of defensive coverages. He challenged coaches to stuff as much information as possible in the game plan.

Does Manning ever run out of questions?

"That," Broncos assistant Adam Gase replied, "would be a firm 'No.'"

As the team's quarterbacks coach in 2012, Gase walked into every meeting with Manning as if there were going to be a pop quiz. And the answers often required the perception to read between the lines of X's and O's in the Broncos playbook.

"His questions are always productive and great questions. When he asks questions, you're sitting there going, 'Gosh, that's a great question.' You're sitting there thinking, and you almost want to say to yourself, 'Why didn't I think of that? That's a great question to ask.'"

"You've got to find answers. And, if you don't know the answers that second, you better go investigate and find out."

OK, riddle me this:

Where on earth did the Broncos find the inspiration to think a broken-down quarterback, unwanted by the Indianapolis Colts, was the answer to their Super Bowl problem?

For centuries, the purple mountain majesty of the Rocky Mountains has inspired moments of 1,000-mile clarity for artists, from western frontier painter Albert Bierstadt to pop musician John Denver, who sat around the campfire, with everybody high, singing about it raining fire in the sky.

In a state with 53 peaks that tower more than 14,000 feet above sea level, it is not hard to get a natural high. The fourteener straight west of Denver that serves as the city's backdrop is Mount Evans. Mount Evans is the centerpiece of a stunning view out the windows of the executive offices on the second floor at the Broncos' Dove Valley Headquarters.

Mount Evans was not always Mount Evans. Way back in 1863, Bierstadt hopped a crude wagon alongside journalist Fitz Hugh Ludlow and took a rocky ride to Idaho Springs, in search of an alpine vista fit for framing. The painter found his inspiration while traveling up Chicago Creek, where Bierstadt was awestruck by the natural beauty of a yet unnamed peak standing tall among gray, threatening storm clouds.

Ludlow, his companion on the trip, was notable for two reasons: (1) the publication of an autobiographical book extremely provocative in the 1800s, because it was titled "The Hashish Eater" and detailed experimentation with cannabis extract, and (2) his hot young wife, a society woman named Rosalie Osborne, who had definitely caught the wandering, artful eye of Bierstadt.

With every masterstroke of his brush, Bierstadt revealed the turbulent, covetous, adulterous emotions roiling inside his heart. Bierstadt called the resulting painting: "A Storm in the Rocky Mountains, Mount Rosalie," thus christening a 14,000-foot peak in the name of a married woman he secretly desired.

By 1866, that cad Bierstadt had wooed Rosalie away from Ludlow. "In 1895," according to Denver art historian Tam O'Neill, "the Colorado legislature decided that the majestic peak should not be named for a scandalous divorced woman, and so changed the name to Mount Evans, honoring John Evans, the second territorial governor of the state."

In 2012, the inspirational powers of the peak formerly known as Mount Rosalie were again messing with affairs of the heart. In fact, you could blame the same mountain for causing the Broncos to cheat on Tim Tebow and dump him for a more attractive quarterback.

The man in the Broncos organization to first propose the bold masterstroke of bringing Manning to Denver never scored a touchdown in the NFL and was not classically trained in football. But a brilliant idea can come from anywhere. The wild-and-crazy notion that Manning could lead the Broncos back to the Super Bowl was originally uttered by Joe Ellis.

Ellis, a 1980 graduate of Colorado College, is the franchise president. His areas of expertise are wide-ranging, from fiscal planning to marketing to stadium development. But watching football videotape? Not so much.

Ellis is a business guy, known primarily as the team executive who took the blame for the hiring mistake and the rocky coaching regime of Josh McDaniels. Ellis could walk down the 16th Street Mall in downtown Denver alongside Elway and barely get noticed. In the Broncos' huge media guide, the biography of Ellis is tucked away on page 44.

But you can take this to the bank. In his imagination, Ellis painted the image of Manning wearing a Broncos uniform before anybody else of power in the franchise did. This is absolutely true, as no less an authority than Elway has confirmed it to *Denver Post* reporter Mike Klis.

Elway said: "Joe Ellis was the first one to talk with me about Peyton Manning."

The Manning Solution was not born in a high-level, dusk-to-dawn, catered-lunch meeting of Broncos front-office executives brainstorming at the demand of franchise owner Pat Bowlen. The image of Manning throwing a touchdown pass to Demaryius Thomas did not startle Ellis awake from a dream in a cold sweat. There was no eureka moment. "To be honest, I approached this more from a fan's perspective," said Ellis, poking fun at himself. "It wasn't like Albert Einstein thinking about the wonders of electricity."

So I had to ask: How did the thought of Manning playing for the Broncos originally cross Ellis's mind? What was he doing?

"I was looking at Mount Evans," Ellis said. "I was staring at Mount Evans. I was. I distinctly remember being in John Elway's office. And I wasn't even looking at him. I was looking out the window."

The idea of Manning came to Ellis out of the clear blue sky, delivered to the Broncos from the 14,265-foot summit of Mount Evans.

OK, brace yourself, Tebowmaniacs.

Here is a dead giveaway of the thought process by the Broncos brain trust that is almost certain to irritate every man, woman, and child in the legion of Tebow fanatics.

By the time Tebow delivered the signature moment of his Denver career and shocked the NFL world with that gorgeous 80-yard touchdown pass to beat the Pittsburgh Steelers 29–23 in overtime on January 8, 2012, his fate with the Broncos was all but sealed. Days earlier, the team had begun thinking in earnest about a better alternative at quarterback, before Tebow even had a chance to win a playoff game in dramatic fashion.

Despite the fact that Tebow had rallied a team that started the 2011 season with an ugly 1-4 record to postseason contention, an air of melancholy occasionally hung like a brown cloud over Dove Valley during the holiday season. After reaching eight victories, the Broncos lost their final three games of the regular season to New England, Buffalo, and Kansas City by the aggregate score of 88–40. It appeared NFL defensive coordinators had figured out how to put a cap on Tebow's magic. On New Year's Day in Denver against the Chiefs, Tebow completed only six passes for 60 yards.

"We backed in the playoffs after we lost to Kansas City, in a game where we never really crossed midfield, save for one turnover," Ellis said. "I don't know how many yards we had passing against the Chiefs. But it was well under 100, I am quite sure. And I think there was exasperation that we weren't advancing as an offense."

The date that changed Broncos football forever was January 2, 2012. At the time, it did not seem like any reason to circle the first Monday of the year in red ink.

Sometime during the 24 hours after every game, Ellis and Elway honor a little ritual. The president of the business side of the team drops by the office of the executive vice president of football operations. Elway and Ellis chat. Nobody takes notes. It is all very casual.

"It was a Monday morning, and we weren't in the best of moods," Ellis recalled. "I think John [Elway] was stunned by how much trouble we were having moving the football."

Elway was plopped behind his desk, attention fixated on video of the 7–3 loss to the Chiefs. Ellis took a seat in a chair, but could not get comfortable. He got back up. Intense competitors often seem to move with a caged tiger's uneasiness after a failed hunt for victory.

Ellis looked to the west, out the window of Elway's swanky second-floor office, seeking a little serenity in the majesty of Mount Evans. Without any deep reflection, or anything close to the formality of a PowerPoint presentation, he asked a question. It turned out to be *the* question.

"Do you think," said Ellis, his words coming out more as an exhale than an intense business proposal, "we could get Peyton Manning?"

Elway barely grunted a reaction. He was stuck in the stinky tape of the loss to Kansas City. But it was clear Elway had heard Ellis. Rather than jump to a conclusion or blurt out a response, Old No. 7 was slowly digesting the bold idea.

Before walking out the door, Ellis left Elway one more juicy tidbit to chew on.

"If you think Manning is an option," Ellis said, "we can find a way to make it work."

On the second day of January, as the Denver coaching staff focused on some way to upset Pittsburgh in the playoffs, the Broncos could not be certain Manning would be available on the open market. But the word on the streets of Indianapolis was the Colts were going to reshape their future with Andrew Luck, a ballyhooed prospect from Stanford.

"We knew the Colts were having a tough season and they might have the number one pick in the draft, so they were going to have a tough decision to make at quarterback. That was in the news," Ellis said. "We were struggling as a team throwing the ball. And this is a passing league."

What did the Broncos do? They zipped lips, rolled up sleeves, and went to work.

Weeks before Indianapolis owner Jim Irsay found the gumption to formally tell Manning the Colts wanted a divorce, Denver began plotting, scheming, and asking questions about how the Broncos could stay ahead of the pack in the chase for the most famous free agent in NFL history.

"We weren't allowed to contact Manning, because he was still under contract to the Colts. So there was no meddling," Ellis said.

So riddle me this:

What's rule number one when thinking outside the box?

The best answer might never be found, unless you're brave enough, bold enough, and maybe just crazy enough to keep relentlessly asking the next question.

The answer to what had seemed like the Broncos' search for a worthy successor to Elway? Ellis found it during a stream-of-consciousness flight of fancy on a blue Monday after a disheartening loss.

Ellis changed the course of franchise history with these dozen words: "What do you think our chances could be of getting Peyton Manning?"

You never will know if you are afraid to ask.

When Manning went looking for a new employer, he needed to a find a work environment where it was safe to ask anything. And everything.

In good fun, Manning handed out a homework assignment to young backup Brock Osweiler, asking the rookie to memorize the funniest lines from actor Steve Martin in his classic 1979 movie *The Jerk*, so the two quarterbacks could have something in common to chuckle about. In a more serious vein, Manning also unabashedly asked the Broncos to step up their game, from darkened film rooms to the bright lights of the stadium.

"Every little detail of the football operation to Peyton Manning is important," Ellis said. "And because everything is important to him, it makes every little thing more important to everybody else on the team than it might have been if Peyton weren't here. Does that make sense?

"What I'm trying to say is Manning's influence carries beyond the other 52 players in the locker room. It influences the trainer. It changes the way you think and approach a problem, whether you're the equipment guy or the team president or the nutritionist. It is all because everything matters so much to Peyton. It matters so much to him, because it is all about the team. And it is all about winning for him. That attitude rubs off everywhere Peyton Manning goes. And it puts everybody else on notice."

Who is the quarterback who tweaked the way the Broncos organization thinks by always asking one more question?

The Prince of Puzzlers. The Count of Conundrums. The Truthsayer of Touchdowns.

Now playing quarterback for the Broncos, number 18: The Riddler.

4

HE'S PFM. YOU'RE NOT.

Let's get this out of the way. Manning can be a real a pain in the ass. He is Peyton Freaking Manning. You're not.

Got it? Good.

A perfectionist can be hard to live with. In Chicago, the Bulls adhered to the Jordan Rules, set down by Michael. While winning four Stanley Cups from Montreal to Colorado, goalie Patrick Roy was far from a saint when perturbed.

Teammates feel genuinely honored to stand in the huddle with Manning. There will never be a Build-A-Bear named in honor of Peyton, though. He is not cuddly. He is demanding. It is nice to be liked, but for a quarterback it is far better to be respected.

On any given Sunday, catching touchdown passes from Manning can be the coolest job in America. But the other 349 days of the year? Working for the NFL's most demanding quarterback might be a more thankless task than being Donald Trump's apprentice. Or comb.

"It's not easy. He stays on you," Broncos receiver Demaryius Thomas told me after a practice when he stayed for extra tutoring by Manning. "He stays on you. But the more Manning stays on you, the better football player you become. I like it. When somebody stays on me, sure, it might bother me. But, at the same time, it makes me better."

Like any professor who practices tough love in the classroom, when a receiver blows a route, Manning might meet him back on the team bench after the punt, and ask his teammate if the hard cut in the route was supposed to be at nine yards or seven yards, when both the quarterback and the receiver damn well know the answer.

"Sometimes, it stings," Thomas said with a smile. "But I'm the type of guy that doesn't say anything. I just go back on the field and do my job."

At the NFL Combine during the winter of 2013, it seemed as if University of Southern California quarterback Matt Barkley showed up a year too late. Once projected as the top selection of the entire draft, Barkley's star had fallen. During his final season at USC, the Trojans finished 7–6, the most disappointing team in college football. And Barkley was their leader. NFL personnel executives took Barkley to task at the combine, showing him endless video of his mistakes. When the difficult process was done, Barkley sat down for an interview with respected *Sports Illustrated* writer Peter King and made a confession: Quarterback is a bad job for Mr. Congeniality.

A tough senior year at USC had driven home advice that should have been taken to heart when Barkley attended the Manning Passing Academy during the summer of 2012. "I learned a valuable lesson from Peyton," Barkley told King, "about sometimes you have to be a dick."

Only a fool challenges the authority of PFM. Dan Patrick, the best sportscaster in the business, once made the mistake. He gave me a word of caution, a little something to keep in mind when Manning came to Denver. Ask Manning a question he does not particularly like, as Patrick once did, and the quarterback might give you the cold shoulder. For years.

Got it? Good.

In a city that bleeds orange and blue during NFL season, more than 75,000 Broncomaniacs make Sunday pilgrimages to Sports Authority Field at Mile High. While chowderheads in Boston or wannabe cowboys from Dallas might argue the point, there is no better sports town in the United States than Denver, Colorado.

There are no sunnier fans anywhere. Win or lose, Denver leads the country in the most cheers per capita. The Rockies play baseball in a park where blue skies are the main attraction and the score is usually forgotten two minutes after the final out. The Nuggets and Avalanche turn the heat up in an arena that allows an escape from the chill of a Colorado winter. Only the Broncos, however, are religion in Denver. And the stadium Broncomaniacs call home is their church, although it is seldom quiet and is often unholy.

Wearing jerseys adorned with the numbers of football heroes past and present, fans squeezed onto RTD light rail make NFL game days one of the few times when commuting in automobile-obsessed Denver really feels like a community activity. I like riding the light rail, even though as kickoff approaches, the railcars often are packed tighter with bodies than a clown car at the circus. The guaranteed claustrophobia or an occasional toe squished by a stranger is well worth the trouble, though, because the peeps heading to the stadium give an accurate emotional weather report for Broncos Country, during the hot streaks or cold spells of any season.

On the first Sunday of December 2012, the train was light as laughter and rocked with giddy anticipation, with fans buzzing about plans for Christmas and the playoffs as the doors opened to unleash an orange flood at the Mile High Station across Interstate 25 from the team's 11-year-old home. The Broncos had won six games in a row, wrapped an iron-fisted grip on first place in the AFC West, and invited the Tampa Bay Bucs in town for the honor of becoming victim number 10 of an increasingly exciting regular season.

The walk from the rail station to Mile High, on a path that winds beneath the highway overpass and a bridge spanning the narrow South Platte River, was the football version of a Mardi Gras parade. Toasts to good fortune were made with cans of Coors Light. Vendors lining the route sang "Burritos, burritos!" The rare, brave supporter of Tampa Bay wearing Bucs gear caught an earful of good-natured heckling.

Then, the parade hit a speed bump. Folks stopped in their tracks. Gawked. Pulled out the smartphone to click a photograph. And for what reason?

A man selling T-shirts.

But not just any old T-shirt.

"Who needs one? Right here, guys. They're going fast," pleaded salesman Carlos Farmer. He enticingly waved a cotton, short-sleeved shirt dyed neon orange and painted on the front and back with big blue lettering in profanely blue language that repeatedly coaxed a spontaneous, laugh-out-loud reaction.

"Oh yeah! How much?" said a young fan, who was keeping his head toasty warm under an orange hunting cap adorned with wonderfully tacky and fuzzy orange earflaps.

"Twenty-five dollars. What size do you need? Large?" replied Farmer. "And if you don't buy the shirt, I need a donation for that picture you're taking. This is not a photo shoot, my man."

Farmer then proceeded to drum up more business by revealing the reason for all the fuss being caused by his custom-made attire.

"Peyton Fucking Manning," Farmer said, reciting the words printed in block letters on the front of the T-shirt.

And the message on the back of the shirt was even more politically incorrect. But the slogan was delivered proudly by Farmer, in the irresistible staccato rhythm of a street-corner rapper: "If you don't bleed navy and orange, take your bitch ass home."

The T-shirt was crude, rude, and socially unacceptable.

But the message struck a chord with ticket-buyers who had developed a big orange crush on the new quarterback in town. From his earliest days in Denver, Manning quickly acquired a nickname that gave a nod to his past as a Broncos Killer, but also let him know Broncomaniacs were damn glad to finally have another Hall of Fame quarterback on their side.

In Denver, he was PFM from the start. Social media made the call, and there was no turning back. The people had spoken. Throughout the Rocky Mountain region, with fans passing instant judgment on all things Broncos, the shorthand for the $18 million QB became as popular on Twitter as SMH or LMAO.

Thomas Edison did not actually invent the lightbulb, but he gets the credit. Vic Lombardi, lead sports anchor at the CBS affiliate in Denver, might not have been the first man to dub Manning "PFM." Lombardi, however, put the edgy acronym of endearment squarely in the local sporting vernacular, and did so without incurring the wrath of any Federal Communication Commission censors. It was beautifully subversive. Whenever asked what the F in PFM stood for, Lombardi would cleverly reply: "Peyton Freaking Manning. Birth name."

PFM made throws that Tebow could not dream. Broncos coach John Fox gave credence to the PFM craze during an interview with the *Los Angeles Times*, when reviewed the performance of Manning by declaring: "What Peyton is doing, in my brain, is not just remarkable, it's freaking historical."

PFM was the football equivalent of a Chuck Norris joke. Peyton Freaking Manning doesn't need to check the scoreboard clock; he decides what time it is.

"To refer to PFM simply as PM is shortsighted, disrespectful, and quite demeaning," Lombardi once tweeted.

"No Plan B" was immortalized on a T-shirt as the unofficial motto of Manning's debut season in Denver. It was only a matter of time before "PFM" garnered the same honor of 21st-century pop culture.

The seller of the PFM shirts harbored a dirty little secret. A large part of the appeal in the football flea market that sets up outside Sports Authority Field is sticking it to the man. Plunk down a buck for peanuts on the street, and that is money never seen by an NFL franchise owner who had his stadium subsidized by the taxpayers' dime. Buy a stocking cap or a bottled water from a rack along the Broncos Walk and you can feel good about helping out a small local businessman. Know what I mean, Mr. Farmer?

"Well, I'm from Ohio. Cleveland, as a matter of fact," said Farmer, lowering his voice to keep his admission from spreading. "You know, the Broncos have been tearing my heart out my whole life. But I come up here and sell T-shirts for the money. I come in to Denver for the game. Sell the shirts at every home game on this exact spot. And, when the game's over, I go right back home."

There was a temptation to rat out Farmer. I suppressed it. Hey, even a dude from Cleveland needs a way to put food on the table. But here was a Browns fan, profiting at the expense of Broncomaniacs? Only in America. Before Farmer could continue with his story of entrepreneurial success, however, two more customers interrupted.

"We're not even going to the game," announced Jameson France, looking as if finding these orange shirts was a more historic discovery than Indiana Jones getting his mitts on the Holy Grail. "We parked in the lot behind the REI store and walked over here for only one reason: To get this shirt!"

France was on a quest. He did not grow up loving the Broncos. But his grip on a wad of cash was tight, and France braved the game-day traffic jam to complete a mission that had been on his to-do list for more than two months. For him, buying PFM T-shirts wasn't a whim. Those orange shirts were an absolute necessity for a red-blooded American football fan, a necessity like air . . . a high-definition television . . . or cold beers in the fridge.

"I'm from Tennessee. I grew up in Johnson City, and have always been a huge Peyton Manning fan," confessed France, a 2009 University of Tennessee graduate. "I had tickets to the Raiders game in September, but didn't have enough cash on me. So I came back. I'm sending shirts home to my family."

Hey, nothing says Merry Christmas like a PFM T-shirt.

"See?" said Farmer, creator of the gift on everyone's list. "I've got a cult following."

On his way to becoming the most beloved sports hero in Colorado history, John Elway picked up a handle accurately reflecting the gunslinger mentality that made him the last hero standing during wild west shows in the fourth quarter. He was affectionately called the Duke for winning more shoot-outs on the field in the final reel of highlights than John Wayne ever did in the movies.

Manning is far from a gunslinger. He is clinical, carving up the will of a defense with surgical precision. He is PFM. It fits him perfectly. He is the freaking boss.

When Manning talks, even rowdy Broncomaniacs shut up and listen.

Chuck Norris doesn't read books. He stares them down until he gets the information he wants. That is nothing, however, compared to the spell PFM cast on Denver.

Back in the day, Moses parted the Red Sea. Only Peyton Freaking Manning can stop the wave in his home stadium.

He told Broncomaniacs to pipe down. They obeyed faster than you can move a finger to your lips and say "Shush!" Guess we know who gives the orders around here.

The Tampa Bay Bucs were in town on that pleasant late-autumn afternoon, apparently summoned so Manning would have a defense to toy with, as he added more impressive factoids to his PowerPoint presentation as a Most Valuable Player candidate.

Manning completed 27 passes for 242 yards against the Bucs, including a touchdown throw to Thomas that appeared as if the football vaporized out of the quarterback's right hand, not to be seen by anyone again again until the end zone during D.T.'s celebration, as if instead of being thrown, the pigskin had been dematerialized and beamed up to its intended target, like something straight from the imagination of Gene Roddenberry.

For comic relief, Manning picked up another first down by scrambling from the pocket with all the grace of a man tumbling down the basement stairs in the dark. But as he stumbled toward the Tampa Bay sideline, Manning somehow spotted Broncos running back Knowshon Moreno, who had aborted his pattern by falling on his rump beyond the first-down stick.

With a delicate touch, Manning dropped a pass softly into the lap of Moreno, as the running back sat nonchalantly on the grass. A second later, when the whistle blew the play dead, Manning unexpectedly found himself looking directly into the eyes of Bucs coach Greg Schiano on the Tampa Bay sideline. Schiano responded involuntarily, in the manner any good football coach does when witnessing unexpected greatness on the field. He excitedly patted Manning on the helmet, the way you see a coach applaud a peewee QB in Pop Warner League.

"That's the first time I've ever had an opposing coach tell me that was a good play in the middle of the game," Manning admitted.

Early in the fourth quarter, with the Broncos in possession of the football and a commanding 15-point lead, it was all over except the shouting, the nacho-munching, and the playful, mindless hijinks of the crowd. In his relentless perfection, Manning had drained all the drama from the proceedings to the point his audience was bored.

With a one-two-three, fans stood, threw up their hands and shouted, as the wave flowed from section to section in the stadium. Sure, the wave is a cliché. But it is mindless good fun, a stadium tradition that reaches back at least 30 years, when a professional cheerleader known as Krazy George Henderson began the craze by accident at a hockey game in Canada.

As the wave crashed around him, Manning operated the Denver offense from the no-huddle attack, completing a short pass on third down to Eric Decker and kept the drive alive.

Manning, however, was ticked. And when he gets miffed, we all know what happens next: a bad case of Peyton Manning face. This time, it was directed at every man, woman, and child in the crowd.

Before hurrying to give teammates instruction, the quarterback turned away from the line of scrimmage and with both hands, gestured with agitation at Broncomaniacs to stop the stupid wave. On the Fox television broadcast, color analyst John Lynch quickly dissected a replay of Manning's objection to the wave and hilariously observed: "He tells the fans: 'Please! C'mon, I'm trying to do some work out here!' He's staring at them. Look at him!"

Responded play-by-play commentator Dick Stockton: "You think he's in charge?"

Lynch: "I think so."

The camera panned the people in the stands, all looking as guilty as kids waiting in the principal's office.

"Fans doing nothing," Stockton noted. "Folding their arms."

"You would, too," added Lynch, "if he told you to be quiet."

Got it? Good.

When the wave began rolling, what words crossed the mind of Manning?

"Oh, I don't know. I probably can't repeat it," confessed Manning, suppressing a grin. That is the beauty of PFM. Everybody knows he means business, without Manning needing to say a single word.

Does a theater audience do the wave when a Shakespearean actor launches into a monologue from *Macbeth*? Tiger Woods demands silence when he lines up a 20-foot putt for a birdie. We all know better than to burp in church.

"I'm all for excitement, but in a no-huddle offense, when you are calling something at the line, the quieter the crowd can be, it is certainly helpful," Manning said. "But I appreciate the spirit, so I don't want to tame that at all."

At the exact moment when that beautiful hush enveloped the stadium, Tebowmania tippy-toed unnoticed out the exit gates, never to be seen or heard from again in Colorado.

"He's a first-ballot Hall of Famer," said Tampa Bay's Schiano, setting aside his competitive ire after a tough defeat long enough to show reverent appreciation for Manning, "and there's a reason why."

Manning told 76,432 Broncomaniacs to sit down and shut up.

And they liked it.

This was the house that Elway built on the basis of back-to-back Super Bowl victories. This was the house that Tebow brought back to happy life after years of football that sometimes made fans cover their eyes in disgust.

But the day he stopped the wave, the new quarterback in town took possession and the stadium officially became Peyton Freaking Manning's House.

Keep quiet when the master is at work.

Behave yourself. Or else.

Only a fool messes with PFM.

Got it? Good.

5

MR. NOODLE ARM

Manning heard. Oh, he heard the whispers that screamed: As a quarterback, he was toast. The accusation? His throwing arm was as sturdy as overcooked fettuccine. But that did not mean his brain had turned to mush. The wit of Manning remained as sharp as infinity knives.

"Watch out," Manning warned reporters standing behind the end zone, as he and the Broncos worked on a passing drill during the early stages of a practice in late September. "Those wobblers still hurt if they hit you in the head."

The message of the zinger was delivered with the velocity of a Justin Verlander fastball. Looking in the direction of his pals in the Denver media, Manning pointed to his helmet and gave a visual clue: Be smart. Manning knew: A man has to use his noodle, especially if his passing arm is dissed as no more threatening than Mom's spaghetti.

Maybe the most remarkable aspect of Manning's comeback is how much he relied on guile, as he adjusted to his body's limitations.

"I am what I am. It is what it is," Manning once said, at the height of his exasperation over the unending speculation on the strength of his passing arm.

Look, the truth is, the Broncos had a pretty good idea they were signing Mr. Noodle Arm, yet offered Manning a $96 million contract with full confidence the best QB mind in the business would find a way to adapt.

Fewer than 72 hours before Manning telephoned Elway on a Monday morning with that happy news of his choice to join the Broncos, Denver management flew from Colorado to North Carolina on a secret mission to inspect the quarterback at Duke University. There was a big stack of franchise owner Pat Bowlen's money on the line. So the Broncos airlifted the best minds in their organization to the East Coast, bringing in everybody from Elway and general manager Brian Xanders, to offensive coordinator Mike McCoy and trainer Steve Antonopulos.

After the private workout, Elway tweeted: "He threw the ball great and looked very comfortable out there." The positive review got Broncos Country geeked. But those glowing words were less than the 100 percent truth. Had Manning been a rookie being poked, prodded, and evaluated at the NFL Combine, his grade would not have matched the expectations of a franchise quarterback. Only months removed from watching the Colt's 2011 season-opener from a hospital bed, Manning's passes were still a work in progress of a long, difficult rehabilitation.

"The way he threw the football when we saw him at Duke? That wasn't what sold us," Elway admitted to me months later. "He looked fine there at Duke. But he wasn't ready to go out and play in an NFL game there. He wasn't ready to go."

The Broncos would have to take it on faith that Manning could be the same as he ever was, a worthy foe for Ben Roethlisberger, the Pittsburgh Steelers quarterback who was scheduled in Denver for the 2012 season-opener, fewer than six months down the road from this workout at Duke. The medical chart pointed upward, but the only 100 percent solid promise was Manning's word to give the comeback his best shot.

So you mean to tell me, I asked Elway, that he changed the direction of the team and bet his reputation on a damaged quarterback, not so much on what Manning physically did, but on the conviction with which he talked to you?

"Absolutely," Elway replied.

Elway invested millions of dollars, not on the strength of Manning's arm, but the strength of Manning's word. Now that took cojones.

"I just knew in my heart, knowing him and his career and what he's about, if any quarterback was ever going to make this deal work, it was Peyton Manning." Elway said.

The question was not so much if Manning could stay on the field for 16 regular-season games with the Broncos, but how many times he would resemble the legendary quarterback that Denver fans would expect.

"There were never any worries with me about his neck. Before John Lynch came to Denver, he had the same surgery with his neck. [Former Tampa Bay star] Mike Alstott had the same surgery. In Lynch and Alstott, you're talking about a strong safety and a fullback, players who get hit hard all the time. If those guys were fine, then, believe me, a quarterback was going to be fine. I was never worried about the neck," Elway said.

Fans and media obsessed about that first hard, blindside hit, to see if Manning could take a licking and keep on ticking. The hearts of those concerned about Manning's well-being were in the right place. But they were focused on the wrong issue. What makes Phil Mickelson such an astounding golfer is his touch around the greens. What makes Manning so amazing is his uncanny feel for the football, a skill that allows him to loft a pass delicately over the outstretched arms of a linebacker. Nerve damage had robbed Manning of that magic touch.

"All I was worried about with Peyton was the nerves. And the doctors told us the nerves would come back," Elwy said. "It was just a matter of when."

In the uncharted galaxy of the Twitterverse, and a TV landscape where the never-ending infotainment scroll screams for attention before a couch potato mindlessly reaches for the remote control, however, there is no time for context and nuance, much less contemplation. Fire the shot of a loud opinion, attract the Internet hits, and ask questions later. Hey, as a newspaper columnist unafraid to offend and intent on staying relevant in the modern media circus, I have done it myself, without apology.

But too many sports commentators have descended into the basement with bloggers for whom they once professed contempt. It is easy
to offer analysis from 1,000 miles away, without the mess or effort of
actually doing anything that resembles reporting from the stadium or
the locker room. But if a potshot from a crackpot draws clicks on a
mainstream website, who cares, especially if it is good for business? All
that suffers is the football IQ of America.

A month before the Colts released Manning, outstanding *Indianapolis Star* columnist Bob Kravitz got the pasta metaphor cooking with an
appearance on Tony Kornheiser's radio show, where Kravitz declared:
"The guy's arm is a noodle; he can't throw like an NFL quarterback."
Within days, Kravitz backpedaled from his harsh diagnosis, graciously
apologizing, by admitting his thoughts sometimes fall short of being
cogent prior to the first cup of coffee in the morning. But if the sound
bite sticks, there's no turning back. In a podcast with ESPN's Bill Sim-
mons, Mike Lombardi of the NFL Network upped the ante, spreading
the notion that Manning could not throw to his left.

The legend of Mr. Noodle Arm was born.

In the competition to bust the Broncos for wasting $18 million on
Manning's salary, the shouting game reached a crescendo in the hours
after Denver lost by six points at Atlanta in week two of the NFL
season. Against the Falcons, Manning came out on the field and looked
lost, disoriented by Atlanta's defensive scheme. He threw interceptions
to end each of Denver's three truly offensive possessions in the opening
quarter. He did not look like Peyton Manning. This was a quarterback
who did not seem to trust his throws.

Despite a furious rally led by Manning that fell just short, his demise
became a trending topic from coast to coast. And sentimental tears are
the first thing cut from a 140-character football obituary. "Manning
can't throw the ball accurately or with zip more than 20 yards. Manning
is toast," wrote Jason Whitlock in his popular NFL Truths column for
the Fox Sports website.

Whitlock blasted *Monday Night Football* analyst Jon Gruden for
gutlessly and willfully ignoring the elephant in the room during the

telecast. His theory? Manning was being propped up, in a conspiracy to fool television viewers too dumb to see the ugly truth. "I get that Manning is ratings gold for TV networks, but Gruden took a dump on his own credibility shilling for Manning in such an obvious manner. Manning used to make the opposition defend the entire field. That's over. He can't take the top off a defense," Whitlock insisted.

The reports of the slow football death for Mr. Noodle Arm were not only premature, but greatly exaggerated. The interceptions Manning threw against the Falcons were to his right. That was supposed to be his good side, was it not? Or were analysts unable to tell their left from their right, while grasping for theories out of thin air, unable to find an insightful assessment with both hands?

"When I see the ball coming out of his hand, what I see is a little wobble on it. That's not what you want to see. We like to see that thing spinning really nice, tight on a spiral," former Philadelphia Eagles quarterback Ron Jaworski observed on ESPN's *SportsCenter*, after a loss to Houston dropped the Broncos' record to 1-2.

The complaint was Manning could not throw a football that looked as pretty in flight as the passes zinged by Green Bay's Aaron Rodgers or Detroit's Matthew Stafford. Well, meaning no disrespect, but neither could "Jaws" in his prime.

Manning was declared done as a deep threat. This Hall of Fame quarterback, it was openly feared, had been reduced to an expensive game manager.

Well, surprise, surprise, surprise.

Six weeks after being declared toast, Manning was sweeter than a tall stack, covered in syrupy praise as the leading candidate for most valuable player, along with Minnesota running back Adrian Peterson.

The scope of what Manning dealt with, both mentally and physically, in returning to the loftiest level of NFL stardom after a serious injury was best described by Marshall Faulk, the main event in "The Greatest Show on Turf" with the St. Louis Rams.

"You're never going to be perfect again. You're only going to be repaired," said Faulk, a running back enshrined in Canton, Ohio, during the summer of 2011.

As a player finally forced to retire after gaining nearly 20,000 yards from scrimmage as a dual threat running or catching the football, Faulk can give a peek inside the head of an athlete whose confidence has been shaken by a serious injury. The fear is not of pain. The real fear is the fear of failure, born of the body's betrayal.

"For Peyton, I'm sure by far the biggest thing was the unknown. He didn't know how his body was going to react. That has to be the biggest fear. As a football player, your body is your precise gauge of how you react to every situation in the game. You don't get to put a test dummy out there on the field in your place, and say: 'How does that feel?' It's trial-and-error with your own body, under the stress of a game," Faulk said.

"Mentally, it has to be both scary and frustrating. At any point in time, in the middle of a play, as you're looking downfield and throwing the football, your body can let you down. Or it can surprise you, where you say, 'Whoa, I didn't know I still had that in me. How did I make that throw?' It's like flying an airplane with no gauges."

Barack Obama won his second term as president of the United States in November, not only beating rival Mitt Romney, but trouncing the Republican challenger 332–206 in the Electoral College tally, by a margin that surprised many prognosticators who had called the contest a toss-up.

Whether the football is political or pigskin, it is all a game. Except football makes for melodrama for a couch potato to enjoy with his chips and salsa, and the race for MVP was no exception. There were two worthy candidates as the top NFL player of 2012, igniting a hot debate among their supporters.

On a surgically repaired knee, Peterson was not only carrying Minnesota to a berth in the NFC playoffs, he was taking dead aim at the single-season rushing record of 2,106 yards, a feat still standing 28 years

after Eric Dickerson established it, way back when the Rams called Los
Angeles home.

But week after week, as the Broncos dispatched foe after foe, Manning certainly looked like the best player on the field. After the Broncos
routed Cleveland for their 10th consecutive victory, Browns defensive
end Frostee Rucker endorsed the candidate from Colorado, declaring,
"We played the best quarterback in the league."

So two days before Christmas, near the conclusion of a 16-game
regular season that reminded him that the best gift really is health,
Manning was asked if a stack of 300-yard passing games convinced him
he was playing as well as in his Hall of Fame prime.

"I don't," said Manning, lining me up squarely in the scope of his
earnest eyes. Then, to underscore the certainty of his response, he
repeated: "I do not."

It was a startling admission from a leading MVP contender.

But was Manning telling the whole truth, or was he merely downplaying his remarkable achievements with false modesty? I leaned toward the latter explanation, because Mr. Noodle Arm compiled gaudy
statistics that Tom Brady or Rodgers would take in a heartbeat. Certainly when he looked in the mirror, Manning had to recognize a quarterback the equal of the superstar who won his fourth MVP award in 2009.

"I don't." Manning insisted. "I'm trying to be as good as I possibly
can be at this state: A 36-year-old quarterback, coming off a year and a
half, playing with a new team. I'm trying to be as good as I possibly can
be in this scenario."

At the risk of incurring the veteran quarterback's wrath, I called B.S.
on Manning.

"I know you guys don't believe me when I say I'm still kind of
learning about myself physically and what I can do. It's still the truth,"
Manning said, with grace so pure its source could have only been genuine humility.

"I still have things that are harder than they used to be and things
that I continue to have to work on, from a rehab standpoint to a

strength standpoint. And that's just the way it is and maybe that's the way it's going to be from here on out for me. I don't know."

Flying without any gauges, Manning operated against the most basic fear in us all: the unknown. And that, more than anything, was the triumph of No Plan B. If reinventing himself as a quarterback did not work, there was going to be no way for Manning to fake it.

The return of Manning and the rebirth of his career in Denver were shot nonstop through different lenses, all searching for fresh angles. It was Manning versus Andrew Luck, the QB who replaced him in Indianapolis. It was Manning versus Baltimore linebacker Ray Lewis, two grizzled warriors who stared at each other across the line of scrimmage, the intensity in their eyes matched only by the respect. It was Manning versus Philip Rivers, to see if the best quarterback in the AFC West was now in Denver rather than San Diego. It was Manning versus Peterson, waging a campaign for MVP.

It was all good theater. But it all seemed a little contrived. Perfectionists measure themselves only against the guy in the mirror. And what Manning saw in the mirror was a middle-aged dude with a hint of a middle-aged paunch and a middle-aged hairline, left to wonder if what he had left was good enough to win.

The comb-over that hides a man's inevitable concessions to age is humor. During week 15 of the NFL season, with rain in the forecast for a game at Baltimore, Manning experimented wearing a glove on his throwing hand during practice. At midweek, he was asked: Could a quarterback whose NFL home was a dome until moving to Denver be concerned about the forecast of wet weather? "Who's giving that weather report on Wednesday? Denver local weather? National weather? You?" Manning cracked. "Do you dabble in the meteorology field?"

He did not wear the glove against the Ravens. Manning, obsessed with preparation, was practicing for winter. No lie: This is a man who would stick his right hand in a cold tub of ice to prepare for freezing conditions. He broke out the gaudy orange glove for the final two games of the regular season, and completed 53 of 72 passes for 643 yards and six touchdowns. Manning loved the glove, and he was not trying to make a fashion statement.

The glove Manning donned for the first time in his NFL career was the ultimate tell. Touch, not velocity, touch was the real issue with Manning's return to health. "I was surprised to see it. Because you just don't see quarterbacks wear gloves," Broncos cornerback Champ Bailey told Mike Klis of the *Denver Post*. "But honestly, the way he's throwing it? I wouldn't be surprised if we do start seeing more of it. I know when I'm just throwing the ball around, I throw better with a glove on."

The glove gave Manning a stronger grip, but it also let it slip that the regeneration of nerves after four neck surgeries was not complete. In his 15th professional season, a superstar practiced the theory of evolution, adapted and learned to love the glove. "I certainly don't think I would have had to wear the glove had I not been injured," Manning said. "It's part of my injury, some things that I've had to adjust."

The biggest adjustment for any athlete who must confront the signs of athletic mortality is to ignore the bitter taste that often accompanies pride being swallowed.

At the Manning Passing Academy his family holds every summer, there were teenagers with more zip on throws. In the weight room at Dove Valley, rookie Broncos quarterback Brock Osweiler pumped iron with such authority that it made Manning feel old. But here was the tricky part for Manning: Deep down inside, he slowly had to accept compromise, a tough deal cut with the realities of a right arm that ain't what it used to be. "You've got to fight carrying that burden," Manning said.

Fair or not, the curse of Mr. Noodle Arm lives.

Manning will have to live with the doubts until he can erase the memory of his last critical error in the 38–35 double-overtime loss to Baltimore in the playoffs.

The last pass he threw that really mattered for the Broncos was an interception, and a stark reminder that the hero who led the Colts to a Super Bowl victory in 2007 is just a quarterback that Manning used to know. "When you play a game where the temperature is 10 degrees, that chronic injury is going to be affected by the cold," Faulk said.

Late in the first overtime of the playoff game against Baltimore, Manning rolled to his right and threw across his body. Manning might not particularly like playing in the cold, but the problem here was brain freeze.

The pass never reached its intended target, Broncos receiver Brandon Stokley. It lacked the velocity to get past Ravens cornerback Corey Graham, whose interception set up Baltimore's game-winning field goal from 47 yards.

"Bad throw. Probably the decision wasn't great," Manning said. "I think I had an opening, and I didn't get enough on it. I was trying to make a play and it's certainly a throw I'd like to have back."

The bummer of the deal is also the compelling challenge of solving a mystery. At age 36, the challenge every morning for Manning is for an old dog to figure out a new way to trick 'em.

"Old dog is right," Manning told me. We have all heard that song by the Rolling Stones on classic-rock radio. What a drag it is getting old.

But what you gonna do? Go sit on the porch? Or run with the pups, as long and far as you can?

"An old dog," said Manning, long in the tooth, but able to muster a bemused smile at the folly that age eventually makes of every man's ego. "That's for sure."

6

THE DAY TEBOWMANIA DIED

Sacking God's quarterback is an unforgivable sin, at least in the eyes of his most devout followers. Denver traded Tebow to the New York Jets on March 21, 2012, receiving two draft choices and $2.5 million in cash. From listening to the righteous rage of Tebowmaniacs, however, you would have thought Elway had sent God's quarterback straight to hell.

Dr. Pat Robertson—octogenarian televangelist, a first lieutenant in the Christian Right army and unabashed fan of Tebow—ran for president of the United States in 1988. So, in the aftermath of the Tebow trade, maybe it should have come as little surprise that Robertson was not hesitant to tell the Broncos how to run their business. Trade Tebow, after obtaining a Hall of Fame quarterback to take his place? Heavens, no!

"The Denver Broncos treated him shabbily. He won seven games. He brought them into the playoffs, for heaven's sakes. I mean, they were a nothing team. He rallied them together with spectacular last-minute passes and, you know, when they beat Buffalo—I mean Pittsburgh, excuse me—it was a tremendous story," said Robertson from the studios of *The 700 Club*, where he preaches to a flock of loyal television viewers.

Robertson did make one unassailable point. The trade was a bummer deal for Tebow, who earnestly, and perhaps a bit naively, believed he could win Elway's enduring trust.

Without the heroics of Tebow, the Broncos would have been unable to overcome a 1-4 record to start the 2011 season and make the playoffs. Without the success of Tebow, perhaps Denver would have failed to attract serious attention from Manning, who preferred joining an NFL team with legitimate championship aspirations after he was dumped by Indianapolis.

Once Manning was signed by Denver, however, keeping Tebow on the Denver roster made zero sense. What was at issue involved more than a conflict of playing styles. The rough-and-tumble Tebow, whose inability to read defensive coverage often resulted in him running around the pocket like a headless chicken, was a bad fit as the understudy to a traditional pocket NFL quarterback the likes of Manning, one of the more precise passers in league history.

But here is the real reason Elway needed to knock down the circus tent and move Tebow out of town. Too many Tebow supporters were red-hot ideologues, casting stones from their high moral ground at anybody who dared to doubt the skill set of a Bible-thumping quarterback. No different than abortion or gun control, once a debate on Tebow began, it was hard to find safe middle ground. "It's because he's a Christian that most sportswriters won't give him a chance," insisted David Rice, a good-hearted Tebow disciple from Durango, Colorado. Countered Detroit Lions cornerback Chris Houston, when asked to evaluate Tebow: "He's no Peyton Manning or Tom Brady or no Michael Vick or none of that. He's got a long ways to go as far as being a quarterback."

As when Dr. Frankenstein created his monster, the Broncos were unprepared for the havoc they would wreak by unleashing Tebow on Denver. I called it the Tebow Thing. It was alive, a phenomenon born of social media, jersey sales, and religious conservatives who stood up and cheered a right-to-life quarterback. He was the child of a difficult pregnancy that his mother refused to abort, so it makes sense his family is pro-life. Tebowing became a verb in the American football lexicon, born of amateur photographers from Denver to the Great Wall of China clicking snapshots of common people saluting the quarterback's ritual of taking a knee and bowing his head in prayer on the field. "I believe in a big God and special things can happen," Tebow told me.

There were other members of the 2011 Broncos who were devoutly religious and unafraid to show it, from Pro Bowl safety Brian Dawkins to third-string quarterback Brady Quinn. Other than ending every interview with "God bless," Tebow seldom brought faith into his public conversations without being asked. Although labeled by pundits on the left and right as a polarizing figure, what draws people to Tebow is a happy bounce in a step that makes him as instantly likable as a Labrador retriever rather than any secrets-of-the-universe insight. Football coaches like Tebow because in a regimented sport, here is a quarter-back who obediently thinks what he is taught on the chalkboard. So coachable, in fact, that manipulative friends and preying foes alike expected Tebow to carry a political football for them, to advance social agendas that revealed as much or more about the opportunists than what was in the heart of the quarterback.

Despite giggles behind his back when he acted as if the winner of wind sprints to end practice won a gift certificate to Dairy Queen, Tebow won over teammates with a relentless energy and a positive attitude that never took a day off. "I call him Baby Jesus," Broncos running back Willis McGahee said, with tongue planted firmly in his cheek. When the website Poll Position conducted a telephone survey of 1,076 football fans across the United States, a startling 43 percent testified to a belief that divine intervention played a role in a string of amazing comeback victories by Tebow. Or as late-night comedian David Letterman once said while revealing the Top Ten Little Known Things about Tim Tebow: "Can turn water into Gatorade."

Behind the closed doors of the Denver locker room, however, Tebow worked religiously to make the Broncos believe that God was on their side. In the hour before a Thursday-night kickoff against the New York Jets on November 17, 2011, as the Broncos prepared to take the field for warm-ups, Denver linebacker Wesley Woodyard looked up from his locker stall and saw Tebow walking toward him with a purpose.

"Tebow came to me and said, 'Don't worry about a thing,' because God had spoken to him," Woodyard recalled. At first, the linebacker found the message from Tebow "kinda weird," because quarterbacks rarely mingle in the end of the locker room where defenders dress.

"I gave him a big hug and told him thank you," Woodyard said. "God speaks to people to reach other people."

After completing only one of eight passes in the third quarter, Tebow and the Denver offense took the field trailing the Jets 13–10 with five minutes, 54 seconds remaining in the game and 95 long yards between the Broncos and the end zone.

With suddenly perfect accuracy on his throws, Tebow marched Denver into range for a tying field goal during the last minute of the fourth quarter. But the miracle comeback was just getting warmed up. On third down from the New York 20-yard line, Jets coach Rex Ryan called an all-out blitz. Tebow slipped the pressure, broke to the left sideline, and bulldozed his way into the end zone for the winning touchdown. As the visitors waited to board a charter plane back home, an emergency medical service unit from the Denver Fire Department was dispatched to Denver International Airport. The reason? Ryan had a tummy ache.

"For all the Tebow haters: You better start believing," Woodyard told me after the improbable 17–13 Denver victory against the Jets.

Later the same season, it was Woodyard who would reach out and rip the football from the grasp of Chicago running back Marion Barber to allow a wilder, wackier comeback against the Bears that required the suspension of all disbelief. Was that Woodyard who caused the fumble? Or the hand of God? To claim their sixth straight victory, the Broncos had to overcome a 10-point deficit in the final 2 minutes and 15 seconds of regulation, then won on a 51-yard field goal by Matt Prater in overtime. The Mile High Messiah had struck again.

Even after Tebow caused grown men to cry with joy at the sight of an overtime victory in the playoffs against Pittsburgh in January, Elway was not a convert, despite the hallelujahs echoing nationwide in praise of God's quarterback. On the night Tebow stunned the Steelers with an

80-yard touchdown pass to Demaryius Thomas on the first snap of overtime, true believer Jonathan Cannon snapped a photograph of an oil-on-canvas-worthy sunset as he entered a pub in Charleston, South Carolina, to watch the Broncos game. The sunset, painted in vivid hues of orange and blue, "took my breath away, and I immediately praised the Lord! Then I thought: 'Hmm, Father, are you going to be up to something wild today in Denver, with a David versus Goliath moment?'" Cannon told me. "Then . . . bam! Tebow and the Broncos pulled out another wild one! This does remind me of how many times through my life and history, God shows up when the impossible is needed against all odds. So many times we just write off the unusual occurrence as coincidental, when, in reality, God orchestrated it to reveal Himself and His Glory!"

With the same impeccable instincts that allowed him to dodge pressure on the football field, Elway inherently understood die-hard Tebow fanatics would never sit quietly as the young quarterback served a lengthy apprenticeship to Manning. Football executives who stand in God's way are condemned as heathens. There was a split in Broncos Country. Within 72 hours after Manning was issued a Denver uniform, Tebow got traded, so the healing could begin.

"It was a tough situation," Elway told Lindsay H. Jones of *USA Today*. "There are Tebow fans and there are Broncos fans. My responsibility is to the Broncos fans, and my responsibility is to Pat Bowlen and what he wants to do, and that's win championships. I base all my decisions on that. It's difficult not to get personal, because every kid that comes in, it's his dream to play. But the bottom line is: My responsibility that Pat's given me is to give him the best opportunity to hoist that trophy."

Pat Robertson was one of those zealots on the topic of Tebow. On television, he chided the Broncos for their risky investment in Manning.

"OK, so Peyton Manning was a tremendous MVP quarterback, but he's been injured," said Robertson, arguing his case to a *700 Club* audience that would naturally be sympathetic to poor, pitiful Tebow being cast into the wilderness by the Broncos. "If that injury comes back, Denver will find itself without a quarterback. And, in my opinion, it would serve them right."

It would serve them right? What in the name of sweet Jesus was Robertson suggesting?

It sounded as if the Broncos would not only have to turn back San Diego, Oakland, and Kansas City to win the AFC West, but also dodge the wrath of God. Every time he took a snap, Manning already was putting his surgically repaired neck on the line, risking damage from a blindside shot by Houston defensive lineman J. J. Watt or a safety blitz by Bernard Pollard of Baltimore. Did Manning also need to beware the possibility of a stack of Bibles falling on his head?

Robertson's tirade, which seemed to openly question a football decision by the Broncos on moral grounds, was so blistering that *700 Club* co-host Terry Meeuwsen could respond on-air with only a single word of pious outrage. "Well!" she harrumphed, her reply as forceful as an "Amen!" to Robertson's football sermon. Was Robertson truly miffed because the Broncos defied God's will? A spokesperson for the Christian Broadcasting Network tried to put a Band-Aid on the raw feelings, with this statement: "Dr. Robertson is in no way advocating an injury to Peyton Manning, who he regards as a tremendous MVP quarterback."

An impossible question to answer remained: If Tebow was actually God's quarterback, why would he not be closer to perfect than his lousy 46.5 completion percentage while making throws during his 2012 season in Denver?

The subject of Tebow caused Manning to gaze at his shoes when he joined the Broncos. The truth hurt. Manning knew the pain of being told by the Colts to get lost. He genuinely despised taking a fellow quarterback's job.

"I know there are great fans of the Denver Broncos. And a lot of times they're fans of the quarterback. There are great reasons for them to be fans of Tim. There's what a great guy he is and what he did (for the team). I'm in the quarterback fraternity," Manning said. The truth was: He hated the prospect of taking the job of a fraternity brother. For Manning, it was the worst part of his recruiting process as an NFL free agent, knowing that if he signed with Tennessee, quarterback Matt Hasselbeck would probably lose his job, or if Manning joined San Francisco, the 49ers might well decide to trade Alex Smith. "But I wanted to go play somewhere else," Manning said. "I don't know there was any easy way to do this."

Manning was no Mile High Messiah. But he was big enough to silence Tebowmaniacs. When number 18 jogged onto the field at 8:44 AM for his first practice at training camp on July 26, 2012, you would have thought Bruce Springsteen had taken the stage. "Everybody's here to see Manning," Maxwell Totten of Littleton said. "Everybody knows this is our Super Bowl team." The rowdy crowd of 4,372 spectators, who started to form a line outside the gates before sunrise and set a single-day record for Broncos summer camp, saluted the new quarterback in town with chants of "Manning, Manning, Manning."

Some would argue Tebowmania was buried that summer day.

In a football town spoiled by the success of Elway, however, there's only one way for a quarterback to earn respect: Win. It took Manning a while to get warmed up, as whispers grew his arm wasn't right and he might not be worth $18 million per year.

Denver had been warned, by none other than Broncos coach John Fox, that it was going to be a long, bumpy ride to the playoffs. "I've been of the school of understate, overproduce," Fox repeated until he was hoarse, in the weeks leading to Manning's regular-season debut. "We're obviously pleased to have Peyton, yet we're still trying to get ready as a football team, and we're definitely not there yet." The Broncos required the one thing nobody wanted to hear about: Patience. It required a clutch 43-yard interception return for a touchdown for Denver to seal a victory in the final two minutes of the home-opener. The stumblebum Oakland Raiders graciously gave Manning what amounted to an early bye week that also counted as a W in the standings.

Dissension crept into the ranks of paying customers in Section 505 of Sports Authority Field as early as September 23, when the Houston Texans came to town and won 31–25. From the nosebleed seats, the cascade of booing rained early on a sunny afternoon. As the approval rating of Manning began to slip, the crowd was so lifeless during much of the second half that the only sound to be heard from the upper deck was a lone protester mournfully crying, "Tee-Bow! Tee-Bow!"

During the final moments of a 27–21 loss in Atlanta, rookie quarterback Brock Osweiler had been spotted warming up near the Broncos bench. Gossip ensued. "I was going in for the Hail Mary," Osweiler told Mike Klis of the *Denver Post*. The Falcons, however, saved John Fox from the delicate situation of yanking his Hall of Fame quarterback by running out the clock on the back of Michael Turner.

After getting run over by a red, white, and blue bus driven by New England quarterback Tom Brady, Denver owned a 2-3 record. "They move at NASCAR speed," said linebacker Joe Mays, after eating the Patriots' dust during a 31-21 loss. Added cornerback Champ Bailey: "Right now, we aren't good enough."

The moment of crisis arrived early in the Manning era.

And then the situation got worse.

On the road in San Diego, facing what Manning called a must win, the Broncos fell behind 24–0 at halftime.

But what happened next will be remembered for decades in the future, when white-haired men grab a tattered number 18 jersey from the attic, gather grandkids around the fire, and tell tall tales from the night when Peyton Manning officially became a Broncos legend.

"I've never seen a football game turn on such a big wave," said Bailey, after Denver scored five straight touchdowns, all in the last 30 minutes of the contest, to stun the Chargers 35–24 as the NFL world watched on *Monday Night Football*.

It was stunningly beautiful. Stunning because the Broncos appeared clueless while falling behind 24 points in the opening half. The mindless offensive game plan seemed as if it was borrowed from the Tebow era. A failure to communicate between Denver receiver Matthew Willis and Manning resulted in an embarrassing interception returned 80 yards for a San Diego touchdown. On what appeared to be a certain six points for the Broncos, Eric Decker tripped over a blade of grass on his way to the end zone.

"It was no mystery words of wisdom at halftime," Fox said.

When your QB is PFM, panic is not part of the vocabulary. "You can never count that guy out," Broncos receiver Brandon Stokley said. "Everybody in this locker room knows, and we all believe, that when you have him behind center, we can come back from any deficit."

In all his glory, Tebow never created a greater football miracle. But this was not a miracle. Miracles are not sustainable. Talent endures. Manning has something Tebow does not: Hall of Fame ability. Elway, the king of all Denver comebacks, never was part of a more improbable victory. During the second half, Manning was the picture of near-perfection, while completing 13 of 14 passes.

"I'm in shock right now that we just did that," Broncos defensive tackle Justin Bannan admitted to Mike Klis of the *Denver Post* after a comeback for the ages was in the books. "I'm just glad I was part of it. That's one you will remember forever."

The weird, wacky turn of events began with an Elvis sighting. Broncos defensive end Elvis Dumervil, who had struggled during the early season to justify his $14 million salary, turned the momentum by stripping the football from San Diego quarterback Philip Rivers late in the third quarter, with the visitors trailing by 17 points. The fumble was scooped up and returned 65 yards for a score by defensive back Tony Carter.

"That's the play we had to have to make a comeback," said Manning, downplaying his contribution, which included three touchdown passes, the most important a 29-yard strike to Thomas on Denver's opening possession of the third quarter. A 21-yard throw and spectacular catch by Stokley put Denver ahead 28–24 with nine minutes, three seconds remaining in the final period.

On an evening when the Broncos were on the verge of being run out of the AFC West division race and straight into the Pacific Ocean, they emerged with as much inner confidence as any team with a 3-3 record could possibly possess. Recent rallies that had sputtered in the end against Atlanta, Houston, and New England were forgotten. A feeling of invincibility took seed, and would blossom with each passing week, as the winning streak got on a roll.

The Broncos had PFM on their side. "We unraveled," Rivers said. In one night, the momentum of the season and the course of history in the AFC West changed forever. The Chargers were clinging to a glorious past already gone. Denver posted first notice it was ready to rejoin the league elite.

Outside the press box after game's end, as reporters scurried to the locker rooms, chasing quotes against deadline, and the *Monday Night Football* crew began breaking down all the apparatus of its dazzling television circus, there was chaos at the entrance to the elevator that served the upper reaches of the stadium.

A team of emergency medical technicians talked with urgency, wheeling a gurney through the elevator doors. An expectant mother who had attended the game was out in the parking lot, going into labor. Oh, baby.

Mention of an impending birth immediately brings a smile of recognition to any father who has experienced the blood-pressure spike on delivery day. There is no cheering in the press box, but everybody takes a rooting interest for a child entering the world. Ink-stained wretches and celebrity broadcasters alike gladly made room for the medical personnel to hop on the elevator.

Included in the impromptu cheering section were Mike Tirico and Jon Gruden, the announcers who had told a nationwide ESPN audience every thrilling detail from the biggest rally in Manning's illustrious career and the biggest comeback since the NFL started playing games on Monday night in 1970.

"Whether it's a boy or a girl," Tirico called out to the EMTs, wishing them Godspeed, "that baby should be named Peyton."

The hot list of baby names changes every year. In with the new, out with the old.

On the Broncos' charter flight back home, Tebowmania died, with the ashes scattered somewhere over the Rocky Mountains.

7

OLD NO. 7

Nothing sticks to the memory like a song. And the Academy Award for stickiest song in movie history goes to: the theme from *Ghostbusters*.

That song is engraved in the head of Broncomaniacs, impossible to erase and forever linked to a special time. But, in Denver, the tune is not identified so much with green slime and Bill Murray as it is with new cars and a famous quarterback. The most played song of the 1990s in Colorado had to be the *Ghostbusters* theme, rewritten and recast as a commercial jingle for number 7's automobile empire.

Who you gonna call?

John Elway!

Long before he became a world champion, Elway was king of the road.

In 1993, Elway sold more than 7,500 Hondas, Oldsmobiles, Toyotas, Hyundais, and Mazdas. That year alone, dealerships carrying the Elway badge grossed nearly $130 million.

Somehow, it figures that Elway, the fastest gunslinger in the West, would never blink in business, whether crashing and burning as a partner with Michael Jordan and Wayne Gretzky in an e-commerce sports equipment venture, or selling his stake in car dealerships for a cool $80 million.

"You know, John Elway told me one time why he loved the car business," said Jim Saccomano, the team's longtime public relations director, known and revered throughout the NFL as Sacco. Saccomano's work shaping the Broncos' image as an elite franchise was every bit as masterful as the best game plans devised by coach Mike Shanahan.

Saccomano can spin a compelling yarn like you used to hear back in the day, while sitting around a campfire. "Love the car business? Really? I mean, this guy's a quarterback," Sacco said, hooking his listener. "So I asked John why he loved it. And his response was straight to the point: The tote board."

The tote board?

Inside the sales offices of every car dealership, there is an accounting of what cars are moving off the lot, who is selling them, and whether quotas for the week, month, or year are being made. No nonsense. Dollars separate the winners from losers on your automobile team.

Scoreboard, baby.

"Yes, there is a scoreboard. And you keep score every day," Elway said. "That's exactly why I do like the car business. You've got goals, and there's a scoreboard that tells you whether you won or lost."

Elway always has his eyes on the scoreboard, because he is hooked on competition. Seek a cure for this lifelong addiction to winning? Or slow down in middle age? No way. Elway could live comfortably off his fame. But Elway lives for the next game.

No wonder he wept without shame when announcing his retirement from the Broncos on May 2, 1999, fresh off being the grand marshal of a second Super Bowl parade in two seasons. Love hurts, and breaking up is hard to do.

In the opening statement during the retirement ceremony, Broncos owner Pat Bowlen broke the tension with an anecdote. With a sense for the dramatic, Bowlen revealed details of the last supper before Elway hung up his football cleats and walked away from a brilliant 16-year NFL career.

"John went downtown to have dinner with some of his teammates at a well-known restaurant that shall remain nameless. There was no parking around the restaurant. But there was a stall there that said nobody can park here. Except John Elway, I guess," Bowlen told family members, friends, teammates, and reporters who came to say goodbye.

"He came out after dinner, and believe it or not, they towed his car. The king's car! And he couldn't get a cab. So he had to walk three miles, in the industrial area of Denver, to pick up his car. When he got there, the lady said: "Can I see some I.D., please? And I need $100.""

In summation, Bowlen tilted his head toward Old No. 7, and concluded: "So welcome to the world of the retired great quarterback, John."

NFL competition is a heavy dose of adrenaline. Go cold turkey on that and reentry into the relatively mundane life of a retired QB can be a shock to the system.

Blindside hits shook Elway to the core. Jack Elway, his father and confidant, died of a heart attack at age 69, during the spring of 2001. Jana, the twin sister born 11 minutes after her famous big brother, succumbed to lung cancer in 2002. The first couple of Denver, once described to me by Janet Elway as two ordinary people leading extraordinary lives, ended their marriage with a divorce in 2003.

"It was boom, boom, boom," the retired quarterback said.

On an August afternoon in 2007, after not talking to him for more than a year, I caught up with Elway. To tell the truth, it was not hard to catch him. Elway limped across the grass, with a bulky, black brace on his knee, as ominous thunderclouds rumbled overhead. He was coaching the quarterbacks at Cherry Creek High School. Why was he here? The starting quarterback for the Bruins was his son.

"Emotion always comes before business," Elway told me. Coaching his kid during a high school season was obviously a cherished bonding experience for a middle-aged man who had learned how your world is capable of quickly unraveling, without rhyme or reason.

"That's the thing, to be in the football wars with him," said Elway, explaining why he was so delighted to be working on a prep practice field with his son. "Plus, I know a little about the job. It's a way for me to be back around the game again and get excited about the game again."

It was as plain as the strain on Elway's face. He was searching. For something to get his competitive juices flowing. For a place in the game. There were too many years left on the clock to plop down on the sofa and try to kill the time by reviewing highlights of his glorious past.

Life without football can send a man reeling. Is it any wonder Elway understood the controlled desperation of Peyton Manning, when he was scrambling to find a place to begin chapter 2 of his NFL career?

In 2010, a few days before his 50th birthday, the greatest player in Colorado sports history sat down to reflect on his life and times, football victories, and personal defeats, with Woody Paige, the most influential sports journalist in Denver during the entire scope of Elway's NFL playing career.

"I've been a gunslinger in business, just like I was in football. I look at a proposition, consider if I think it will be a winner, and I make my investment. I've always been a risk-taker. You make your best educated guess, and it might fail. But there have been high-fliers. I don't want to just lend my name to a product or a company. I want to be part of winning or losing," Elway said, as two longtime friends swapped stories in the upscale Cherry Creek shopping district, home to a steakhouse named after Old No. 7.

Then, on that summer day, Elway offered Paige a revealing little confession.

"I've got to be totally honest," Elway said. "I was watching TV when [great UCLA basketball legend] John Wooden recently died, and in an interview they had asked him if he was afraid of dying. And he said: 'Absolutely not.'

"That was the very first time I asked myself, 'Would you be afraid to die?' I can't answer yes or no, but, reaching 50, I've started to conjure up thoughts of my own mortality."

Sports columnists are often accused, justifiably so, of engaging in the easiest game in the world: second-guessing. Fifty years after Paige is gone from this earth, folks might remember him only for being the funniest panelist on ESPN's *Around the Horn*. He is destined to be forever known as the cast member of the sports debate show who sat under a chalkboard, where Paige has scribbled wisecracks such as: "I'd make a terrible pessimist" and "Dear Algebra, stop asking us to find your X, she's not coming back."

But let the record show it was also Paige who pushed and prodded, cajoled and led cheers, until Old No. 7 and the Broncos got back together again. Elway was hired January 5, 2011, as the team's executive vice president of football operations.

Just as he had bid farewell to his quarterback with good humor nearly a dozen years earlier, Bowlen welcomed Elway back to Dove Valley with a well-timed quip.

"I can't think of a better job and a better guy to do that job than John Elway, and I look forward to great things in the future. I think John will return this team to a very high level of competitiveness. I think we'll win some more Super Bowls," said Bowlen, patiently setting up his punch line.

The next time Denver won the NFL championship, Bowlen added, he expected Elway to hand him the Vince Lombardi Trophy and declare: "This one's for Pat!"

Sure, Elway was inducted into the Pro Football Hall of Fame in 2004. He had some experience as a football czar, leading the Colorado Crush to the 2005 championship of the Arena Football League. But how much did that really count? Arena football has about as much in common with the NFL as the roller derby does with the Daytona 500.

Elway was walking into a mess, the result of perhaps the most embarrassing stretch for a proud franchise, caused by the mistakes of inexperienced coach Josh McDaniels, who had been fired in December 2010 after a videotaping scandal had shamed the Broncos as bungling cheaters. Elway did not have a head coach. In the wake of a 4-12 season, it might have been kind to say the Denver roster stunk. Was Elway in over his head?

Rather than try to bluff, Elway smartly admitted two things, from his first day on the job: (1) competitiveness was far and away his greatest asset; and (2) he was smart enough to realize there was a lot for him to learn about operating an NFL team, and he would show no reluctance to ask for help.

It is a gross simplification to suggest, but everything Elway needed to know about the slim difference between winning a lot and winning it all he learned the hard way from Dan Reeves.

Reeves was the coach in Denver when Elway entered the NFL in 1983. Many Broncos fans, not to mention Elway himself, chafed at the harness Reeves put on Elway's talent with conservative play calling.

It would be folly, however, to deny that Reeves also taught Elway how a football gunslinger who saves a few bullets for the fourth quarter can survive and become the triumphant hero in the end. "Anytime you have John Elway," Reeves was fond of saying, "you have a chance."

The Broncos Ring of Fame honors the most essential contributors to the franchise. How can the Ring of Fame exist without Reeves, with his 110 regular-season victories and three AFC championships, as a member? That is a cruel joke. Not funny, not funny at all.

But there is also no denying: Reeves graduated from a school as old, traditional, and stuffy as that Stetson fedora his mentor, Tom Landry, wore on the sideline for the Dallas Cowboys. In Denver, Reeves erected a thick wall between his office and the locker room. Coaches gave orders. Players listened. Elway grew sick of it. Somebody had to go. The superstar won.

At training camp in 1993, months after Reeves had been fired and departed town for a job with the New York Giants, Elway ripped his former coach: "The last three years have been hell. I know that I would not have been back if Dan Reeves had been here. It wasn't worth it to me. I didn't enjoy it. It wasn't any fun, and I got tired of working with him."

At the time, at the ugly height of the feud, Reeves snapped back: "Just tell him it wasn't exactly heaven for me, either. One of these days, I hope he grows up."

Time wounds all heels. Nevertheless, realizing bitterness makes for a lousy partner during the long walk through life, Elway has buried the hatchet with Reeves.

His clashes with Reeves made it crystal clear to Elway: In football matters, he would never be a dictator. Elway would surround himself with smart people willing to challenge his ideas. A football executive might be at the top of the team's organizational chart, but his job is to serve.

"The most important people in football are the ones who play," Elway said. "The players are the ones who make it happen on the field. I'm just trying to put the puzzle together outside the lines. Front-office people and coaches who have success in the NFL understand it's the players who make everything happen."

The instant I heard Elway tell me his basic management philosophy, his words sent my mind racing back to informal chats I was blessed to enjoy with UCLA's legendary Wooden through the years at the Final Four. He was the Wizard of Westwood. The magic was in his humility, which prompted an important piece of sports wisdom that stuck. "The better the players I had on the basketball floor," Wooden told me, "the smarter the coach I became."

Elway instinctively understands what Wooden figured out decades ago.

General managers draft, sign, and trade for talent. Coaches draw X's and O's. But only players can turn all the hours of planning into a championship.

For most Broncomaniacs, the most indelible image from Elway's first run to the Super Bowl was a damn-the-torpedoes play now simply known as "The Helicopter."

If you are unable to recite every detail of that famous Elway scramble by heart, your Broncos Country citizenship card can be revoked. It was the defining moment of Denver's 31–24 upset of Green Bay. Needing six yards to keep a drive alive in the red zone, Elway threw caution and his body to the wind, spinning like helicopter blades through hits by three defenders to gain a first down.

It, however, was neither the most crucial play along the long road to that Super Bowl victory, nor the fondest photograph I have kept from the first championship season in Broncos history.

Two weeks before Elway and running back Terrell Davis shocked
Green Bay, a berth in the Super Bowl was on the line January 11, 1998.
As Denver battled Pittsburgh down by the river in Pennsylvania, the
unofficial but extremely emotional play-by-play description of the action on the field was provided to me by Jack Elway and Jerry Frei, two
former coaches whose vast knowledge of the game benefited the Broncos. Elway was the team's director of pro scouting, while Frei oversaw
the college scouting department.

Frei was a spry 73 years old at the time, seven years older than
Elway. They sat a row behind me in the Steelers' press box. It was a
bigger hoot than watching an episode of *The Muppets* from the balcony
alongside Statler and Waldorf.

Late in the fourth quarter, after the Steelers had pulled to within
24–21 on a touchdown pass from Kordell Stewart to Charles Johnson,
the stadium was rocking, as terrible towels waved. Denver was pinned
back at its own 15-yard line, needing six yards to retain possession of the
ball. Sometimes you can feel a momentum shift, and other times it
rumbles louder than an oncoming avalanche.

A punt at this point would have been akin to punching Pittsburgh's
ticket to the Super Bowl. With two minutes remaining in the final
period, the Broncos broke the huddle on third down. Make or break
time. Elway's favorite time.

Before Shannon Sharpe trotted to the line of scrimmage and took his
upright stance in the left slot, the tight end spun quickly, and excitedly
asked Elway: "What route do I run?"

Elway replied: "Just get open!"

Sharpe ran a deep curl. In the instant he turned back to catch his
quarterback's attention, a pass arrived like a wrecking ball intent on
knocking a hole in Sharpe's massive chest. Somehow, the tight end held
on to the football for an 18-yard gain. The most important play in
franchise history could not have been more improvised if it had been
drawn in the dirt.

Great players can make a coach look like a genius.

Up in the press box, my head swiveled away from the spot on the field where Sharpe made the most clutch catch in team history. From the second row of the press box, Jack Elway looked at Jerry Frei and with pure unbridled joy exclaimed: "You know where we're going, don't you?"

The Super Bowl.

Then, the two old football coaches hugged as if their winning lotto numbers had hit.

Manning was born to play quarterback.

Jack Elway raised his son to never surrender.

During the late 1990s, as his golden years coincided with the Broncos' glory years, the elder Elway would often cross my path in the hallway at team headquarters. He would nod hello, and if there was an educational message to convey to a *Denver Post* sportswriter, the legendary QB's father would grab my elbow and talk in a voice as hushed as a police informant.

"John really did not like that column you wrote for today's paper," Jack Elway might tell me, his words accompanied by an impish grin that tickled him all the way to the funny bone. "Don't tell John. But I thought what you wrote was great . . . even if I didn't agree with a word of it. Bad press gets his competitive juices flowing. Keep it up."

Most NFL players are thankful if they have one game of a lifetime. Elway had 50. At least.

But perhaps the most telling Elway performance occurred during his rookie season. Not as a ballyhooed rookie draft with the Broncos, but as a peewee player in Montana.

Although I was far from the first to hear the story, Jack Elway's eyes twinkled when he introduced me to the tale. Once upon a time, in a faraway land, where the deer and the antelope play . . .

Young Elway was a fourth grader. His favorite team was the Dallas Cowboys. His hero was Calvin Hill. So the kid wanted to be a running back when he joined a youth football league in Missoula, Montana, where his father was an assistant football coach at the local university.

The schedules of the University of Montana Grizzlies of father Jack and the Little Grizzlies of young John were often in conflict during the autumn. So Jack did the smart thing. He enlisted a set of trained and trusted eyes to keep notes on his young running back.

The trusty scout in question? A Montana basketball coach named Jud Heathcote, whose nose for talent would be undeniably confirmed years later, when he would recruit Earvin "Magic" Johnson to Michigan State.

Now, ladies and gentlemen, boys and girls, you are about to learn where the Elway legend began, with a competitive ball of fire that could not be contained.

Fresh off work, Jack Elway arrived at halftime for a Little Grizzlies game. He went straight to Heathcote in search of a quick synopsis of the opening two quarters of football.

"Well, there are two possibilities here," Heathcote said. "Number one: Most 10-year-old boys in this state can't walk and chew gum at the same time. Or . . . number 2: Your son is the greatest football player I've ever seen in my life."

What had Dad missed? Oh, nothing much.

Unless, of course, you think the four touchdowns scored by his kid in the first half were worth mentioning.

At age 52, with his eyes on the prize and No Plan B, Elway is still running as fast as he can.

Know what?

They ain't gonna catch Elway before he scores.

8

THE BROTHERS ORANGE

OK, it is time to test your sports knowledge with a trivia quiz.

Question No. 1: Name the athlete who has hit a home run in Wrigley Field, thrown a pass in the Rose Bowl, and shot a duck with Peyton Manning.

"Todd Helton," said Manning.

Yep, Helton. We are talking about the same Helton who crafted a .320 lifetime batting average through 16 major-league seasons as a first baseman for the Colorado Rockies.

Question No. 2: Who was the quarterback ahead of Manning on the depth chart when the University of Tennessee Volunteers opened the 1994 college football season against UCLA in the Rose Bowl?

Helton.

Question No. 3: And who was the first receiver to catch a pass from Manning in Denver?

Helton.

Notice a pattern?

"Helton?" said Manning, pausing to assess how they came to be best friends forever. "We both love the University of Tennessee. We both played quarterback there. We're kind of the same age and have been playing sports at a high level for a long time. We know how much work it takes, and how much time you put into it."

Helton and Manning are the classic rockers of Colorado sports. They are the Brothers Orange, twin legends born on Rocky Top, Tennessee. Of all the reasons Manning chose to start chapter 2 of his NFL career with the Broncos, it would be unwise to underestimate the friendship of Helton.

Amid the dog days of the 2011 NFL lockout, when Manning was hurting and unable to use the training facilities in Indianapolis during the labor dispute, he needed a place to test his throwing arm, left weak from surgery on his neck. Helton invited Manning to Denver. Long before the veteran quarterback ever imagined he would need a place to play football after the Colts, Manning made himself at home in Colorado with an old college buddy.

"I came out to Denver for a week during the lockout, and he opened the Rockies clubhouse to me. There's no way I could've let a baseball player in our facility for a week during the NFL season. And Todd said: "Here, have at it.' For the friend he was to me on that, I'm grateful," Manning told me on the day he signed with the Broncos.

You will hear it from everybody who knows Manning well, from his father to former Indianapolis coach Tony Dungy to a graduate assistant who met him nearly 20 years ago at Tennessee. They all say familiarity is what the quarterback craves, seeks, and needs to succeed.

When Manning could not throw a pass 20 yards without risking major embarrassment in June 2011, where did he find the desired privacy? Well hidden from public view, at the last place anybody would think to look: inside the indoor batting cages at Coors Field. And who was trusted to catch those humbling passes?

"The first pass I threw in Denver was to Helton," Manning told Judy Battista, who covers pro football superbly for the *New York Times*.

It would be more than 20 months after the wobblers caught by Helton that the Broncos would haul in the most high-profile catch in the history of NFL free agency. What was among the first major sporting events Manning attended after signing a contract with Denver?

By much more than coincidence, it was a Rockies baseball game at Coors Field. Manning sat alongside new Broncos teammate Eric Decker that April afternoon, as the home team fell behind 4–0 against the New York Mets.

Down to their last six outs, Colorado loaded the bases in the eighth inning. It was rally cap time. Getting in the spirit, Decker wore his cap with the bill pointing straight up from the middle of his noggin. Left-handed reliever Tim Byrdak was summoned from the bullpen to face Helton. The veteran Rockies slugger, often criticized in recent years for declining statistics and a hefty salary, worked the count to two balls and two strikes. Byrdak tried to sneak a slider past Helton.

Big mistake. Helton crushed the 84 miles-per-hour pitch, sending the baseball soaring off his bat, until a home run smacked the facing of the second deck in right field. Helton's grand slam tied the game. Befitting a bad team that lost 98 times in 2012, the Rockies would waste Helton's heroics and get beat in extra innings. But the shot off Helton's bat was a big, beautiful blast, and nobody had a bigger blast witnessing the homer than Manning. He pointed his right index finger to the sky as the ballpark rocked with the Rocky Mountain thunder for which local fans are famous.

The cheers honored Helton's fourth dinger of the young season's opening month. The 38-year-old first baseman flipped his bat as he briefly admired the shot, and as he circled the bases it was like watching a home movie from a happier time. Helton is the greatest player in Rockies history. Or at least he used to be.

If the baseball gods are keeping score, Helton will be the first player in franchise history enshrined in Cooperstown, New York, alongside Babe Ruth, Bob Gibson, and the game's other legends. But Helton's record of greatness has gathered dust in recent seasons. He led the National League with a .372 batting average in 2000. He pumped fists to the sky, framing the iconic photograph of a city's euphoria, when the Rockies beat the Arizona Diamondbacks to clinch a berth in the 2007 World Series that the baseball world never saw coming.

But chronic back pain sapped his power and tested his confidence, forcing him to seriously contemplate retirement, and that was before his hip gave out on him in 2012. Helton walked tall through it all. Thanks, in no small part, to a longtime friend he could lean on.

"What Todd went through with his back a couple years ago was real. Everybody realizes how hard it was," Manning said. "And I could tell he wasn't sure there for a while."

Helton and Manning understand each other's pain, and have stared down the fears that could have pushed either one of them to go sit on the porch forever. The trust they share required nearly two decades to build. Way back in 1994, in Knoxville, Tennessee, the skinny son of a famous quarterback stuck out his hand and said: "Good to meet you, I'm Peyton Manning." It is a greeting Manning offers new acquaintances to this day, never assuming fame precedes him or excuses a lack of proper manners.

"Yeah, his parents raised him right," Helton told me, his voice ringing with admiration. Then, with the comedic timing that would do the late, great John Belushi proud, Helton raised an eyebrow. There was something more that needed to be said about Manning.

"But as soon as you turn your back, he will give you grief," Helton deadpanned.

According to the unofficial book of guys, that pretty much is the very definition of a true friend: He is a person who can rip you in a way that might get a stranger punched in the mouth, but instead has you rolling on the floor with laughter.

"We've lived similar lives, so we can relate to each other. And we're both obsessive about our jobs," Helton said.

As Helton talked about Manning, he kept taking a peek at the batting cage on a back diamond on the Rockies' perfectly manicured spring training campus in Scottsdale, Arizona. The hint was obvious. Helton was aching to take a few more hacks before the season began. Hall of Fame hitters all have the eye of a hawk and the processing speeds of a supercomputer. But that is seldom enough. Helton is obsessed with the minute details of his swing; he is a teeth-grinder who chews the furniture over every hitless game at the plate.

"I'm a guy who has never been sure of myself, and that's what drives me," said Helton, making a confession that sounded a little odd, coming from a five-time National League all star.

But blessed to do a job that has taken me into the workplaces of Cal Ripken Jr. and Lance Armstrong alike, watching Helton's never-ending desire to improve makes perfect sense. The great ones do not need a push. They are driven 24/7.

Then, Helton said something that startled me.

"Peyton Manning is way more driven than I am," he said.

"Way more?" I stammered. It did not seem humanly possible, to tell the truth. "Are you kidding?"

Helton's eyes narrowed. "Way more," he repeated, as if Manning's intensity also was capable of startling him. "We're not even in the same universe."

Helton, who hates talking about himself, certainly will not say it.

So I will: The Rockies first baseman is a far superior athlete to Manning.

"Don't get me wrong. I was the high school player of the year in football in the state of Tennessee and went to college to play two sports," said Helton, who turned down $450,000 to sign with the San Diego Padres out of high school. "But when I got to school, Heath Shuler was the quarterback. You remember Shuler, don't you? He went in the first round of the draft to the Washington Redskins. So I knew what an NFL quarterback looked like. And I knew it didn't look like me."

In the recorded history of great American multisport athletes, the legendary names that come readily to mind are Jackie Robinson, Jim Brown, Bo Jackson . . . and Helton?

Todd knows baseball. But football? Anybody have a scouting report on Helton as an NFL prospect?

"Todd Helton," former Vols coach Phillip Fulmer once joked to a crew filming an ESPN documentary, "was no more ready to go and be our quarterback than the man in the moon."

But, in the opening game of the 1994 season, looking for a quarter-back to substitute after Tennessee starter Jerry Colquitt seriously injured a knee while running the football early in the game against UCLA, Fulmer looked up and down his bench in the Rose Bowl. He picked Helton over Manning.

At the time, the choice seemed logical. Manning was an 18-year-old freshman, just hoping to get his face on the ABC broadcast long enough for friends back home to catch a glimpse of him. Although Helton had only nine passes on his college football resume, he was a junior. Furthermore, as a star slugger and relief pitcher on the Vols baseball team, Helton was used to walking cold into trouble of somebody else's doing.

Much to his parents' amazement, Manning did get a shot to play against the Bruins, albeit briefly. ABC broadcaster Keith Jackson, who always sounded more like a college football Saturday than a brat sizzling on the grill, took a look at Archie's kid warming up on the sideline and boomed: "There's one pair of sweaty palms right there. That's number 16, Peyton Manning."

Welcome to the big time, kid.

Trotting onto one of the most famous football fields in America, Manning recalled paternal advice. The quarterback, especially a new quarterback, must take charge of the huddle.

What happened next is a story Manning has enjoyed telling many times, a tale he shares because the punch line wallops him squarely between the eyes. We will use the version he relayed to Dan Patrick during an interview for *ESPN the Magazine*.

"I don't think I'm nervous, but all the hair on my arms is just sticking straight up," Manning told Patrick. "We're getting beat 21–0, I think. The team's kind of down. Anyway, I'm jogging in and right then I remember old Dad's pep talk.

"So I get in there and say: 'All right, guys, I know I'm just a freshman, but I can take you down the field right now and lead you to a touchdown.' I'm fired up. And, this left tackle, Jason Layman, grabs me by the shoulders and says: "Peyton Freshman, shut the fuck up and call the fucking play!' No lie.

"I said: 'Yes, sir.' And called the play . . . and I didn't say another word the whole season."

Three times, Manning took the snap. Three times, he handed off the ball for a running play. The Volunteers punted. Manning took a seat. Even stories with fairy-tale endings sometimes begin with a yawn.

No dummy, Fulmer got Helton back in the Tennessee huddle before his freshman quarterback got run out of the stadium by his own teammates. It should be duly noted: Helton rallied the Vols for 23 points in the fourth quarter, ultimately completing 14 of 28 passes for 165 yards and a touchdown, in a narrow, two-point loss to UCLA. Not bad for a first baseman.

During the fourth game of the '94 season, however, as Tennessee fell out of the national rankings, Helton banged up his knee against Mississippi State. This time, Manning checked in the huddle again and never departed. This time, Manning did make it his football team. There were absolutely no hard feelings. Helton had other dreams, soon to be fulfilled by the Rockies making him the eighth overall selection in the first round of major-league baseball's 1995 draft.

With pride as vibrant as the orange worn by the Tennessee Volunteers, the friendship of Manning and Helton runs deep. But not quite as deep as a post pattern. In fact, the very fact that Helton and Manning keep it real between them explains why the first baseman had to quit the quarterback's football team, before he got cut.

"I can't catch. Catch a football? No way," Helton said. "Now, you give me a first baseman's glove, and I can catch a baseball. But when [Manning] throws a football? That's not for me. It hurts your hands too much."

After the spinal fusion surgery that forced Manning to miss his final season in Indianapolis and ultimately led to his release from the Colts, Manning went to work at Duke University with coach David Cutcliffe, the same coach who had recruited him to Tennessee long ago. The program Cutcliffe put together was a brilliant combination of 21st-century rehabilitation techniques and old-school woodshedding. All in the name of getting Manning's act together. A handful of friends came down to North Carolina to help Manning find his groove.

Among the private receiving corps was Helton. How does a middle-aged first baseman run a skinny post route?

"Very slowly," said Helton, chuckling at the memory.

Manning, however, had no time to do anything slowly. He was in a hurry to get back in NFL shape. And Helton quickly felt the sting of the perfectionist that burns at 500 degrees in the belly of Manning.

"Baseball is a totally different mind-set than football, and for good reason. I mean, in his sport, they're trying to kill each other," Helton said. "I was lost on a few of the routes. [Manning] tells you one time how to do it, and expects you to know what you're doing. He kept calling for a check down. And I didn't know where to go. I kept telling him: 'What the hell are you talking about?'"

In the most essential way, a pro locker room is no different than the one you knew in high school. Blood, sweat, and tears adhere stronger than Crazy Glue. Humor is the male defense mechanism to mask the underlying affection.

"I didn't know anybody when I got drafted to Indianapolis. And that wasn't easy," Manning said. "When I got to Denver, it was easier. Why? Because of Todd."

The wrinkles and the grays in the mirror are much easier to laugh at when you have a sidekick to help stare down your athletic mortality. Helton is the Sundance Kid to Manning's Butch Cassidy. They hear the clock ticking. It's all borrowed time and stolen memories now. But, as long as Manning and Helton are on the way out, they figure it might as well be in a blaze of glory.

All summer long, Manning was a regular in the seats at Coors Field. "I probably went to a dozen Rockies games," he said.

And when the Broncos started playing at Sports Authority Field, who was sitting alongside Ashley Manning, as she cheered her husband? Helton. "I don't think Todd missed one game," the quarterback said.

After a Denver victory, it would often be Manning and Helton, sitting around the dinner table, breaking bread, cracking up, sharing the aches and pains of growing old.

"We've always had a good friendship," Manning said. "But it obviously has been strengthened this year. And I really, really appreciate the value of a good friend."

In June 2011, Manning tentatively threw a football to Helton in the Rockies batting cage, a pass with so little oomph it crash-landed so pathetically into his old buddy's arms that at first the first baseman thought it was a joke.

In February 2013, the plan was for Helton to watch Manning throw a beautiful spiral for a touchdown at the Super Bowl in New Orleans. But, as comedian Woody Allen once said: "If you want to hear God laugh, tell him your plans." Yes, even if they are the best-laid plans of a Hall of Fame quarterback and stellar first baseman.

That was Baltimore linebacker Ray Lewis whooping and laughing as the Ravens wrecked the Super Bowl dream of Manning and his famous sidekick with a shocking 38–35 overtime loss in the NFL playoffs.

So, as the city of Denver cursed and moped, Butch and Sundance hightailed it out of town. Helton bought some ammunition, packed up the truck, and dragged Manning along to do some hunting on a cross-country road trip.

The silence of a dawn hunt helps empty a guy's noggin of any of the regrets rattling around in there.

"He's trying to get over it. I don't know when that happens, or how," said Archie Manning, who told the Associated Press that his son killed a duck in Colorado and a deer in Mississippi during a stretch of 24 hours.

Picture this: Helton and Manning watching the birds fly, anticipating the perfect moment to squeeze the trigger.

In fact, there is a photo of the first baseman and the quarterback standing together and grinning alongside a pickup, with the tailgate down, and truck bed ready to be stacked with dead ducks.

If you cannot go get a Super Bowl ring, what is a man to do?

Clean the rifle, grab a buddy, and go shoot dinner.

9

WHO'S IN CHARGE?

John Fox stopped the insanity.

Shortly after sunrise on a summer morning shortly before one of Fox's first preseason workouts as the Broncos' new coach in 2011, I stood in grass still wet from the overnight sprinkling and asked a sleepy-eyed player: "What's the biggest difference between training camp this year and when Josh McDaniels was in charge?"

"Well," the player said, a sly grin prefacing his answer, "I guess you could say we have an adult coaching the team now."

Everybody likes Uncle Foxy.

The 14th head coach in Broncos history will not go down in NFL history as a great innovator in the mold of Paul Brown or as a towering sideline presence as intimidating as Vince Lombardi. In fact, anybody who thinks Fox knows X's and O's better than his predecessor, Josh McDaniels, is nuts.

But coaching is about way more than drawing up a game plan. Pro football can be a stressful world defined by uncertainty and anxiety, from sudden-death overtime to nonguaranteed contracts. Fox has a gift. No matter how crazy it gets, Foxy exudes a simple thought as soothing as the chorus of a Bob Marley reggae song: "Don't worry about a thing, cuz every little thing is gonna be all right."

Fox's coaching mantra: Under-sell. Over-deliver.

Get out of the way, and let whatever talent is inside a player shine, whether it is Tim Tebow running around like a headless chicken until he bumps into a miracle or Peyton Manning directing every detail as if all movements between the white lines are controlled by the Matrix.

John Elway hired Fox in January 2011 for a reason. He was a silver Foxy, with gray in his hair, a coach well past his fiftieth birthday. No doubt, part of the appeal was Fox had been around the block, to the Super Bowl and back, from an apprenticeship he took with Pittsburgh Steelers icon Chuck Noll in 1989, to nine years running his own shop as head coach of the Carolina Panthers.

Elway went counter to what had been a long-standing tradition in Denver, a city that had seen, from McDaniels to Mike Shanahan to Dan Reeves, more than its share of bright young offensive minds who brought to town no shortage of ideas or ego. Fox was not only a defensive coach, but downright avuncular. No, check that. After a lengthy meeting with Fox on the day he was introduced to Colorado, I walked away thinking of another coach with a homespun wit and a gentle touch: Jack Elway, father of the greatest player in Broncos history.

Fox immediately fulfilled the number one purpose of his hiring. He returned the sanity to Dove Valley, after McDaniels drove everybody to distraction during his tumultuous stint of chaos, which was akin to being stuck on a roller coaster for 23 months.

At Harmon's Pub in Canton, the pigskin-obsessed Ohio town where a young McDaniels had thrown passes in a prep stadium across the street from the Pro Football Hall of Fame, the friendly barkeep's name is Matt Cunningham. He owns the joint, which is a perfect mix of Cleveland Indians games on TV, chicken wings so spicy they burn your lips, and sing-along anthems from Bon Jovi or Journey thumping through the sound system.

A pal of McDaniels since childhood, Cunningham needed to ask a visitor from Denver a serious question. But the inquiry could wait. There was a drink to shake and shot glasses to fill with a diabolical combination of Captain Morgan, Coke, and Red Bull. This specialty of the house is called a Ric Flair, named in honor of the flamboyant pro wrestler, better known to his legion of fans as The Nature Boy.

Why name a drink after Flair?

Because after you throw back the shot, it makes you shout Nature Boy's trademark catchphrase: "Woooo!"

As soon as my head stopped spinning, Cunningham asked: "OK, why couldn't McDaniels ever catch a break with Broncos fans? They would've liked Josh, if they got to know him."

There, in a nutshell, was the downfall of the McDaniels regime.

Players never knew which McDaniels was going to show up to Dove Valley. A buddy who wanted to exchange fist bumps and play rap during the team stretch. Or the raving lunatic caught by NFL Network cameras during a victory over the New York Giants in 2009, dressing down his offense by shouting: "All we're trying to do is win a mother-fucking game!"

He was the baby-faced Kid McD, hired by the Broncos at age 33, looking like a mere child dressed up like an NFL coach for Halloween. McDaniels arrived in Denver from the New England Patriots, wearing his hoodie. He came off as a Bill Belichick wannabe.

The real issue with McDaniels, however, was not arrogance, as often presumed by detractors who never took the time to get under the hoodie, where a whistle-twirling bundle of nervous energy hid behind his insecurities. McDaniels knew football, but did not know how to act as an NFL coach.

"You react as your leader reacts," former Broncos linebacker Mario Haggan once told me. "If your leader is a guy who's out there cursing and making life hard, it trickles down to the players. If your leader is having fun and makes work fun in a way that coincides with what his players like to do, that shapes how his guys will be."

Fake anger or fake authority does not work in an NFL locker room. Pro football players can smell phony baloney from 100 yards away. McDaniels never let the Broncos, much less the team's fans, see what was genuinely inside his heart for more than a few, fleeting seconds at a time. He never gave anybody in Denver a compelling reason or real chance to root for him.

McDaniels could F-bomb a player straight to hell.

Fox, on the other hand, has the uncanny knack of being able to make an F-bomb sound like he just let you in on a private joke, with him as the punch line.

"You gotta love Foxy," said Patrick Smyth, the team's savvy executive director of media relations. "He's a real beauty."

Maybe the real beauty of Foxy is this: In a voice as raspy dry as vodka shaken on the rocks, his coaching sneaks up on you. And the message goes down as smoothly as the contents of a $12 martini. Next thing you know, it seems as if his idea was yours in the first place.

So it was by plan, not coincidence, that Fox placed the opening telephone call to Manning, on the very day the veteran quarterback was released by the Indianapolis Colts. There was no hard sell. Fox merely wanted Manning to know the Broncos would love to have him come out to Colorado for a visit, no rush, whenever the quarterback was good and ready.

Is the picture coming into focus? Smooth as a $12 martini, with a twist, no olives.

St. Patrick's Day is the wedding anniversary of Peyton and Ashley Manning. On a Saturday morning, March 17, 2012, with NFL teams anxiously awaiting word from the free-agent quarterback and the Manning family facing one of the biggest decisions of their 11 years of marriage together, Fox texted a simple message to both the groom and his lovely bride: "Happy Anniversary." This is the oldest trick in the recruiting playbook. Win the mother's heart and the player will follow.

A gentle tug on the heartstrings in the direction of Denver with happy anniversary wishes makes for a cute story, but the important question was adroitly asked by *Sports Illustrated* pro football expert Peter King: Where did Foxy get Ashley Manning's cell number? "Top secret," Fox told King. "I recruited for 10 years in college. I was pretty good."

Beginning to understand? Smooth as a $12 martini, shaken, not stirred.

But Foxy is seldom confused for Agent 007, as Manning gleefully told his teammates on the charter flight back from a road victory against Kansas City in November of the quarterback's first season with the Broncos.

With a comedic touch honed by his work on *Saturday Night Live*, Manning made a habit of grabbing the flight attendant's microphone and giving a quick review of team performances during the 11-game win streak to close the regular season. According to one of my spies on the plane, Manning noted the Broncos beat the Chiefs 17–9, despite some intelligence provided by Foxy on Kansas City personnel that proved to be erroneous.

"Nice work, James Bond," Manning announced over the loudspeaker, as everybody in the traveling party laughed. And nobody thought it was funnier than Uncle Foxy.

In a profession where many coaches act as if they invented the game, Fox is comfortable enough in his own skin to do what serves his team rather than his vanity.

"My biggest advice for somebody who's going to be a head coach would be: 'Just be you. Don't try to be somebody else.' Most of us aren't smart enough to be somebody else," Fox said.

After the Broncos opened with only a single victory in the opening five games during his debut season, Fox handed the keys to the offense to Tim Tebow in October 2011. Cynics suggested it was to show knucklehead fans the stupidity of their demand that Tebow get a shot. Balderdash, insisted Fox, who added that setting Tebow up to fail would have been akin to "buying a Ferrari and pouring sugar in the gas tank."

Undeterred by the knowledge that failure would make him the target of derision, Fox ripped up his playbook in the middle of the season for Tebow, then asked his players to turn back the clock 60 years and drop the forward pass like a bad habit. "Put in this offense and some quarterbacks in the league would look at you like you had three heads. Tebow feeds off it," said Fox. His trust in Tebow was rewarded with an unlikely playoff berth, but only two votes in the 2011 NFL Coach of the Year balloting.

There is no hiding his conservative nature. Rival NFL coaches know it. As you might expect from the son of a U.S. Navy Seal, Fox carries out the mission. He rarely colors outside the lines of the game plan.

Here is a prime example: Leading New England 13–7 in the second quarter of a regular-season game in December 2011, Tebow scrambled inside the 10-yard line of the Patriots, setting up a fourth-down-and-one situation. The Broncos were flagged for holding on Tebow's run. Rather than push back Denver with the penalty yardage, New England's Belichick let the play stand, daring Fox to be bold and go for it on fourth down.

But, sure enough, Fox sent in the field goal unit, eschewing the opportunity to score an early knockout blow. A 26-yard chip shot by Matt Prater put the Broncos ahead 16–7. The Patriots would score 27 unanswered points. And Denver lost the game. It would be unfair to pin the defeat solely on Fox, especially on a day the Broncos' defense was torched by quarterback Tom Brady. Fox's conservative nature, however, allowed an ample window of opportunity for New England to climb back in the contest.

Yes, there is some fuddy-duddy in the Broncos coach. What else would anyone expect from Fox, whose coaching principles were nurtured at the hand of no-frills, no-fuss Noll? "You are what you eat," Fox has often told me.

In an interview with Gary Dulac of the *Pittsburgh Post-Gazette*, Fox revealed why he is a reasonable facsimile of Noll, detailing the attributes he admired in the Steelers coach: "I think he's the greatest guy I've ever been around. [Noll] is very calm, very technique-oriented, very fundamental-oriented. He is not a screamer. He wasn't up or down. I think the biggest thing is that he was the same guy every day. He was not an ego guy like, 'Look what I'm doing.' I thought he was a great mentor."

When Manning decided to join forces with Fox in Denver, the move was blasted as a dumb business decision by *MarketWatch*, which

screamed this headline: "Peyton Manning blew it by picking Broncos."
Columnist Jon Friedman insisted: "He should've signed instead with
the San Francisco 49ers." The reasons given were: (1) too many bliz-
zards in Denver, (2) Broncos not contenders, (3) Tim Tebow backlash,
and (4) Frank Gore carries the rock in San Francisco.

Which only goes to prove: Wall Street pundits are even worse at
analyzing football than keeping your 401(k) out of harm's way.

San Francisco's Jim Harbaugh is a brilliant coach, maybe the best in
the NFL. But he also is an arrogant, loudmouthed lout (not that there's
anything wrong with that). His type A personality and Manning's obsessive perfection would have never peacefully coexisted.

Sometimes, it is hard to tell who is in charge of the Broncos. During
games, nobody does more coaching on the Denver sideline than Manning. That is precisely why Fox was a much better choice for this partic-
ular quarterback than Harbaugh, whose demeanor from the opening
kickoff to the final gun is half-man, half-Doberman.

"My impression of what's most important for a football coach is: Can
you get guys to play hard for you? There are different ways to do that,"
Manning told Mike Klis of the *Denver Post*. "There are scare tactics,
fear tactics where you're scared if you don't make this tackle they may
cut you next week. That's worked. I've had coaches where you just like
them so much you don't want to let them down. I'd say Fox is in that
category. I think players really like him. He's very fair to players.
There's no reason guys shouldn't be going out there laying it on the
line."

Players break rocks for Harbaugh. Manning works in concert with
Fox.

Foxy is far more concerned with winning than reminding everybody
who is the boss.

"It's all about winning. Football is only fun if you win." said Fox, who
wouldn't dare think of coloring a single gray hair on his 57-year-old
head to make himself look like somebody he is not.

Everybody at the team's Dove Valley headquarters can read and
understand the organizational chart. But, just as Elway learned the

painful way with Dan Reeves, it gives a team a better shot at the fun that accompanies winning if a veteran quarterback and an experienced coach can both shelve the egos and work as peers, rather than wrestle over power.

"Peyton is a great player, there's no argument to that. But he's also a guy who wants to be coached and wants to do it the right way," Fox said. "He has one Super Bowl ring, so he has an understanding of how it gets done. That allows a great understanding between us, as coach and quarterback. Because, you know, this isn't my first rodeo, either."

Maybe it was Elway's charisma, or the common bond between Hall of Fame quarterbacks, that initially attracted Manning to Denver. But contrary to the analysts who cavalierly treated this decision like a fantasy football transaction rather than drilling down to inspect the core issues of an effective business relationship, Manning did not blow it by choosing the Broncos over San Francisco or Tennessee. Why? Give credit to Foxy. The way he does business works for Manning.

"Everybody has got his own way of coaching. And there are a lot of ways to have success coaching," Fox said. "Me? I'm comfortable with empowering players to lead the team."

Beneath his aw-shucks veneer, however, Foxy is fiercely competitive. Suggest he might rank more at the middle of the pack among the NFL's 32 head coaches rather than at the top alongside Harbaugh or Belichick and Fox will retort: "When you're one of 32, or whatever, in this profession, I think everybody's pretty much gold standard."

During training camp, when some knucklehead suggested in the pages of the *Denver Post* that the Broncos' defensive personnel were more suited to a three-down lineman and four-linebacker alignment than the defense Fox was employing, he shot down the criticism with a joke.

"Did Vince Lombardi come back and write that?" Fox asked, knowing full well the column was penned by me. Fox playfully stuck the needle in my funny bone, when other NFL coaches might have angrily gone for the jugular.

With a laugh, Fox added: "I think everybody's entitled to their opinions, but I think we have some fairly proven minds on our staff. We appreciate the suggestions. But I think we might know a little bit more."

Uncle Foxy gives the impression that when he turns out the lights at Dove Valley, he goes home, puts a chew between his cheek and gum and commences to whittle. The reality? He is a reader. Books. Serious books. *Lone Survivor*, the tale of one U.S. military hero who escaped alive from a bloody battle on the Afghanistan-Pakistan border, is definitely not a page-turner for the fainthearted, but it fully engaged the mind of Fox.

Although raised in a military family, Fox seldom shakes an iron fist. He does, however, firmly believe that once men pull on uniforms, they are all equals.

It was that guiding principle that led Fox to a rather unorthodox way of holding his players accountable. When the Broncos watched video of their games during 2012, coaches were not present. Placing trust in veteran leaders such as Manning and cornerback Champ Bailey, players switched off the lights in the meeting room, turned on the tape, and corrected their own mistakes.

"We watch the game film together, just the players. Coaches aren't in there," Manning said. "It's each player's job to speak up on what he did wrong."

Players in charge? Really? Can you imagine McDaniels allowing that to happen?

In the NFL, which has the reputation of being as flexible as a straitjacket, the idea sounds almost as wacky as putting Jack Nicholson in charge of the Cuckoo's Nest. But it is simpler than you think, Chief. This crazy notion was thoroughly thought out before Fox implemented it.

"A very common thing in the military is debriefing. They spend a lot of time in the preparation of their mission, then they debrief. It's a process that's rankless. What your name is doesn't matter," Fox said.

"One of the dysfunctional aspects of any football team can be unhealthy conflict, or even the fear of conflict. Now, I know conflict can be a rough word that scares some people. But, if you're going to win in this business, guys have to own up to their errors."

Bailey blows a coverage? He hears about it. Tackle Ryan Clady misses an assignment? His Pro Bowl pedigree gets zero credit from his peers.

"Everybody is held accountable, from the top to the bottom. We take our stripes off in the defensive meeting room, and we go after each other," Broncos linebacker Wesley Woodyard said.

There is one adage respected by all who wear an NFL uniform: The eye in the sky does not lie. The All-22 videotape of a football game sees all, knows all, and reveals all. Oh, Fox and his staff dissect the film. They hand grade sheets to the players.

Then, however, old Uncle Foxy departs the meeting room and leaves his conservatism at the door.

"We, as coaches, trust our players to take ownership of getting better. In the end, this is their team," Fox said.

"It sounds simple, like a lot of things in football do. But it's not easy. Nothing in the NFL is easy."

10

SIGNED WITH RESPECT

Let's go for a ride on the way-back time machine, rewinding the years at warp speed to 1997. We take this trip as a reminder of how quickly lives can be turned upside down. The world spins so fast, it can be hard to hang on, let alone keep pace with all the changes.

With a crazy notion that people would buy a hybrid automobile, Toyota gave birth to the Prius in 1997. Princess Diana died in a car accident, and a worldwide television audience of two billion grieved during her funeral. Steve Jobs returned as interim CEO of a quirky but struggling company, in the hope he could save Apple Computer from financial doom. In a college football preview issue published August 18, 1997, the *Sporting News* adorned its cover with a photograph of the quarterback for their preseason number one team, a superb athlete named . . .

John Hessler, quarterback of the Colorado Buffaloes.

"Yeah," said Hessler, as he slid a copy of the old *Sporting News* from '97 across a table. "But I want you to open up this magazine and see the story of another college quarterback who wasn't on the cover. Tell me his name."

Peyton Manning.

"Just one of the guys" was the headline on the Manning feature, written by David Climer, whose portrait of the University of Tennessee senior holds up remarkably well 16 years later. As I read a handful of paragraphs aloud, Hessler suppressed a cat-that-ate-the-canary grin in his seat across from me in a suburban Denver restaurant.

"For three years, Manning didn't have time to find the roses, much less stop and smell them. He ran from classroom to football field to speaking engagement to the library," I said, reciting the words on page S-8 of the 16-year-old magazine, its pages beginning to turn yellow with age. "[Manning] now has learned the fine art of the post-lunch nap, which, come to think of it, is something normally mastered by the greenest of freshman instead of the orangest of seniors."

Hessler laughed out loud. "I know one thing: I was way better at naps than Manning. Way better," said Hessler, now 38 years old and a Northglenn resident, living in a cozy house a stone's throw away from Interstate 25. "Remember what they called me? Mad Magazine. Friends started calling me that long before I got to CU, because I looked like Alfred E. Neuman. What! Me worry?"

But, in 1997, Mr. Mad Magazine made the cover of one of America's most-respected sports publications. Ranking every major football program in the land, the *Sporting News* predicted the Buffaloes to be number one. Dead last in the preseason rankings was a football school that seemed doomed to be famous for little else besides potatoes and a home field covered with blue Smurf turf: Boise State.

The story celebrating the nation's top-ranked team was written by Terry Frei, who focused on Rick Neuheisel, building a name for himself with his rock 'n' roll spirit, his great offensive mind, and his lack of patience with slackers who cruised through life like Alfred E. Neuman.

"While working with quarterbacks, Neuheisel is like a perfectionist music professor who wants to make his pupils into prodigies and blows his stack when pupils don't share his obsession," wrote Frei, nailing the personality of one of the rising stars in the coaching game during the 1990s. "Last fall, Neuheisel was irate when Hessler—who was solid as a '95 fill-in for [Koy] Detmer—couldn't seem to get his brain out of low gear. When Hessler was oblivious to the slight adjustments, Neuheisel exploded in practice."

The big bang theory was built on matter and antimatter. Well, here are two theories about building a football team. Get yourself a quarter-back as obsessive as Manning, where every detail matters. Or find a QB who forgets about the dangers and thinks of the fun. Hessler was the anti-Manning.

Hessler, a coach on the field? Not exactly. But Hessler could have taught Manning a thing or two about not sweating the small stuff. May-be he could never read a defensive alignment with the instant recogni-tion that Manning did, but Hessler had the 20/20 vision to see life is good, even when a coach is spewing venom in your face. "Nobody could make Coach Neuheisel yell like I did. Nobody," said Hessler, with a mischievously twisted sense of pride. "Know what? Most of the time, I deserved it. But every word that Coach Neu shouted at me? It was love. Pure love."

You don't have to be a weatherman to know: Tomorrow pays no heed to predictions.

Manning led Tennessee to 11 victories in 1997, including a scrap-book-worthy comeback from 13 points down to beat Auburn 30–29 in the Southeastern Conference championship game that earned the Vols a berth in the Orange Bowl. The trophy case haul for Manning included the Maxwell Award, the Davey O'Brien Award and a second-place fin-ish behind Michigan cornerback Charles Woodson in the Heisman Tro-phy balloting.

On his way to the Heisman ceremony in New York, Manning stopped by the set of *Late Night with David Letterman*. He threw a perfect spiral across 53rd Street into an open second-story window on a dare by Letterman, and joked about having a bursa sac injury checked out in Manhattan. "It was the same doctor you went to eight years ago," Manning told Letterman, "for your knee, I think." Amazed and amused at the depth to which a college senior had studied the comedian's biog-raphy in preparation for the show, Letterman cackled and quipped: "The kid's got writers."

In fact, Manning might have taken home the Heisman as a souvenir from that trip to New York, if not for Hessler. During Michigan's season-opener, Woodson started the last successful campaign by a defensive player to win college football's biggest prize. What was Woodson's first Heisman moment? Leaping high to intercept a pass underthrown by Colorado's senior quarterback. The Wolverines won the game 27–3. CU's national championship designs were shattered. And the Buffaloes never figured out how to put the pieces back together again. Colorado finished with a disappointing 5-6 record, when a gritty fourth-quarter rally against Nebraska led by Hessler fell three points short of redemption.

"Wanna know the truth? My head was never right all season long," Hessler told me. Hidden from the headlines was the real nitty-gritty of why Hessler was so distracted. On November 4, three days after the Buffaloes lost to Missouri in Boulder, Hessler became the father to a son, a child born out of wedlock. "Being a dad is a blessing," Hessler confessed, "but at the time, I was a mess."

Manning had no such drama. He was the first player taken in the 1998 draft, by Indianapolis.

Hessler began the same odyssey experienced by many young men fresh out of college, with no map for the rest of life. Hessler chased dreams on both sides of the Atlantic Ocean, briefly playing quarterback for vino and pizza in Europe. He also spectacularly failed in an attempt to get back together with his true sports love, as a minor-leaguer with the Colorado Rockies baseball organization. "Lost my fastball while playing quarterback in college. And I never did find it," Hessler said.

His glory days had passed Hessler by. Early in his college career, after Hessler had come off the bench to rally the Buffaloes to victory against third-ranked Texas, Neuheisel proclaimed: "John Hessler is going to go down in Colorado football history as the Comeback Kid."

Little did Neuheisel know how prophetic those words would ultimately be.

Settled in a thoroughly adult routine as a seventh-grade social studies teacher and an assistant football coach at Regis Jesuit High School, Hessler was driving down Highway 76 near Denver in October 2003 when he got blindsided by a hit that nearly killed him. A Chevy Blazer clipped Hessler's Honda Accord, sending him careening across the median and into the path of a pickup truck. The driver of the SUV stepped on the gas, ran like a coward, and has never been caught.

Hessler was lucky to get to the hospital alive. He slipped into a coma that lasted 33 days. "There was a time when the doctors gave me 24 hours to live. Do you believe it? That's one thing that blows my mind," Hessler said.

His weight dropped to 143 pounds. A titanium plate was used to patch his skull. Hessler felt trapped inside his broken body. A quarterback who once threw two touchdown passes in the Cotton Bowl was told extremely depressing news: Relearning to walk would take years.

Why get out of bed and out of the house, if there was no place to go, no job waiting, no real hope? Hessler stopped dreaming. He forgot how. At one point, there was a do-not-resuscitate order taped to his refrigerator door. He cursed God and cried. "We're not talking little tears," Hessler said. "I was flat-out bawling, crying so hard to the point where I couldn't breathe."

Nearly a decade after being left for dead at the side of the road, a guy who never sweated the small details still has difficulty getting the trivial details of life to stick in his brain, a lingering effect of the accident. For example: Regardless of how many times Hessler visits his favorite neighborhood lunch spot, he never recalls whether or not flavored ice tea is on the menu, and checks each visit with the waitress, as if asking for the first time.

But, from his personality to his fondest memories, everything that is essential to making him "Hess" survived the tragic accident, stronger than ever. The lyrics of a favorite song by Rascal Flatts? Every word is chiseled in Hessler's brain. "Hoping I would find love along the broken road," Hessler will croon, tears of joy unabashedly streaming down his cheek. Or ask what date changed his life forever, and without a second of hesitation, Hessler will respond: "April 20, 2007."

That is the spring day a physical therapist named Sarah Bindel walked into his life and took a sledgehammer to the metal walker Hessler used more as an emotional crutch than a tool to support his weight.

Bindel was the first person able to make Hessler stop the pity party, get off his lazy butt, and stand on his own two feet.

No wonder Hessler fell so hard in love with her. They married in February 2010. "Who would have thought I'd ever get married? Well, to tell the truth, nobody," Hessler said. "As Sarah was walking down the aisle toward me at the wedding, I cried. I thought the day would never come. It was a better feeling than anything I ever did playing sports. Why? Football is only temporary. Being married is forever."

These days, Hessler volunteers as an assistant coach in football and baseball at his neighborhood high school. He has taught himself to play golf. He watches Colorado or the Broncos with as unblinkingly tough, analytical eyes as Neuheisel ever watched him. But the childlike wonder for sports has never left Hessler, which is why he digs memorabilia: a T-shirt brought back to the United States from the Summer Olympics in London; a baseball cap from the Traverse City Beach Bums, an independent team of misfits based in Michigan; an autograph from a pro athlete. All tickle him. But, when it comes to an autograph, not just any name scribbled on a scrap of paper will do. Hessler only collects autographs from the best.

Manning was raised by a famous quarterback. Archie taught his son more than how to play a quarterback, he taught him what it meant to be a quarterback. By example, the elder Manning also demonstrated that being a quarterback also required a man to serve as a goodwill ambassador for your team, your city, and your sport.

From Knoxville to Indianapolis to Denver, the current Broncos quarterback has passed too many milestones to count. But, without doing an official count, Manning can be pretty confident he has signed his name on a ticket, T-shirt, or football more than twice for every one of his 60,000 passing yards in the NFL.

"Growing up with a dad who got asked for a lot of autographs, I used to see it a lot after games," Manning said. "After wins or after losses, he always took time to sign. It makes an impression on a young kid."

It does not require more than a few seconds to create a lifetime memory. During one of the earliest days of his first training camp with the Broncos, Manning spotted a young boy carrying a plastic water bottle and asked the kid if he could lend a thirsty NFL quarterback a swallow. Wide-eyed, the boy watched one of the all-time great players squeeze the bottle, as Manning sprayed a stream of cool refreshment into the same mouth that had been barking signals to Demaryius Thomas only minutes earlier.

Before handing the bottle back to the kid, Manning secretly gave the lid two quick turns. When his new, young friend raised the bottle and squeezed, the lid popped off, and a small waterfall splashed the boy's face. Got ya! This classic, harmless football prank gets them every time. Punked by an NFL legend. For a Broncos fan, it was a story guaranteed to bring laughter in the retelling for a lifetime.

Rather than head for the showers, Manning gladly signs under the heat of the summer sun. During the week of the Pro Bowl, when a tropical rainstorm not only put an early halt to practice but also made a tourist wonder if Oahu might sink into the Pacific Ocean, I got as drenched as Carl Spackler during his "I don't think the heavy stuff's gonna come down for quite a while" scene in the movie *Caddyshack*, as Manning signed for a line of admirers that went on forever. With every stroke of his pen from Denver to Hawaii, Manning built a relationship with a new fan base, adding a line to the second chapter of his NFL life.

"Sometimes I hear, 'So and so is a jerk,'" said Manning, repeating a frequent fan lament about some "stuck-up" athlete. "I'm like, 'Why is he a jerk?' And they say, 'Well, he was sprinting to catch his flight and I asked him for an autograph and he wouldn't sign.' I go: 'Well, maybe he had to catch his flight.'"

After beating the Chiefs 17–9 in Kansas City on Thanksgiving weekend, Manning was walking toward the Broncos team bus when he was stopped by an autograph hound. It was Chiefs starting running back Jamaal Charles, running an errand for his mother, who was too bashful to ask Manning. "She was shy. So I told my mom, 'Give me the paper, I'll go do it for you,'" Charles said.

A television crew caught the scene on video, and it became a source of controversy among the crabbier faction of Chiefs Nation, with critics complaining that if Charles was not so starstruck by Manning, Kansas City might have had a better shot at beating the Broncos quarterback. Newsflash: Football is a violent and competitive, but it seldom resembles the 100-yard war we saw in the larger-than-life myths created by NFL Films. "I don't think it was a big deal," said Charles, absolutely unashamed about getting a signature from Manning. "People do it every week. We're like brothers, a fraternity in the game."

Once you're in the football brotherhood, that fraternity membership is good for life, no matter where life might take you. Random acts of kindness are not only permitted in the league, but take place on any given Sunday.

During his 11th NFL season, Justin Bannan wrestled in the trenches as a defensive tackle with the Broncos. Way back in 1997, during that lousy senior season Hessler had with the Buffaloes, Bannan was a freshman from California on that Colorado team. The quarterback made Bannan feel at home.

And the football fraternity never forgets. Out of a sense of modesty, Bannan will probably hate the world knowing, but he left two tickets for Hessler to attend every home Broncos game in 2012.

"I never met Peyton Manning in college. But I knew about him, and I knew he was stinking good. Now, I sit in the stadium, and as I see Manning come to the line of scrimmage and do his checks, I'm thinking along with him, predicting what he will do with the football in my mind. In my head, I'm playing quarterback along with him. I love watching Manning, and here's what I admire: I bet Peyton Manning had to completely relearn how to throw a football after those neck surgeries. When he first picked up a football, it had to feel foreign in his hand. But look at him now. He's amazing," said Hessler, who has a hard-earned appreciation for the rigor, stress, and uncertainty of major rehabilitation.

"I know one thing: Just because a guy's an NFL quarterback doesn't mean he's any good. Manning is one of the greatest of all time. But I can't even believe Tim Tebow is in the dang league. I used to hear people in Denver say, 'Thank God for Tebow.' And I thought at the time: 'If God's a Broncos fan, then why are we stuck with Tebow?' If

God had a plan for the Broncos, then it must have been for Tebow to leave town, so we could have Peyton Manning as our quarterback. Thank God."

Every true orange-and-blue Broncomaniac has a game-day ritual. In 2012, this was what Hessler did every Sunday that Denver played at home, without fail. He would rise early, pack a lunch with his wife, then ride to the stadium, arriving four hours before kickoff. Then, Sarah and he would claim a spot near the players' entrance to the locker room.

Hessler was on a mission. He wanted Manning's autograph. The quarterback signs before games. Week after week, from the home-opener against Pittsburgh to a late October date against New Orleans, Hessler and his spouse would stake out Manning. Week after week, they would fail to get his attention.

But give up? No way.

The security guards at the stadium recognized the former CU star. Hessler asked a friend on the Broncos' staff to tell Manning to look for him. Finally, on November 18, when Hessler shouted to number 18, Manning stopped.

Two of the premier college quarterbacks of 1997, face-to-face after all these years.

Gripped tight in Hessler's hands was one of his most cherished pieces of sports memorabilia: A 16-year-old copy of the *Sporting News*, with his face on the cover.

"My words to him were: 'Hey, Peyton Manning, do you remember this magazine from your senior year at Tennessee?'" Hessler said. "Peyton looked at the magazine cover. And he looked at me. And then Peyton looked back at my photo on the magazine again. He got a weird look on his face and said: 'What the heck?'"

Hessler implored Manning to open the magazine to a page marked with a paper clip. The Broncos' quarterback took a gander at the *Sporting News* story on him as a far younger man. Next to a photograph of a young QB throwing a football in a Tennessee uniform, Manning signed his name, and handed the magazine back to Hessler.

"Thanks, man," said Hessler, his voice full of gratitude. But the Alfred E. Neuman inside him couldn't resist. And, peer to peer, Hessler needled Manning, the way athletes do: "The *Sporting News* put me on the cover and not you, buddy. You've got to love that."

Manning shook his head and chuckled.

"I remember Hessler well from playing at Colorado. But until Chris Valenti, our equipment guy with the Broncos, who's also a big Buff supporter, told me about everything Hessler has been through since he left CU, I was not aware of it," Manning told me, vividly remembering the scene weeks after crossing paths with Hessler in the parking lot of Sports Authority Stadium at Mile High. "I've got to say, it was good to finally meet him. He's a quarterback from my era. We had just a short visit, but it will be hard to forget. I would say in the autograph world, nothing surprises me any more. But when Hessler handed me a magazine with his face on the cover? That was a new request I had not ever seen. A first for me. That was definitely a new one."

There were skeptics who wondered if Manning could ever walk back on an NFL field and command the same respect as before his neck surgeries.

After his auto accident, there were nights when Hessler wondered if he would ever walk again without fear of falling.

Once a quarterback, always a quarterback.

It's the best fraternity in sports.

Every autograph by Manning is signed with respect for how lucky he is to be a quarterback.

Once in a blue moon, an autograph might even be the signature moment forever linking the lives of two strangers.

11

GENIUS AT WORK

Peyton Manning sees a different game than you or me. On the football field, he sees dead people. Oh, they are still breathing. But the defenders are dead before the football is snapped, with no chance to prevent Manning from throwing another dagger to the heart.

Touchdown, Denver.

Manning has a beautiful mind, but the eye of an artist.

To break down every nuance of a game and grade the performance of players, NFL coaches rely on the eye in the sky, a camera placed high above the stadium floor that provides an unblinking view called the All-22, which tracks every movement and mistake of all the athletes on both sides of the football.

The genius of Manning? When he walks to the line of scrimmage to call a play, change the blocking scheme of his offensive line, or make an audible, it is as if the All-22 is playing in his head on a continuous loop.

The processing speed of his eyes slows down everything on the field, to the point where it sometimes seems as if Manning can see the future with 20/20 vision.

Or as one NFL coach told me: "You know what's most amazing about Peyton Manning as a quarterback? Here's the thing: He is able to take what has been studied for hours on film, process all that information, and instantly recognize a situation in the split-second heat of a game, then get the offense in the perfect play for the situation and complete a throw that makes a real difference. The football he throws might not always be pretty. But the ball he throws has eyes. Manning sees things on the football field other quarterbacks don't."

The eyes are what make him PFM.

From inside Manning's head, he sees ways to win in all 64 vibrant hues in the crayon box. And he colors outside the lines.

How awesome must it be to see what Manning sees?

Here are three plays from the 2012 season, dissected for me in the super-slow motion of videotape by trained NFL observers. Here are three prime examples of a genius at work.

Date: September 9, 2012
Opponent: Pittsburgh Steelers
Location: Sports Authority Field at Mile High, Denver
Game clock: 8 minutes, 13 seconds to go in the second quarter
Situation: 2nd down and 6 at Pittsburgh 41-yard line
Score at the time: Pittsburgh 3, Denver 0

The curtain went up on the NFL season. Enter Manning, stage right, wearing number 18 for the Denver Broncos. In his opening act, there was a big surprise. One of the greatest quarterbacks in league history changed the course of this game against the Steelers on a play where Manning used . . . his feet.

What the heck? Tim Tebow was long gone from Denver and riding the pine for the New York Jets, was he not? And we are supposed to believe that Manning's first beautifully heartbreaking work of staggering genius in a Broncos uniform occurred when he carried the football?

Believe it.

After his opening three possessions as the Denver quarterback ended with the whimper of a punt, fumble, and punt, when the Broncos got the football back in the second quarter, they put the maestro to work, with Manning directing a no-huddle attack.

Each time he lined up in the shotgun formation behind center, there were two plays on the Manning menu. A primary option and an audible call, depending on the look presented him by the Pittsburgh defense.

Manning operates the no-huddle the way Leonard Bernstein conducted the New York Philharmonic. After wrapping four completions around a short run by Willis McGahee, the Broncos had advanced to the 41-yard line of the Steelers in five plays.

Manning called signals from the shotgun. The ball was snapped. Pittsburgh linebacker Lawrence Timmons shot a gap on the right side of the Denver offensive line. Under pressure, running back Knowshon Moreno freaked out for an instant, stepped the wrong way in the backfield, and missed the assignment of picking up Timmons, who was hurtling toward a veteran quarterback playing his first game back from four neck surgeries.

As an act of self-preservation, Manning smartly darted to his right, scampered around end, and gained seven yards to pick up the first down, before stepping out of bounds in front of the Pittsburgh bench.

Well, well, well. The old QB proved his wheels still worked.

Take that, Tebow.

But the scramble was not the act of genius.

The genius was what Manning detected about the Pittsburgh defense while running for his life.

At halftime, Manning suggested the coaching staff make a small adjustment. During the first half, when the play choice being supplied by a coach talking through the speaker in Manning's helmet was between a run and a screen pass, the run was the primary call, with the screen as an audible.

But on the blitz by Timmons, Manning noted a defensive vulnerability that could be exploited by a screen pass. So the veteran quarterback made a very simple, very subtle change. He flipped the order of play priorities, making the screen pass his first option when supplying the code words to teammates at the line of scrimmage.

With his amazing football ESP, Manning had seen the future. If Pittsburgh was caught showing the same blitz in the third quarter and Denver had a screen pass dialed up, Manning promised his coaches: I have the Steelers exactly where we want them. And the result is going to be a home run.

As the Pittsburgh defenders jogged on the field for the second half kickoff, they were in big trouble, blissfully unaware of how much their future was going to hurt. Quarterback Ben Roethlisberger guided the Steelers on a 16-play, clock-chewing drive to open the third quarter with a field goal that put the visitors ahead 13–7.

It had been nearly an hour of real time since Manning had thrown a pass. But the Broncos offense came out in the no-huddle. And on the second play of the drive, the quarterback saw precisely the future he had foretold to Denver coaches at intermission.

A screen pass was the call. The throw by Manning barely traveled an inch past the line of scrimmage, where receiver Demaryius Thomas grabbed the football, as tight end Jacob Tamme applied a crisp seal block on Pittsburgh cornerback Ike Taylor in the left flat.

Manning had the Steelers precisely where he wanted them. Here is what boggles the mind. Manning did not check into the play when he detected a safety tipping off the blitz prior to the snap. That would have been amazing. But what Manning did was spooky brilliant. He had anticipated that exact blitz coming at him for more than an hour, and patiently waited to ambush Pittsburgh's Dick LeBeau, one of the finest defensive coordinators in the NFL.

How well did Manning see what the future held?

Without a defender so much as placing a fingernail tip on him, Thomas bolted 71 yards for a Denver touchdown. The Broncos led 14–13 and were on their way to a rousing victory in Manning's debut.

Thomas was asked to identify the short route he ran to produce the 400th touchdown pass of Manning's illustrious career. Would it best be described as a bubble screen?

"No," replied Thomas, laughing. "It was more like a smoke screen. It was something we saw at halftime."

As Manning trotted toward Denver teammates celebrating the Thomas touchdown in the stadium's south end zone, the quarterback briefly swiveled his head toward the Denver sideline and flashed an I-told-you-so-smile so huge it could shame a Cheshire cat.

A genius, doing work.

Date: October 15, 2012
Opponent: San Diego Chargers
Site: Qualcomm Stadium, San Diego
Game clock: 9 minutes, 32 seconds to go in the fourth quarter
Situation: First down and 10 at San Diego 21-yard line
Score at the time: San Diego 24, Denver 21

A genius resides in his own private world, sometimes so lost in the complexities of his work that he forgets what time it is.

Maybe that explains why the most memorable touchdown pass of Manning's first season with the Broncos almost did not happen.

Instead of the defining moment of the remarkable 24-point comeback against the San Diego Chargers, it was nearly a delay-of-game penalty by the nutty professor. While gesticulating, orchestrating, and basically telling everyone else on the field for the Broncos how to do their jobs, Manning almost forgot to complete his most basic assignment: Get the ball snapped before the 40-second play clock expired.

"What a catch! What a play! What a comeback!" ESPN play-by-play broadcaster Mike Tirico would succinctly shout, perfectly honoring the biggest Denver score of 2012. Broncos receiver Brandon Stokley had leapt higher than any 36-year-old man should be able to hop and hauled in a 21-yard pass, then landed barely inbounds with a touchdown that not only blew the minds of the Chargers, but signaled a change in the power structure of the AFC West. With that throw, Manning wrested control of a division long owned by San Diego quarterback Philip Rivers.

But here is what was left unsaid and largely went unnoticed until the game video could be reviewed frame by frame: Only the quick, level-headed thinking of center Dan Koppen saved the fourth-quarter touchdown from being a forgettable little disaster. As the "shot clock" dwindled to four seconds, Koppen told Manning to shut the hell up and play football.

From a spot on the sofa back home, it is sometimes hard to detect how keenly aware NFL players are about the small details that can make the difference between winning and losing. Manning lifts the IQ of all his teammates. But Koppen might be able to whip his quarterback in a Sudoku showdown. The dude is smart.

"Let's go! Let's go!" Koppen growled, as Manning hastily retreated to his position in the shotgun formation and the veteran center snapped the ball with one slim second to spare before a yellow flag would have flown, blowing the play dead for delay of game.

Up to the point where Koppen needed to jump his case, Manning had been as flawless as a quarterback can possibly be during the second half, completing all dozen of his pass attempts for 146 yards.

The Chargers owned a daunting 24–0 lead at halftime. But by the time the fourth quarter began, they were choking. Sometime after intermission, Rivers had lost his poise, not to mention two turnovers, via a fumble and interception. Taking over at the 50-yard line and trailing by only three points with 11 minutes and 11 seconds still remaining on the clock, Manning smartly marched the Broncos to the doorstep of the red zone with three quick plays and the help of an encroachment penalty by San Diego.

The time was right for Denver to go for the jugular.

At such a critical moment in the game, how could a quarterback as fastidious as Manning possibly lose track of time?

He tried to do everything at once.

As the play clock began to wind down, Manning looked to his right, immediately recognizing how desperate the Chargers defense was to force the issue in a contest the jittery home team realized was slip-sliding away. San Diego defensive backs Marcus Gilchrist and Quentin Jammer were in double-press coverage, lined up so close to Stokley and Eric Decker they could smell what the Denver wideouts ate for lunch.

After stamping his left foot twice, looking as if he were ready for the snap, Manning broke out of his stance in the shotgun formation and walked toward his receivers. With a simple hand signal, Manning altered the routes for Stokley and Decker to run, ordering a deep crossing pattern. Decker would now drive downfield and switch to the inside lane with a hard cut, while Stokley would break out toward the pylon at the goal line.

The time on the play clock had dwindled to ten seconds. But with the nonchalance of a safecracker, Manning decided he needed to change his offensive line's blocking scheme. The middle linebacker was indentified.

Six seconds, five, four . . .

And Koppen could not take it any longer. With a dismissive wave of his left hand, Koppen swatted at the nuisance of his quarterback's incessant chatter and gruffly ordered Manning to get back in position to take the snap.

Somehow, Manning set his feet and opened his palms before Koppen knocked him over with the football.

And there was no doubt where Manning was going with the pass. He looked immediately toward the spot in the end zone where Stokley was running. Before the receiver could turn his head, Manning let rip a high, soft spiral.

Matching Stokley stride for stride in exemplary man-to-man coverage, Gilchrist reached with his right hand to swipe at the football. Swing and a miss.

Stokley jumped halfway to the moon and grabbed the pass just inside the sideline chalk.

Falling to his butt, Gilchrist sat up and waved incomplete, begging an official for a call.

But there was no doubt. Stokley got both feet inbounds. The football was adhered to his palms.

It was touchdown, Broncos. They had come all the way back to take a 28–24 lead.

Good night, San Diego. Drive home safely.

Stokley's catch was literal proof that teammates go above and beyond to make plays for Manning. If the quarterback delivers a perfect pass at the perfect time, a receiver is not going to drop Manning's work of art.

"Without him, I wouldn't have played this year," Stokley said of Manning, who has thrown him touchdown passes from Indianapolis to Denver. "There's no doubt I would be retired . . . and probably about

20 pounds heavier. So, yeah, I owe him a lot. For this year, and a lot for my career in general. Playing with [Manning] kind of sparked my career. I owe that guy a lot."

Stokley waited 14 NFL seasons to catch a football so spectacularly thrown. For the second-oldest wide receiver in the league, the wait was well worth it.

Real genius cannot be rushed.

Date: December 2, 2012
Opponent: Tampa Bay Buccaneers
Site: Sports Authority Field at Mile High, Denver
Game clock: 4 minutes, 45 seconds to go in the third quarter
Situation: 2nd down and goal at Tampa Bay 10-yard line
Score at the time: Denver 14, Tampa Bay 10

It took until week 13 of the NFL season for an observation Thomas offered me way back in June to sink in: "The more Manning stays on your case, the better football player you become."

While other Broncos hit the showers at the conclusion of that late spring practice, Manning held a one-sided, animated discussion with his receiver. But not before the quarterback paused to make certain no television cameras were rolling. Praise in public. Work out the kinks in private. It is smart business.

A quarterback's primary duty is to lead touchdown drives. Along the way, Manning is also driven to teach talented teammates how to become even bigger winners.

After discovering that Manning's pearls of wisdom are a strand stretching to infinity, Thomas might never graduate from Professor Peyton's class. But, on December 2, 2012, weeks shy of his 25th birthday, the physically gifted receiver earned a gold star for academic achievement.

Thomas began thinking like PFM does.

Have you ever watched the wonder of cherry flowers blossoming with time-lapse photography? That is almost as cool as watching the football IQ of Thomas spike through the ceiling on a play in the third quarter of Denver's 31–23 victory against Tampa Bay.

With the football resting on the 10-yard line, the Broncos emptied their backfield and gave Tampa Bay a mouthful of trouble to chew on. This offensive formation was not a good look for the Bucs in the red zone. To Manning's far left flank, lining up near the sideline was Moreno, a running back. Standing in the left slot, creating an instant mismatch, was Thomas.

Manning did not immediately grasp the obvious opportunity to hurt the Bucs. He was taking care of details in his blocking scheme, paying no attention to Thomas.

Rather than straining to be noticed with the annoying urgency of a teacher's pet, Thomas calmly caught the eye of Manning. The message from Thomas to his quarterback was direct and to the point: Check this out. You're going to love it. Do you see what I see, Professor?

The Tampa Bay defense had bracketed Thomas with two defenders. On the inside was rookie linebacker Lavonte David. On the outside, standing near the goal line, playing too soft to be a serious threat, was safety Ahmad Black.

The way Thomas had it figured, there was no way either Bucs defender could hang with him.

What Thomas did next demonstrated that when the lightbulb goes on for a star pupil, it shines brightly. Without being prompted, Thomas flashed a hand signal to Manning. The receiver, not the quarterback, was the Denver player calling the audible here.

Hit me on a square-in pattern to the post, Thomas silently informed Manning, and this double-coverage will be made to look stupidly inept with an easy touchdown.

What was so beautiful is that Manning instantly recognized that his receiver had solved a problem with the efficiency worthy of an A+. Manning lifted his left index finger in the direction of Thomas. No words accompanied Manning's gesture, but his subtle finger wag of acknowledgment absolutely shouted to Thomas: Eureka! You've found it!

When Manning no longer needs to do all the thinking, he can concentrate on throwing a spiral through a window so slightly cracked that a 20-dollar bill might not slide through the opening. When teammates start analyzing football on the level of PFM, then the Broncos have matured into an offense that can reasonably expect to score 30 points against any defense.

The play went as Thomas had predicted. He beat the Tampa Bay linebacker in one quick and easy move and left the safety slowly shaking his head in disgust as Manning delivered the throw. This 10-yard touchdown pass was indefensible.

When he entered the NFL as a rookie from Georgia Tech in 2010, the quickie scouting report on Thomas read: "Genuinely blessed athlete, painfully raw at the art of football." But look at him now: Student of the game, all grown up.

"We go out every day and try to get better at what we do, get better at our craft," Thomas said.

The student pleased his professor. Big time.

"What I liked about the touchdown was Damaryius was seeing the same thing I was seeing," Manning said. "He was kind of looking for something. He had another route and we changed it at the line. We were kind of thinking along the same line. That was good to see—that kind of communication and growth."

The ultimate payoff for the Broncos with Manning as quarterback?

A genius, passing on his knowledge.

12

NO LAUGH TRACK REQUIRED

We should have known Peyton Manning would be almost as unbeatable on *Saturday Night Live* as he is on Sunday afternoons.

When he removes his helmet, Peyton Manning looks a little like a Conehead.

Sharing much in common with Stuart Smalley, this NFL quarterback is good enough. He is definitely smart enough. And, doggone it, people do like Manning.

The point is: "Da Bears" were worshipped by Bill Swerski and his merry band of superfans. But even "Ditkaaa" would have to agree.

The funniest athlete ever to grace the television soundstage of *Saturday Night Live* is Manning. In this contest, there is no second place.

Here is what's so remarkable. It is easier for an athlete to knock down the door of the Hall of Fame than score an invitation to host *SNL*. The NBC-TV production is the most famous brand in the history of American comedy, created by Lorne Michaels, launched in 1975, and still going strong.

A jock must possess rare skills, not to mention an off-the-charts Q score, to land the gig as host. The roster includes: John Madden, Joe Montana, Michael Jordan, Jeff Gordon, Lance Armstrong, and two brothers named Manning.

But enough about Eli.

The show is built on comedy sketches that have become woven so tightly in American pop culture that classic scenes can instantly bring smiles with the mention of two little words ("More Cowbell!"). Manning will be forever linked to the most surprising performance of his career. And it had nothing to do with completing 25 passes while leading the Indianapolis Colts to victory in Super Bowl XLI.

To discover the quarterback's best chance at pop-culture immortality, all anyone needs to do is Google this phrase: "Manning United Way." Hundreds of thousands of people already have done it.

With assistance from the beautifully warped minds of *SNL* writers, Manning stars in the most hilarious—and quite possibly the most dastardly—public service announcement ever recorded. It debuted in March 24, 2007, on the occasion of Manning's 31st birthday, and a few scant weeks after Manning claimed his only NFL championship. The parody of the NFL's well-known United Way commercials is more perfect than the shine on the Vince Lombardi Trophy.

The scene opens in a city park. Wearing a blue V-neck sweater, Manning jogs in to play football with adorable young children. His mission is to graciously share life lessons on teamwork. The voice-over announcer tugs at our heartstrings by earnestly declaring: "Being a kid can be harder than it looks. So it helps to have an adult around. This is why Peyton Manning takes the time to volunteer with local youth groups."

Manning gathers his young admirers in a huddle, lines them up, and calls signals as the quarterback in a game of two-hand touch. Aw, isn't that sweet?

Madness ensues. Profanity happens. Manning's flawless image is ripped to shreds.

From the first snap, frustration at children unable to meet a perfectionist's standards angers Manning. "Get open, get open," the quarterback mutters at a 10-year-old boy running a short down-and-out pattern.

Then, Manning fires a pass that nails the offending kid in the rump, the football knocking the boy to the ground in a puddle of pain and humiliation.

"Get your head out of your ass! You suck!" Manning declares, adding insult to injury.

The fuming football star demands that his team return to the huddle for remedial instruction.

"Except for you!" Manning screams at the boy who ruined the quarterback's completion percentage by allowing the game's first pass to hit the ground incomplete. "I can't even look at you. Go sit in the Port-o-Let for 20 minutes. Just stay in there!"

With Manning more intense than a Little League parent from hell, the football game is a spectacular failure. So he offers them a lesson every big-city kid can use: How to break into a car.

As police sirens wail, Manning cocks his head and warns his young apprentices: "I'll kill a snitch. I'm not saying I have. I'm not saying I haven't."

Oh, boy.

The PSA has driven home the point with the wallop of a two-by-four upside the head. There is no more important work an adult can do than shape the character of a child. The announcer leaves us all with one final thought:

"The NFL and United Way urge you to spend time with your kids, so Peyton Manning doesn't."

What made the sketch pure comedy gold was the way it blew all preconceived notions of Manning's sterling reputation to smithereens. The skit had more bite than a Land Shark. And the most precise quarterback in football executed the game plan to absolute perfection.

"He didn't buckle under the pressure. I told him to go kill a 12-pack and make it happen," cast member Jason Sudeikis told the *Indianapolis Star* on the night of Manning's bravura display of comedic timing. "I see an Oscar within the next five years. Maybe not even in acting. Maybe in directing."

Now that is funny. The kernel of truth is comedy gold. Manning constantly directs. And it is no act. As Broncos wide receiver Demaryius Thomas once told me: "I think Manning has run the show for every team he has every played on, from the time he was a kid to when he goes to Hawaii for the Pro Bowl."

Manning prods and pushes teammates to performances they did not think possible. If it requires 99 takes to get down the timing of a pass route, then Manning is going to rehearse the play 100 times. At the very least.

The writers at *SNL* could not have known how faithfully their art replicated life. Dallas Clark was a rookie tight end in the Indianapolis training camp of 2003. In a scene recounted by *ESPN the Magazine*, Clark got off on the wrong foot with the perfectionist playing quarterback.

The issue was Clark's lack of flexibility. Every time the rookie ran a quick-out route toward the sideline, he had trouble swiveling his torso to be a ready target for Manning's crisp spiral. As frustration built, Manning refused to wait for Clark to catch on. Instead, Manning drilled Clark with beautiful pass after beautiful pass in the back of the tight end's helmet.

That little kid in the *SNL* skit certainly could identify with Clark's pain. While the young tight end might not have been too fond of Manning's unforgiving approach to teaching, he learned. Maybe Clark should have considered himself lucky he was not banished to the Port-o-Let.

In other words: Manning can be a real pain in the ass.

But teammates never tune Manning out. Why? His way wins.

When Manning departed the University of Tennessee in 1998, he owned the Southeastern Conference record for career victories by a quarterback, with 39 to his credit as a starter for the Volunteers.

With his NFL record as a starting quarterback now sitting at 154-70, Manning has surpassed John Elway's mark of 148-82-1.

Who can forget the Manning commercial for NFL Mobile from Sprint? In the spot, he played a fan of . . . Peyton Manning. Standing in a garage, he wore a fake mustache, poorly adhered above his lip, and a Colts jersey. The sales pitch: Every football lover needs game highlights on the cell phone. Especially, this imposter dressed like a fan suggests, if your favorite player is "Peyton Manning. That guy's pretty good. If you like 6-5, 230-pound quarterbacks with . . . laser-rocket arm."

It is more than a track record of success to sell his message, though. Manning can be hilarious in front of one of the toughest crowds to impress: an NFL locker room.

Asked about the quarterback's habit of borrowing the flight attendant's microphone and performing an impromptu stand-up routine as the Broncos traveled back from road games on their chartered jet, Denver veteran Champ Bailey said: "I can't give all of his secrets away. But Peyton Manning can be a very funny man. He knows you can't be serious all the time. He knows how to keep it light.

"But you can tell he thinks about it before he gets up and tries to be funny. Peyton Manning always does his homework. And, whether he's throwing a pass or telling a joke, his timing is always perfect."

As dry as a shot of top-shelf tequila and packing as much bite, the best shots of comedy by Manning do a nice, slow burn.

A funny thing happened on the Broncos' way to routing the Oakland Raiders 37–6 in Sports Authority Field at Mile High on the last Sunday in September. Leading by a touchdown in the second quarter, a Denver drive faced fourth down at the Oakland 36-yard line.

Contrary to his conservative nature, Broncos coach John Fox decided to go for the first down. And why not? Denver needed to gain only a single, silly yard to move the chains.

With one of the more dangerous offenses in the league, the options seemed limitless. Running back Willis McGahee could be handed the rock, so he could churn for positive yardage behind the block of star offensive tackle Ryan Clady. Or perhaps Manning could play a simple game of catch with longtime pal and slot receiver Brandon Stokley.

What did Fox choose? Something off the menu: a fake field goal, which required both Denver's punter and placekicker to pass the football.

The snap went to punter Britton Colquitt, the regular holder for field-goal specialist Matt Prater, who was lined up for a 54-yard attempt, well within his range, especially at 5,280 feet above sea level.

But instead of placing the point of the ball in the turf, Colquitt tossed it to Prater, who took the lateral and rolled to his left, out of the pocket and out of his element. Since when did the Broncos mistake a 5-foot, 10-inch kicker for Jake "The Snake" Plummer?

Well, Prater pointed out, in his flag football league back home, he is undefeated in the games where he is allowed to be the all-time quarterback for both teams. But the guys he is schooling on that field are accountants and barbers.

The play was designed as a run-pass option. Less than three strides into the run, however, Prater determined there was one tiny problem: He is too slow to catch a bus, much less sprint past an Oakland defensive back looking to cause some mayhem.

So Prater went to Plan B: self-preservation. Spotting 305-pound Broncos guard Zane Beadles chugging down the field, the kicker launched something that more closely resembled a helium balloon release than a Hall of Fame throw.

"I tried to give him a 50-50 ball," said Prater, as if his target were Randy Moss rather than an offensive guard. "Might have overthrown him a little bit. Had a little extra adrenaline. I'm not used to having the ball in my hands."

Beadles tripped over his shot at glory. The pass crashed to the turf, with a sound as uncomfortable as china in a five-star restaurant hitting the floor.

"We probably won't see that one again for a while," Fox admitted.

Manning was asked to critique the genius used by Broncos coaches to make this bit of football trickeration.

"I kind of told them to maybe give Manning to Stokley a chance, maybe before Prater to Beadles," said the quarterback. His voice dripped with sarcasm. And he was just getting warmed up.

"It's one of the all-time great combinations right?" added Manning, thinking of the most dangerous quarterback-receiver tandems of his generation, from the Buffalo Bills to the San Francisco 49ers. "[Jim] Kelly–[Andre] Reed . . . [Joe] Montana–[Jerry] Rice . . . Prater–Beadles. You know?"

For those of you keeping score at home.

Career pass receptions: Rice 1,549. Beadles? Zero.

Career pass completions: Manning 5,082. Prater? Zero.

Whenever within shouting distance of Manning, the listener better be ready to catch some good-natured grief. Teammates. Media members. It makes no difference. If you leave yourself open as a target, Manning will find you.

In May of 2012, after a spring practice during which Manning got his first real chance to inspect the work of 6-foot, 8-inch rookie quarterback Brock Osweiler, Manning was asked for an expert evaluation.

"Is it weird looking up to a taller quarterback?" said 104.3 FM reporter Brandon Krisztal, who could be approved for a spot in a 6-feet-and-under basketball league without ever consulting a tape measure.

Krisztal is short. Manning is tall. So the intrepid radio reporter wanted to know if Manning felt small next to Osweiler.

"That doesn't happen too often to you, does it?" Krisztal asked.

Replied Manning: "Happens to you all your life."

Then, to emphasize the point, he gave Krisztal a gentle pat on the head.

Who said it was the No Fun League?

In October of 2012, at one of the more disheartening junctures of the Broncos' season, with Denver trailing 10–0 on the road at San Diego, Manning lofted a perfect pass beyond midfield to Eric Decker, who hauled in the football with nothing between him and the end zone.

At the 40-yard line, Decker tripped. Nobody touched him. He flopped, head over heels, on the ground coming to rest with a forward somersault, preventing a certain Denver touchdown with nothing except his own inexplicable clumsiness.

Former Broncos safety Brian Dawkins immediately tweeted: "Turf monster got 'em!"

Denver came back to beat San Diego 35–24, so it was safe for me to ask Manning after the fact: What the heck happened to Decker on that embarrassing play in the first half?

"That guy made a great tackle," Manning replied, before giving it some thought. "I mean, the piece of grass made a great tackle."

On his Twitter account, Decker offered his own theory: "If y'all didn't see, they had a trip wire out there tonight. I reported it to the NFL so an investigation is pending. #humblingmoment."

What is the best way to rid your nightmares of a turf monster? Kill him with laughter.

Although obsequious admirers might think a star quarterback is always funny, Manning works without a laugh track. He does not need canned chuckles. The great ones never do.

During the telecast of the Academy Awards in 1979, master of ceremonies Johnny Carson scanned the room of beautiful Hollywood stars, many of them anxiously waiting for a call from Oscar. Carson quipped: "I see a lot of new faces . . . especially on the old faces."

Contrary to popular belief, snark was invented before the birth of the Twitterverse. Snark is a time-honored comedy tradition, older than Don Rickles.

Manning can do snark.

In fact, Manning does snark every year, as the unofficial master of ceremonies at the Pro Bowl.

When the most talented players from the American and National conferences gather for the opening meeting at a ritzy resort in a private little corner of Oahu, Manning routinely stands up and warmly welcomes them to one of the coolest fraternity houses on Earth. He has hosted the party more often than Billy Crystal has served as emcee to the Oscars.

On this Tuesday night in 2013, Manning gave an impassioned plea to raise the Pro Bowl's level of play, or else face the consequence of NFL commissioner Roger Goodell following through on his threat to cancel the game and everyone's all-expenses-paid trip to Hawaii.

His primary mission accomplished, Manning lightened the mood with an ego-popping zinger for nearly every star in the resort's ballroom. Andy Fenelon was present and recorded some of the best, clean shots by Manning for NFL.com.

Checking off the first task of any veteran social chairman, Manning wanted to make certain nobody got in trouble. "Couple of rules, couple of reminders," Manning said. "Let's just keep the pictures and autographs at the pool to a minimum. It's an area for the guys to hang out, get to know each other. [The rule] is not for guys like me. I'll sign whatever. It's for guys who get bothered for autographs all the time. Guys like Dustin Colquitt, Phil Dawson."

Colquitt is the punter for the Kansas City Chiefs. Dawson kicks field goals for the San Francisco 49ers. About the only time these two guys get asked for a signature, a waiter is holding a check for dinner.

"These guys," insisted Manning, "can't go anywhere."

After roasting the dubious achievements of players with lengthy Pro Bowl backgrounds, Manning eventually turned his sharp tongue on himself.

"Peyton Manning," the Broncos quarterback announced, reading from the all-star game's dusty annals, "holds the record with nine interceptions in the Pro Bowl. I want to thank PR for looking that up for me."

Manning paused, searching for NFC cornerbacks in the crowd.

"I want to keep that record," Manning deadpanned. "So, on Sunday, [Charles] Tillman, [Tim] Jennings and [Patrick] Peterson, look out. I'm going to throw it every time."

Maybe Manning's best line was saved for Minnesota running back Adrian Peterson, who had recovered from serious knee surgery to lead the league with 2,097 yards rushing and become the primary rival of the Denver quarterback in the race for Most Valuable Player.

With the reminder that the Pro Bowl should be more than a game of two-hand touch, Manning cracked: "Everyone should play like Adrian Peterson. The guy does everything at full speed: The Pro Bowl. Promoting himself for MVP."

Everybody laughed. Nobody laughed harder than Peterson. "I thought it was funny, man," Peterson told me. "Manning is always pulling somebody's chain. This time, he got me. That's just the way he is. And I have a ton of respect for him."

As we walked together toward the locker room where the AFC squad of Manning would meet the NFC squad of Peterson, the Minnesota running back got an unmistakable look in his eyes. Peterson was looking for an opening. Who was I to disappoint the man?

"So," I asked Peterson, "who is going to win the MVP award. You? Or Manning?"

"Oh," replied Peterson, "I'm going to win. I will get it."

Touché.

On February 2, 2013, the loudest noise at the NFL Honors Ceremony was the sound of the last laugh by Peterson going down. In a vote of a 50-person panel assembled by the Associated Press, Peterson won the MVP. He received 30.5 votes to 19.5 for Manning.

In recognition of the 37 touchdown passes against 11 interceptions he threw during his first season as Denver's quarterback, Manning had to settle for the Comeback Player of the Year award.

But Manning was not even slightly disappointed.

"I used to say this was an award I never wanted to have, because it meant having a significant injury and missing some time. I will say for any young player out there, if they do get injured, I wish they would be as fortunate as I was to receive the kind of help and support from all kind of people from all different places. Denver, Duke University, coaches, trainers, doctors who have supported me. Family members," Manning told the *Denver Post*.

"I'm very grateful to be back playing this game."

Comeback Player of the Year?

For Manning, it was far more than a nice consolation prize.

For a guy fired from his job a year earlier, it was sweet redemption.

13

LAST OF THE DINOSAURS

Darwinism does apply to football. Adapt or die. The NFL is known as the Not For Long for good reason. From the salary-cap restrictions on rosters to schedules slanted against elite teams, the league is rigged in favor of turnover and parity. Stealing is the ultimate form of flattery. This is the ultimate copycat league, from cheerleaders dancing on the sideline to zone blitzers sacking the quarterback.

The current flavor of the month in the NFL is the read-option offensive scheme. The read option is the bastard son of a wildcat and the father of invention. Please do not take that as an insult. The read option is ingenious. There was a glaring need in pro football, and the read option filled it, at least long enough for San Francisco 49ers quarterback Colin Kaepernick to become a household name across America.

In a sport where it seems all the rules are designed to make quarterbacks rich and famous, know what is a bummer? There are never enough quality quarterbacks to go around. Teams without a reliable quarterback tumble to last place, then reach into the draft for a quality signal caller faster than you can say Ryan Leaf.

The read-option play is nothing new. It's older than the veer, the wishbone, and wing-T formations. Nevertheless, a quarterback whose legs are stronger than his throwing arm has long been an outlier in the NFL.

The league never really trusted Steve Young until he was over 30, as the pro game relentlessly drilled conformity into him. But Young had the last laugh, taking the long way home to the Pro Football Hall of Fame in Canton, Ohio, with Super Bowl trophies riding shotgun.

Before his ugly entanglement with dogfighting sent him to prison, Michael Vick was lauded by every pixel-loving kid of the early 21st century. Young boys admired Vick as the most unstoppable football force on the video-game landscape. Vick was Super Mario in shoulder pads. NFL coaches, however, never quite figured out how to harness Vick's freewheeling energy for championship good.

The wildcat formation was a temporary but sharp pain in the posterior for defensive coordinators, forced to deal with a direct snap to a running back standing several steps behind the center. The wildcat owed a huge debt to longtime University of Delaware coach Tubby Raymond, a master of misdirection and one of the more underappreciated offensive minds in the game's history. The wildcat gave Miami Dolphins running back Ronnie Brown his 15 minutes of NFL fame. But the wildcat always felt like a gimmick.

As Peyton Manning donned a Broncos jersey for the first time in 2012, the league took a significant step forward in opening the position of quarterback to more applicants. Now trending on Twitter: RG3.

Robert Griffin III was a world-class hurdler who grew up to win the Heisman Trophy at Baylor University. When Washington traded up for the number two pick in the 2012 draft with Griffin in mind, it ended any possibility of Manning playing for Redskins coach Mike Shanahan, a coach long admired by the veteran quarterback. If Shanahan, among the more innovative strategists in the business, was adapting to the emerging skill set of the modern quarterback, then the movement had merit.

Russell Wilson, who first came on the radar of the Colorado sports fans as a minor-league infielder in the Rockies organization, emerged from the University of Wisconsin with all the abilities necessary to succeed in the NFL save one prickly issue: height. Wilson was shorter than the minimum line required to get behind the wheel of a pro offense.

Listed at 5 feet, 11 inches, Wilson would need to be mobile in the pocket to spot receivers and be efficient against massive defenders. But Seattle sent shock waves throughout the league by naming Wilson the team's starter. An undersized, raw rookie won the job ahead of bally-hooed free agent Matt Flynn, signed shortly before the draft by the Seahawks to a three-year, $19.5 million contract.

The 2011 NFL draft is fondly remembered in Denver as the place where the Broncos selected linebacker Von Miller with the first pick of John Elway's tenure as a front-office executive. Here is the trivia question: Whatever happened to the team's selection at number 36 in the same draft? The Broncos traded the pick to San Francisco. The Niners selected Kaepernick. As a University of Nevada senior, Kaepernick had shaken me from a tryptophan stupor during Thanksgiving weekend of 2010, by leading a remarkable upset against previously undefeated Boise State. But it took until the 10th week of the 2012 season for Kaepernick to get his shot on the big stage, after San Francisco quarterback Alex Smith went down with a concussion.

While Manning posted statistics worthy of a traditional MVP candidate during his first year in Denver, Griffin, Wilson, and Kaepernick not only knocked conventional wisdom on its ear, but made the most unexpectedly beautiful noise of the NFL campaign, by leading the Redskins, Seahawks, and Niners to playoff bids.

It was a back-to-the-future revolution. Quarterbacks capable of running the option became overnight smash success stories. "People say you can't run the option in the NFL, but we're proving you can. It's not something that's our bread and butter, but you can sprinkle it in now and then. Teams have to prepare for it," Griffin told Arnie Stapleton of the Associated Press.

"Coaches take a certain pride in shutting down what they call college stuff. They take pride in that. It doesn't bother me. We can run it two times a game. We can run it 15 times a game."

The experiment worked. The proof rolled in, one rousing victory at a time. It appears Griffin, Wilson, and Kaepernick have invented a new way to be a successful quarterback in the NFL. Charles Darwin would have loved this war between different species of quarterback.

Maybe, just maybe, the drop-back quarterback now has something more frightening to worry about than a brutal blindside tackle by a defensive end. The sport constantly evolves. And, as the late, great Darwin would be the first to tell you: It is not the strongest of the species that survives, nor the most intelligent, but the one most responsive to change. Maybe, just maybe, great field vision and a deft passing touch are no longer sufficient for a quarterback to thrive in the league.

Is Manning the last of the dinosaurs?

"People have been saying for seven or eight years now that the drop-back quarterback is a thing of the past, and the mobile quarterback is the future," Manning told me, as he walked off the practice field one morning.

Manning let his statement sink in my thick skull. He stood as quiet as a statue, which, come to think of it, is exactly how Manning looks in the pocket, when preparing to throw a pass. To call him slow of foot is an insult to molasses.

Proving once again that this man's comedic timing is as sharp as his ability to hit a receiver fresh out of the break with a football between the numbers, Manning hit me with the punch line.

The drop-back quarterback is going the way of the dinosaur?

"Well, this isn't good," said Manning, a mischievous, crooked grin lifting one corner of his mouth.

What happens if there is a read-option revolution?

"I'm going to be out of a job," said Manning, cracking wise.

If Manning can now joke about being out of work, maybe the psychological wounds of being fired from the Indianapolis Colts are beginning to heal.

More important, Manning has done the math and he knows the answer: So long as the NFL desires to entertain the masses by lighting up the scoreboard, a guy who can fling the football will always find gainful employment. Some things never go out of style: Macaroni and cheese. The sweet growl of a 1967 Ford Mustang as it shifts into second gear. A spiral perfectly spun by a quarterback from the old school.

"I admire the versatility of these young quarterbacks," Manning said. "But I certainly think there's still a place in the NFL for the drop-back quarterback. Or at least I hope so. I'd like to keep working."

I'm loath to incite fist-shaking anger from Broncomaniacs with a number 15 jersey banished to the dark end of the closet, but did Denver dump Tim Tebow at the dawn of an offensive revolution?

Innovation hatched in the football research laboratories on university campuses has long enhanced the NFL product. But option football is as old as the hills. Manning was seen operating the Colts offense from a spread formation during his glory days with Indianapolis. Manning did not carry the rock. But the blocking schemes and misdirection plays helped Colts running back Edgerrin James gain more than 9,000 yards on the ground from 1999 through the 2005 season.

"There are not many new things in the National Football League," Broncos coach John Fox said. "The read-option is a college type of run game that has been going on for at least 30 years, whether it was the Southwest Conference with Texas and the wishbone, or the veer that Houston ran back in the day. Mouse Davis, when he was the coach at Portland State, put in the run-and-shoot offense. So this is not new. You know all that is really different now in pro football that did not exist much back in the 1970s? Now, there are more quarterbacks who can run the football as well as throw it."

The Broncos were comfortable with dumbing down their offense for the benefit of Tebow, because Fox had proof it could work. Way back in 2006, when Fox was coaching in Carolina, the Panthers were in trouble. Having lost quarterback Jake Delhomme to injury, they were struggling to generate offense with backup Chris Weinke under center. "The wildcat formation? We actually started that when I was back in Carolina," Fox said.

Desperation fosters innovation. Fox decided to have tailback DeAngelo Williams take direct snaps from a shotgun stance. Darn, if it did not work. Carolina beat Atlanta. Fox would be the last to take credit for inventing the wildcat, but he certainly helped promote the idea it could be effective in the NFL.

While known for backslaps as warm as a hello from your favorite uncle, Fox has seldom been accused of being a cutting-edge coach. But he experimented with Tebow as a run-first quarterback, made the playoffs as Broncos Country adopted Tebow as its favorite son, and then returned to a more conventional offense. Why?

With a voice as down-home as the sound of car wheels on a gravel road, Fox shared the unavoidable reason why he is skeptical that the read-option attack employed by San Francisco will take over and dominate the NFL. Fox needed only one word to state the crux of his case:

"Exposure," Foxy said, repeating the word to underline his point. "Exposure. That's the hard part. It's a long season. And this is a game of violent collisions. When a quarterback runs a lot, it's the exposure he gets against big, fast, physical people who play defense."

Manning was hired by the Broncos in part because Fox and Elway learned the brutal lessons that await any NFL team that takes on the risks inherent with a running quarterback.

From the beginning to the end of a Super Bowl run, a quarterback can be subject to 20 games of violent hits. Tebow won his only 2011 playoff game in Denver, with an 80-yard touchdown pass to Demaryius Thomas that beat the Pittsburgh Steelers. But during a 45–10 loss to New England the next weekend, Tebow suffered a rib injury so severe that it was unlikely he would have been able to play in the AFC championship game had the Broncos somehow managed to beat the Patriots.

"Tebow got whacked pretty good," Fox said. "Anytime you go inside those lines of a football field, you're exposed. Even a pocket passer is exposed. And now you're going to run your quarterback as a regular part of your offense? That only increases the exposure."

While Cam Newton of the Carolina Panthers is bigger, sturdier, and faster than the stuff of Fran Tarkenton's dreams, you can take this to the bank: The rambling, gambling quarterback who makes his living on the option play will never, ever receive unconditional support at the pro game. It is one thing to have the scrambling ability of Roger Staubach.

It is a far more dangerous proposition to embarrass NFL defenders with an offensive scheme they recall from peewee football.

"I view the read option the same as I viewed the wildcat. It can be successful as an offense in spots, with the right personnel," Minnesota defensive end Jared Allen said. "But give NFL minds some time to work on it, and defenses will find a way to negate it. Someone is going to come up with a defense to stop the read option. It's a good wrinkle. But I don't think it can be the basis of everything you do on offense."

Wilson bristles at any suggestion he has benefited extensively from a scheme that is Remedial Football 101. Wilson runs the read-option attack. But when Wilson looks in the mirror, he sees something far more than an immature read-option quarterback who is trying to fool people by wearing grown-up NFL clothes.

A read-option quarterback incapable of throwing the football will not be a starting quarterback for long, Wilson insisted. In other words: Wilson is not Tebow. "The game is changing," Wilson said. "But my ability to succeed is based on being able to throw the football effectively."

Proponents of the read-option attack argue the scheme has legs for multifaceted reasons. It forces defenses to be reactive. It can minimize the pass rush. The read-option scheme can employ a variety of personnel sets. It gives less-polished quarterbacks a chance to play earlier in their careers.

"I think this is the real deal. There are all kinds of ways to hand the ball off, have three wide receivers, have that kind of thing," respected former Cowboys executive Gil Brandt told Mike Klis of the *Denver Post*. "I'm not sure anybody has a way to stop this. They may slow it down, but they're not going to stop it."

To find out what the NFL truly values, however, the path to discovery is tried and true. Follow the money. In 2013, Kaepernick is due to be paid $714,000 for sticking his neck out with San Francisco. Compare that to the $20 million salary of New Orleans Saints quarterback Drew Brees. While Kaepernick started for San Francisco in the Super Bowl XLVII against Baltimore, the championship was won by Ravens quarterback Joe Flacco, a classic drop-back passer. And what earns Flacco great respect throughout the league? It is his throwing arm, such a strong weapon that no safety is truly safe against Flacco rearing back and desperately heaving a bomb deep into the night.

The NFL makes a fortune as an entertainment vehicle that is dependent on the barely controlled mayhem of violent collisions between the white lines and the thinly veiled form of gambling known as fantasy football. The read-option quarterback, however, made us all look for another reason. The read option is just plain fun.

Fun is far down the priority list for NFL coaches, though. They are obsessed with winning. The read-option attack is fun that coaches want to stamp out.

"I think it's the flavor of the day. We'll see if it's the flavor of the year. We'll see if guys are committed to getting their guys hit," Pittsburgh Steelers coach Mike Tomlin said, during the NFL owners meeting in March 2013.

Griffin and the read-option gang fooled the NFL once.

But what happens next could be a painful slap of reality upside the head of this read-option revolution. There are football nerds working overtime in darkened video rooms, planning revenge against any read-option quarterback who caught an NFL team flat-footed. The trail of embarrassment that Griffin left in his wake during a 76-yard romp to the end zone against Allen and his Vikings teammates in October 2012 can keep coaches awake at night and muttering: Never again.

"We look forward to stopping it," said Tomlin, making it sound as if the rise of read-option quarterbacks was an annoyance as easily eliminated as ants in the kitchen pantry. "We look forward to eliminating it."

So watch your back, RG3. The nickname of the Redskins' quarterback makes for a nice hashtag. Griffin proves that big and bold trends on Twitter far quicker than traditional and old.

The final, enduring image of Griffin from his amazing rookie season, however, served as a gruesome foreshadowing. His bold, fearless running took its toll, as RG3 entered the playoffs hobbling like a peg-legged pirate. During the fourth quarter of Washington's 24–14 loss to

Seattle, a low snap caused Griffin to bend awkwardly for the football. His injured right knee buckled. Everything bright about the Redskins' future fell in a heap on the ground, with the quarterback's body as limp as dirty laundry.

For the second time in his athletic career, Griffin had torn the same anterior cruciate ligament in his knee. Like it or not, football pounds conformity into a quarterback with cruel intention and ugly consequences.

Long after the read-option is a footnote in NFL history, Manning will be remembered as a giant of the sport.

The dinosaur, a beast of yore, doesn't live here anymore. In the NFL, the unwritten rule is: Adapt or perish.

Manning, however, is bigger—and way smarter—than *Tyrannosaurus rex*.

The read-option offense is all the rage, with more coaches in a copy-cat league certain to experiment with the scheme. But will pro football sack the classic drop-back passer and toss Manning's old-school skills in some dusty corner of a museum?

That would be harder than throwing away a comfortable old pair of blue jeans.

14

MANNING VERSUS ELWAY

The clock was ticking toward eleven o'clock at night, but the three kings who rule the Broncos' fate were in absolutely no hurry to go home. Quarterback Peyton Manning, front-office honcho John Elway, and coach John Fox stood together around the new Denver quarterback's locker long after the game had ended, like three fraternity brothers standing around the keg on an awesome night nobody wanted to end.

The curtain had risen on the Manning era in Denver to thunderous applause from the home crowd, and after beating the Pittsburgh Steelers 31–19 in the first game of the 2012 NFL season, the reviews were going to be positively glowing.

Down the hall from this private celebration by Manning, Elway, and Fox, journalists with deadlines to meet squirmed impatiently in their seats, waiting for an audience with the evening's star. Nevertheless, Broncos media relations director Patrick Smyth, one of the best and brightest in the business, listened to the laughter bouncing among Elway, Manning, and Fox. Interrupt this impromptu executive meeting so the quarterback could face the cameras? No way. Smyth was way too smart to attempt anything so foolhardy.

"I can buzz the tower," Smyth told a newspaper hack waiting for a word with Elway. "But I'm not breaking this up. Look at these guys. They're enjoying themselves. And they should, don't you think?"

Before taking the field against Pittsburgh on the night of September 9, the four-time MVP who had endured four neck surgeries had not taken a snap in a game that counted for more than 600 days.

Six hundred days of rust. For Manning, it was gone in 60 seconds.

Manning looked as if he had never left the huddle, let alone transferred from Indianapolis to Denver in a move that turned his life upside down and league fortunes inside out. On the second snap of his big debut night, Manning found Eric Decker for a simple and simply beautiful 13-yard gain. Against the Steelers, Manning would finish with 19 completions in 26 attempts for 253 yards and two touchdowns.

As Manning replayed the night with Fox and Elway, it was apparent these three men were not encumbered by the normal boss and employee formalities. They were three peers getting their first real glimpses of how well their dreams of success for the Broncos could actually play out on the football field. And they were loving the possibilities.

As Manning finally departed for his postgame press conference, I approached Elway and told him the one thought that would not budge from my mind throughout that entire evening, when Manning brought back the noise unheard in a Denver stadium since Old No. 7 had retired in the spring of 1999. Cheers come in a variety of tones and timbre. This roar was a sound louder than hope. The fans were again rocking with the knowledge that their Broncos were firmly back in good standing among the league's elite teams.

"Can you believe," I asked Elway, "the Colts cut that guy?"

While shaking his head from side to side, Elway wore the grin of a man with the world on a string.

One more time: Indianapolis did what?

The Colts cut one of the greatest quarterbacks in NFL history.

"And I'm glad they did," said Elway, chuckling.

From Brian Griese to Jake Plummer to Tim Tebow, quarterbacks arrived, quarterbacks went, but the first quarterback to stand taller than Elway's legendary shadow is Manning.

"He's back," said Broncos cornerback Champ Bailey, declaring Manning as good as new. "And he's ready."

Are you ready for this, Broncomaniacs? Could it be that Manning has more skills as a quarterback than Elway possessed? Compare career passing yardage, completion percentage, touchdown passes. Any way you peel back the layers of statistics, the answer is the same: Advantage, Manning.

What Elway achieved as the Broncos' quarterback was bigger than any advanced metric can measure. It was Elway, not 300 days of sunshine per year or teams in all four major professional sports, who transformed Denver from a dusty old cow town to a big-league city.

Denver was not ready yet, and perhaps will not ever fully accept Elway's number one goal for Manning. Before Manning threw a single pass for the Broncos, Elway revealed a dream that showed how comfortable Old No. 7 really is in his own skin. Without question, Elway is confident enough with his place in Colorado sports history to never be envious of what the future holds.

"My goal," Elway said, "is to make Peyton Manning the best quarterback that's ever played the game."

Could it be, I wondered aloud on the March afternoon that Denver signed Manning, that the newcomer already qualified as the most talented quarterback to ever wear a Denver uniform?

"That's up to you guys," responded Elway, talking to the media horde that had assembled for Manning's introduction, but looking directly at me. "I know one thing: Peyton's got a heckuva lot more yards than I ever did."

Quarterbacks, however, are forever judged on far more than their ability to move the chains. Right or wrong, fair or not, a quarterback's place in history is often measured on the number of championships he has won.

Bart Starr led the Green Bay Packers to five NFL titles during the 1960s. Terry Bradshaw and Pittsburgh owned the 1970s, winning four championships. Joe Montana remains cool enough at age 56 to sell the country casual shoes, because he can flash four Super Bowl rings. Would Tom Brady have married a supermodel if not for his three championships in New England?

If the contest is Super Bowl victories, then Elway has Manning beat, 2–1.

Forget the greatest of all time. The lone way Manning can win hearts away from Elway as Broncomaniacs' favorite quarterback is to win championships.

Should Manning win one in Denver for his second NFL championship, the tie would undoubtedly still go to Elway. That only makes sense. While Elway might have started playing football as a kid in Montana and gone to college in California, he is now considered more Colorado than a 1977 Ford Bronco with a weather-worn "NATIVE" sticker peeling at the corners on the rear bumper. Even if Manning eventually owns every Papa John's pizza parlor in Denver, will he ever truly be regarded as a native son?

There is a thought that exists in the dark recesses of Broncomania that Manning should be held at arm's length, viewed as an interloper. In *South Stands Denver*, a popular and often irreverent local sports website, writer Colin Shattuck opened a vein, bled orange, and expressed precisely the deep-set sentiment Manning is up against with some of the team's most devout fans.

"Somehow, signing Peyton Manning feels like cheating—as though the Broncos are taking a short cut the likes of which has never worked before. No QB has won a Super Bowl with one team and gone on to lead another to the promised land," wrote Shattuck, bravely admitting that, for him and Broncos fans like him, seeing Manning wear number 18 in Denver does not quite feel right.

"He's a rental. Or perhaps it's more appropriate to say the Broncos leased him. They won't be able to put too many miles on Manning before it's time to turn him in. Where will they go while they've got him? That's the ultimate question. History tells us that they'll get close, but not quite there, before Peyton reaches the end of his road."

Manning versus Elway is a battle Manning probably will not ever win among the rowdy denizens of the stadium's South Stands. Before joining the Broncos, Manning beat Denver in eight of 10 meetings as quarterback of the Colts, including 41–10 and 49–24 routs by Indianap-

olis in consecutive seasons that were so ugly the losses nearly ran coach
Mike Shanahan out of Denver for a gig with the University of Florida.
Manning has left a scar on the heart of Broncomaniacs that will hurt
forever.

Manning is a welcome visitor in Denver. But this is John Elway's
town.

And there is something else you should know.

Although Elway's reputation as a football executive is directly tied to
the success of Manning, and Old No. 7 warmly regarded Manning as a
friend before handing him a hefty contract with the Broncos, there is a
stubborn chunk of Elway's pride that refuses to concede a thing to
Manning in terms of playing quarterback.

There is zero doubt Elway has the utmost respect for Manning as a
quarterback. But does Elway look at Manning as a quarterback who can
match or better the skills that Old No. 7 brought to the game?

No way. No how.

And I discovered this truth the hard way.

The reminder of how white-hot the competitive fire burns within
Elway hit me with the force of one of his palm-burning, chest-crushing
passes, while I sat in the Dove Valley executive offices across from him.

I was intrigued at how Elway would analyze his and Manning's re-
spective strengths as a quarterback. Sure, they play the same position.
But one was a fireman. The other is a surgeon. Both are heroes who can
come to your rescue in a dire situation. But they get the job done in
very different ways.

Thinking it was an open-ended, unbiased, harmless topic, I asked
Elway: "What's one thing that Peyton Manning does as a quarterback
that's clearly better than a skill you had?"

The answer from Elway was a sigh so heavy it could knock over a
redwood tree. When he was done exhaling, what followed were three
seconds of silence that can only be described as an awkward pause.

Rushing to fill the dead air between us, I blurted: "OK, what's one
attribute of Manning that you would like to beg, borrow, or steal as a
quarterback?"

Elway tried his best to be a diplomat, hide his glare, and not reveal his impatience with my impertinent question. But the competitor in him simply would not allow it. So Elway spoke the truth.

"You know, Mark, that's why you're in the media and not a football player," Elway said. "Because, as a quarterback, I never think that way."

In an instant, the killer instinct in Elway vanished. He launched gracefully into a reasoned, intelligent, calm discussion of how offensive schemes have quickly and drastically evolved from his prime as a quarterback to the way Manning orchestrates decisions at the line of scrimmage in today's NFL.

"It's an entirely different game now," Elway said.

But unable to shake the passion of Elway's brief ready-to-rumble glare, I had to laugh.

The truth was obvious: Elway never, ever allowed himself for one second to believe any NFL quarterback, from Montana to Manning, could get the better of Old No. 7.

His protest against my crazy notion that a quarterback named Elway needed to steal an attribute from Manning was an honestly beautiful moment, one as intensely perfect as anything I had witnessed in close proximity to Michael Jordan or Tiger Woods.

A glimpse at one true thing in the essence of a person is too rare to be ignored. "Where did I mess it up?" I asked Elway. "Did I poke the competitor in you, when I asked if there was one attribute of Manning you wish you could borrow?"

Now laughing with me, Elway replied: "It's always going to be hard, especially in my situation with this team, for me to sit here and compare Peyton Manning and myself. And I don't want to get into that."

Remember when he was hired as the team's executive vice president of football operations, Elway vowed to Broncos Country that his strongest virtue was his competitiveness?

He was not lying.

Elway does not need any of Manning's stinking skills. But believe this: Elway would beg, borrow, or steal for the chance to get back on that field and take Manning's place in the Broncos huddle. A champion never loses his urge to compete, even after a shredded knee needs to be replaced and there are 52 candles to blow out on the birthday cake.

How many NFL cities have been blessed with two of the top dozen quarterbacks to play the game? San Francisco has seen Montana and Steve Young. But they are not Elway and Manning.

Manning turns every masterstroke he brings to the quarterback position into something that could make Paul Cézanne wish he had taken up carpentry instead.

Elway walked into every football fight with such cocksure confidence it could make John Wesley Hardin put away his pistol and slink out of town before dawn, pardner.

"Would I want to do what Peyton does every time he steps to the line of scrimmage? Probably not," Elway said. "I was much more comfortable taking the call that came in from the sideline. I'd trust what would come in from the coach, then go make a play."

At the Pro Football Hall of Fame in Canton, Ohio, there is an exhibit that is a shrine to "The Drive."

Twenty-five years before he brought the Broncos back to championship relevance by recruiting Manning, Elway led the greatest comeback in team history. Trailing the Browns 20–13 with five and a half minutes remaining in the fourth quarter, Elway broke the huddle in Cleveland, with the tying touchdown 98 yards in the distance.

An impossible situation? No way. No how.

Got 'em right where we want 'em.

"I suddenly flashed on something I was thinking about before the game," Elway would later reveal. "Great quarterbacks make great plays in great games. That's what it's all about, isn't it?"

Broncomaniacs know the rest of the story: The five-yard pass on third down to Mark Jackson with the final quarter down to its final 37 seconds. The 33-yard field goal by Rich Karlis that sealed a 23–20 victory in overtime. The legend created, with a story worthy of football immortality.

As a quarterback, Manning is the teacher's pet many C+ students like myself hated in grade school. He does his homework, and checks it twice. He knows every answer in class before the professor can ask. Between the lines of chalk on a board, Manning can read secrets of the football universe using only the letters X and O.

Manning beats NFL defenses before the snap, throwing precisely to a spot his foes fail to realize will be hopelessly vulnerable until it is far too late to prevent a touchdown. His genius as a football player is so celebrated an analyst sometimes lets his SAT scores drool down his chin in an effort to show off pedantic reference points Manning would never dream of using to describe himself.

For example: Here is Stefan Fatsis, in a 2010 ode penned to Manning, comparing an NFL quarterback to the greatest thinkers of the history of mankind.

Without once coming up for air, Fatsis gushed:

> Manning has the attributes of what Malcolm Gladwell has called the popular definition of genius: obsession (notebooks filled with observations on offenses and defenses), isolation (a darkened video room), and insight (a second-half evisceration of the New York Jets' defense in the AFC Championship Game). The 18th-century writer and naturalist Georges-Louis Leclerc (Comte de Buffon), quoted in Nobel-winning neuroscientist Santiago Ramón y Cajal's 1916 book *Advice for a Young Investigator*, put it even more neatly: "Genius is simply patience carried to an extreme."

Whew. Now I would buy a ticket to see if Manning could whip Leclerc in a raucous game of Scrabble, even if the wily old Count of Buffon demanded all the words be spelled in French. But let us not get carried away. In layman's terms, how brilliant a football player is Manning? Well, he can walk over to Demaryius Thomas during practice and tell the wide receiver to solely concern himself with reading the cornerback's moves on an option route, because Manning will take care of worrying about the safeties.

Sure, you could rewind every second of pro football history and not find a more meticulous or cerebral quarterback than Manning. Go to the archives of NFL Films, and you will hear Manning tell his Indy teammates in the huddle: "On my audible, I'll use brown. All right?" At the line of scrimmage, Manning has the mental dexterity to switch plays, using every color in the artist's palette. Orange. Purple. Red.

Manning is admired in the locker room, because he would rather throw himself under the bus than point fingers of blame. After a subpar performance in a preseason game for the Broncos, Manning said: "Every interception has its own story that nobody really wants to hear at the end of the day. The quarterback signs the check on every ball he throws."

His unrelenting perfectionism, combined with uncanny comedic timing, makes Manning a leader teammates love. Yes, he can be an automaton. But Manning is a robot with a sense of humor. "Once you get to know P, you know he's crazy. A funny guy," Colts receiver Reggie Wayne told me.

Manning bristles at any suggestion he is a nerd, that he hates playing in the cold, or his ego intrudes on the decision-making turf of the offensive coordinator. But, in one respect, Manning is reminiscent of former Broncos coach Mike Shanahan, whose two Super Bowl victories and meticulously scripted offensive game plans earned him the nickname Mastermind.

Both Manning and Shanahan are such ardent investigators of the game's nuances that they appear at least three steps ahead of the competition at the outset of the NFL regular season. But, as autumn turns to winter, and the playoffs loom, even the remedial students begin to catch up with Shanahan and Manning. The playing field returns to level. Athleticism increasingly exerts its will on natural intelligence.

And if Manning lacks anything as a quarterback, it is the swagger to match the big moments that made Montana and Bradshaw legends.

Elway exuded a vibe that doing the impossible was his idea of a good time.

Sometimes, Manning appears to be sweating every little detail so hard that he forgets to get up and dance.

From week to week of the NFL regular season, no quarterback has ever painted in more exquisite colors than Manning.

But the NFL playoffs are something less than art. They are a five-alarm fire. Football intelligence does not count as much on the scoreboard as pure athletic instinct. Championship teams are built on heroes stuck in a football crisis thinking all the trouble is fun.

What can possibly go wrong in a playoff game? Everything. All at once, the sky can fall.

15

SKYFALL

No man in Broncos Country better understands the ugly scars left from the shrapnel of shattered dreams. With all the character lines in his 52-year-old face hard-earned through defeat, Elway leaned forward in his office chair to issue a stern warning on an otherwise upbeat afternoon in mid-December. I should have listened. A quarterback who trudged home beaten from the NFL playoffs seven times before lifting the Lombardi Trophy in triumph knows all there is about fear. He learned the hard way, how dreams can take a wrong turn and get lost on a football field.

"There are so many little things that can derail you in the playoffs that I never look ahead now, because I never did look ahead as a player," Elway told me seven days before Christmas, with his Broncos riding the euphoria of a winning streak that had reached nine straight games barely 48 hours earlier, with an utter and complete dismantling of the Ravens in Baltimore. The Super Bowl buzz was everywhere, like flakes in a snow globe. Elway brushed all the hype aside.

"I will remind you of this: I lost twice in the playoffs as a number one seed. And we won a Super Bowl as a number five seed. The bottom line is: Does where you play a playoff game win you that playoff game? Absolutely not. Playing at home doesn't guarantee you anything," Elway said.

It was a foreboding bit of foreshadowing. In the NFL playoffs, play-ing at home is not nearly as important as playing great football.

Unwisely, I did not catch the hint from Elway. And the city of Den-ver was too giddy to see anything ahead except dancing on Bourbon Street for Super Bowl XLVII. And who could blame Broncomaniacs for their runaway optimism?

As the NFL playoffs began, the wise guys in Las Vegas were falling head over heels in love with the team, establishing Denver as the odds-on favorite to win their first championship since Elway retired 14 sea-sons earlier with a victory against Atlanta in the Super Bowl as his going-away present. On New Year's Eve, young Broncos players out celebrating were the toast of the town, which eagerly anticipated the arrival of 2013, because it seemed the time was right for Denver to claim championship rings for the third time in franchise history.

Needing three victories to win it all, fresh and rested off a well-earned bye during the opening weekend of the playoffs, the Broncos' first task seemed almost too easy: Baltimore was not only a nine-point underdog, the Ravens had lost to Manning nine straight times. Denver mayor Michael Hancock, who had worked for $25 per game as Huddles the Broncos mascot in his youth, was so confident his favorite NFL team would advance in the tournament that he offered to do a version of Baltimore linebacker Ray Lewis's trademark "Squirrel" dance in the extremely unlikely event of the visitors pulling off an upset.

To qualify for their trip to Colorado, the Ravens had defeated rookie quarterback Andrew Luck and the Indianapolis Colts during the wild-card round of the playoffs. Lewis, who publicly announced the 17th-season mark as the end of a Hall of Fame career, privately vowed to teammates that they would not lose the final time he strapped on his Ravens helmet and wore a purple number 52 jersey in the shot-and-a-beer town of Baltimore. Marching up the tunnel after trouncing the Colts by 15 points, veteran Baltimore receiver Anquan Boldin loudly asked: "Who are we playing next?"

Nobody had to tell Boldin. He knew damn well a rematch with the Broncos awaited Baltimore, and there was a score to settle.

Boldin was itching for a fight. Who was going to be the first fool to suggest the Ravens had no shot against Denver? The Baltimore media lobbed softball queries to Boldin in the moments after the Ravens dispatched Indy with a no-doubt-about-it victory over the Colts. Somebody had to ask. And, if looks could kill, I would have been six feet on the wrong side of the grass. Boldin buried me with a defiant stare, bristling at the question.

Baltimore appeared helpless in a loss at home to the Broncos late in the regular season. So I asked: What made Boldin believe the outcome could be any different this time, especially on Denver's turf?

"We'll make it different," Boldin insisted.

On December 16, the Broncos had walked into M&T Stadium, exerted their will against Baltimore, and forced the orneriest team in pro football to turn meek and surrender. Denver won 34–17.

Bolden was held without a reception in the humiliating defeat. His frustration was as obvious as a personal foul penalty for going after Denver cornerback Chris Harris, a rising defensive star whose 98-yard interception for a touchdown against Joe Flacco in the final minute of the second quarter ignited the rout.

How bad was the beat down? "We're a 9-5 football team," Flacco said at the time. "And it feels like we're 0-14 right now."

In the NFL, history counts for nothing on the scoreboard. Heading into the Broncos' first playoff appearance in the Manning era, Fox issued the standard coach speak: "Forget about rest, forget about seeds, forget about who you play, when or where."

One day short of four weeks from the moment Denver made Flacco and the Ravens feel like a zero, Baltimore returned the favor when the stakes were much higher.

That's why Saturday, January 12, 2013, is doomed to live in infamy throughout Broncos Country. The thermometer read a frigid 13 degrees. But how Denver lost is what sends shivers down the spine.

There was the obvious pass interference the officials missed when Ravens cornerback Corey Graham returned an interception 39 yards for a touchdown to stake the visitors to a 14–7 lead early in the first quarter.

There was the coverage that Hall of Fame cornerback Champ Bailey blew not once but twice against Ravens receiver Torrey Smith, with the errors resulting in 14 points for Baltimore.

There was the missed 52-yard field goal by Denver kicker Matt Prater that could have staked the Broncos to a 24–14 lead in the final 76 seconds of the opening half.

There was the buzzard's luck of Knowshon Moreno suffering a knee injury that knocked him from the huddle, leaving Denver's running attack with no leg to stand on as the Broncos tried to maintain a late lead.

There was the way Fox nursed the advantage as if his quarterback were Tim Tebow rather than Manning. The Broncos came out of the two-minute warning with a running play by rookie Ronnie Hillman needing seven yards to move the chains on third down in Baltimore territory, rather than giving a quarterback being paid $18 million a chance to clinch the victory with one of those short, accurate passes for which Manning is famous.

Despite all that went wrong, however, the Broncos led 35–28, after punting to the Ravens late in the fourth quarter. Little 5-foot-5 Trindon Holliday, picked up at midseason off the street by Elway and the Denver front office, had cast himself as the biggest hero of the game, by returning a punt 90 yards for a touchdown and a kickoff 104 yards for another score.

The Broncos took the lead, putting the career of Lewis officially on the clock, midway through the final period. A nifty little pass from Manning that Demaryius Thomas turned into a 17-yard touchdown left Lewis facedown, an old, tired man eating dirt in D.T.'s wake. An AFC championship game between Denver and New England, matching Manning versus longtime rival Tom Brady, seemed a near certainty.

Fox certainly must have felt the Broncos needed to do nothing more. At the two-minute warning, with the Ravens unable to stop the clock again, Denver faced a third down at its own 47-yard line. Gain seven yards on the next snap, and the Broncos offense could sit back and laugh, because it would be all over except the crying in the rust belt town of Baltimore. Nobody throws those nifty, safe, little underneath passes better than Manning. This was precisely the situation for which a team pays a Hall of Fame quarterback $18 million per year. But what did Denver do in this situation? Put the football in the hands of Hillman, a rookie running back.

Unbelievable.

Rather than step on the neck of the Ravens, Fox stood back and played beat the clock, satisfied with punting.

"The percentages prove true. Ninety-seven percent, you're going to win the game in that situation," said Fox, who obviously liked his chances as Baltimore's offense took the field, needing a miracle to tie the game.

Out of timeouts, 70 yards from the end zone and regulation time down to its final 41 seconds, all Baltimore had was a prayer. As his offensive teammates took the field, Ravens safety Ed Reed stood on the sideline, shaking his head and mumbling to himself. Lewis buried himself beneath the hoodie of his parka, the way a little kid tries to hide under the covers from the end of grandpa's bedtime story, because once the book snaps closed, there is nothing more to look forward to except the dark.

Strategy gone after a harmless incompletion on first down and an inconsequential scramble by Flacco on second down, what Baltimore did was throw caution into the night sky. Against defenders required to do little on third down except keep the football in front of them no matter how far toward the goal line the Broncos needed to backpedal, Flacco called for four receivers to run four vertical routes.

That is, a Hail Mary. Times four. No matter how you do the math that almost certainly equates to no chance in hell.

After taking the snap, Flacco stepped up in the pocket, dodging severe pressure applied by Broncos defensive ends Elvis Dumervil and Robert Ayers. As the clock ticked, a voice of doubt inside his head urgently suggested discretion called for surrender on this play: Throw the ball away. Throw the ball away. Throw the ball away.

But Flacco told discretion to shut up. "I call him Smokin' Joe," Baltimore receiver Jacoby Jones said. Quarterbacks with big arms are seldom shy at taking a shot. They do not want to be told the odds. Said Flacco: "You have to get a little bit lucky."

Pure dumb luck, however, would have never stood a chance except for the arrogant, unfocused stupidity of Broncos safety Rahim Moore.

As Jones ran behind him at the Denver 30-yard line and Flacco launched a pass with the trajectory of a mortar shot, Moore inexplicably moved without purpose, as if somebody else would do the work for him. Caught too shallow on the route, he was challenging the NFL's strongest arm to blow the football by him. What on Earth was Moore thinking? Or was he thinking at all?

"I think I got a little too happy. I misjudged it, man," said Moore, admitting he was going for an interception that could have cast him as the hero in the final snapshot of the game, rather than playing sound defensive technique that every player learns in elementary school.

As Moore leapt at the pass and made a desperate stab with his left hand, he wore the same hopelessly lost look as a panicky Little League outfielder watching a ball sail over his head.

Near the east sideline of the stadium, in front of the Baltimore bench, Jones caught Flacco's prayer and scampered untouched into the end zone, blowing a kiss to heaven for the 70-yard touchdown that tied the score at 35. Manning stared into space, the road to the Super Bowl suddenly appearing to be to infinity and beyond.

Some way, somehow, the Broncos had to shake off the shock and give hope a chance.

The Ravens kicked off. After the touchback, Denver had possession at the 20-yard line, with two timeouts and the number one quarterback of his generation on its side. Manning had 48 game-winning drives in the fourth quarter or overtime on his sparkling NFL resume. He needed to move the Broncos 45 yards to give Prater a decent shot at a field goal to break the tie.

In Denver's moment of need, Manning took a knee.

Unfathomable.

Tebow would have taken a knee, but only in a short prayer on the sideline, then risen to preach to teammates that faith was invented for crisis.

In his playing days, if Elway had been told by coach Dan Reeves to take a knee, there might have been fisticuffs on the bench.

"No Plan B" does not take a knee.

It felt like a shameless act of surrender. The sky was falling and the Broncos could not find the courage to get up. Many of the 76,732 spectators had a distinct sense this team was doomed the instant Manning assumed the fetal position on the final offensive snap of the fourth quarter. The stadium was filled with dread. No, it was worse than dread. The stadium was filled with booing. In the final seconds of regulation, the Broncos surrendered everything, including the home-field advantage they had worked all season long to gain.

Sports analysts are often accused of second-guessing long after the game is done. At 6:03 PM in the Rocky Mountains, as Denver settled for a coin flip to see which team would receive first crack at avoiding sudden death in the playoffs, I tweeted: "Can't take a knee there, John Fox." On the CBS telecast, Dan Dierdorf beautifully gave voice to what America was thinking: "Am I the only one shaking my head here a little bit? Two timeouts left for Denver, Peyton Manning at the quarterback position and you don't at least give it a whirl?"

Denver lost its nerve.

Big moments call for bold moves.

Denver wimped out.

A leader steps out front and demands action in the face of adversity. The best Fox could offer was a hug and a pat on the rump.

"There is a certain amount of shock value, a little bit like a prize fighter taking a right cross on the chin at the end of the round," said Fox, who detected his players were weak in the knees. "We're looking to get out of the round. That might not be the ideal time to go for the knockout punch."

Rather than pulling egos off the canvas, Fox let his players cede every emotional edge to Lewis and the Ravens, who believed they were on a mission from God. The Broncos got what namby-pamby meekness deserves. In overtime, they were dead men walking.

During the waning seconds of the game's fifth quarter, Manning took a snap at his own 38-yard line, rolled to his right, and probably should have kept running to the concession stands for a cup of hot chocolate. Instead, a veteran quarterback with a history of playoff flameouts suffered total brain freeze, uncharacteristically throwing a pass across his body, into the teeth of the Baltimore secondary.

Although Broncos receiver Brandon Stokley fought for the catch, he got outmuscled for possession of the football at the 45-yard line, and Graham nabbed his second crucial interception of the of the game for the Ravens.

Six snaps later, rookie Baltimore kicker Justin Tucker calmly drilled a 42-yard field goal 1 minute, 42 seconds into the second overtime period to end the Broncos' season with a 38–35 loss.

"Am I the only one in Denver who's happy right now," tweeted Peter Tebow, trolling an entire city in the name of his brother, dumped by Elway so Manning could become the Broncos quarterback.

If God actually cares anything about football, He will penalize you 15 yards for unsportsmanlike conduct for that juvenile display of pettiness, Peter Tebow.

But this is why it will be the name of Rahim Moore that Broncomaniacs will take in vain. Starting with the season-opening game in September against the Pittsburgh Steelers, from rushes to punts and sacks to extra points, Denver took 3,210 snaps to put itself in the best position possible to make a Super Bowl run. And with nothing more than a single 10-second play, all that beautiful work was destroyed.

"I'm taking the blame for it. Hey, I lost the game for us," said Moore, taking full responsibility and never blinking as one question after another cast him as the sacrificial goat of the disheartening loss. "It is what it is."

When Broncos executive John Elway signed Peyton Manning to a $96 million contract in March 2012, the investment paid off handsomely, with two trips to the Super Bowl during the next four seasons. © Eric Lars Bakke/Denver Broncos

Out of the public eye, Manning might have faced his toughest challenge of the 2012 NFL season while rehabilitating in the team's weight room. "Certain things are harder for me than it used to be. It's a different body I'm playing in," he said. © Eric Lars Bakke/Denver Broncos

Manning estimates he has gladly given his autograph to fans more than 100,000 times since college. One caveat: Don't offer him a Terrible Towel from the Pittsburgh Steelers. He won't sign it. © Eric Lars Bakke/Denver Broncos

After the Broncos hired Gary Kubiak as coach, no longer was the team's offense built around Manning's skills, and the veteran quarterback admitted learning a new scheme was extremely difficult. © Eric Lars Bakke/Denver Broncos

With this catch by Demaryius Thomas against the San Francisco 49ers on October 19, 2014, Manning became the NFL's all-time leader in touchdown passes. © Eric Lars Bakke/Denver Broncos

During 58 regular-season games in Denver, Manning passed for 17,112 yards and 140 touchdowns, while also being named MVP of the league during the 2013 season, when he was 37 years old. © Eric Lars Bakke/Denver Broncos

November 15, 2015: A day that will live in infamy in the history of Manning's career. He was benched for Brock Osweiler during a loss to Kansas City, creating a quarterback controversy in Denver. © Eric Lars Bakke/Denver Broncos

While Manning recovered from a painful foot injury, Osweiler stepped in and won five games as the starting QB for Denver in 2015, including a crucial 30–24 overtime victory against New England. Manning was to return to the starting line-up in the last regular game of the season, coming off the bench against San Diego. © Eric Lars Bakke/Denver Broncos

The Last Rodeo: During his final game in 17 seasons as a pro, Manning lifted the Vince Lombardi Trophy after beating Carolina 24–10 in Super Bowl 50 and retired from the NFL as a champion. © Eric Lars Bakke/Denver Broncos

Tell you what it is: The most epic blunder in the history of the Broncos. Since players began pulling on uniforms in 1960, no member of this team has ever made a more monumental mental mistake.

It was an unforgivable mistake by any athlete paid good money to play safety in the NFL. It caused too many sleepless nights to count. It might have cost Manning his last, best chance at another Super Bowl ring. It was a party balloon Moore popped.

"The worst thing about it is," Moore said, "is we're going home. We're going home off a play I could've made, and a play I'm here to make. Coach Fox and the staff, everybody's around me to make that play. And I didn't make it."

In the aftermath of the upset, anybody with an old number 7 Broncos jersey had flashbacks to January 1997. Remember? The irate Jacksonville Jaguars, a second-year NFL franchise disparaged by the *Denver Post*'s Woody Paige as the "Jagwads" in a pregame column, entered Denver a 14½-point underdog, but departed with a 30–27 victory on the strength of Mark Brunell's passing and the running of Natrone Means. "I'm going to go home, sit on my couch and probably cry," said tight end Shannon Sharpe in a sad Denver locker room.

In the sports department of every major newspaper, the copy desk needs at least one person who serves as a living, breathing Wikipedia capable of recalling so many fascinating little-known facts of local athletic lore it could make *Jeopardy!* master of ceremonies Alex Trebek faint. At the *Denver Post* the bottomless well of information is Mike Burrows. Credit—or blame—him for this list:

> To end the 1996 season, Jacksonville beat Elway and the Broncos by three points, the same amount as this stunning setback to Baltimore.
>
> In both instances, the Broncos entered the fateful playoff game with a 13-3 record and the seed in the AFC.
>
> Elway was 36 years old when he lost to Jacksonville. Manning was also 36 when he lost to Baltimore. And what franchise drafted both quarterbacks when they entered the NFL? The Colts.

Mike Shanahan and John Fox seemed to be bound for the Super
   Bowl during their second seasons of coaching in Denver, until
   the Jaguars upset Shanahan and the Ravens beat Fox.

But here is where it gets downright freaky:

In both 1996 and 2012, would you like to guess which team won the
   national championship in college basketball? Kentucky.
The starting running back for the Broncos in both games was a
   proud alumnus from the University of Georgia (Terrell Davis and
   Moreno).
Amy Van Dyken came out of landlocked Colorado to make a big
   splash at the Summer Olympics in Atlanta, swimming to four
   gold medals in 1996. Teenage swimming phenom Missy Franklin
   did Colorado proud at the Summer Olympics in London, winning
   four golds in 2012.

Sixteen years separated two defeats that stole the breath of stunned
Broncomaniacs. Against Jacksonville, Alfred Williams wore number 91
as a defensive lineman. When Flacco lofted a desperation pass and the
sky fell on the Super Bowl dreams of the city 16 years later, Williams
watched as a helpless spectator, while wearing a number 77 throwback
jersey that honored Broncos legend Karl Mecklenburg.

"This loss was worse," said Williams, his eyes glassy with shock as he
trudged down a gray-drab hallway in the underbelly of the stadium.

In those mournful eyes of Williams, the truth was revealed: In defeat, the pain of loving the Broncos is all the same, whether you are a
player on the field or a fan in the stands.

Under the weight of falling skies, hearts break.

As Williams walked past the Broncos locker room, Fox was behind
the closed doors, telling Moore, Manning, and the rest of his disconso-
late team: "Don't let this loss define you."

16

SWIMMING WITH THE SNARKS

On any given Sunday, or any of the other six days in the week, there is a great American pastime growing faster than pro football. It is called snark. Anybody can play, sharp-tongued devils and dumb wits alike.

Welcome to the rise of antisocial media. We the people of the Internet hold this truth to be self-evident: In the wake of any NFL player's knucklehead move, on the field or in a nightclub, the sound of LMAO will be 10 times louder than the comfort the poor fool gets from electronic sympathy cards.

Nasty as we wanna be, full of sarcasm and devoid of context, snark attacks hit and run after 140 characters. Whether directed at the funny bone or below the belt, a cold-blooded snark never apologizes for kicking your sorry hashtag.

If you believe as Baltimore star Ray Lewis does, God suited up in purple and white and took the field as the Ravens' 12th man during the 38-35 upset of Denver on the bitter cold January afternoon that ended the Broncos' season. "God is amazing, and when you believe in him . . ." Lewis preached to CBS sideline reporter Solomon Wilcots after the victory kept the veteran linebacker's retirement tour alive. "Man believes in the possible. God believes in the impossible!"

Lewis praised the Lord. But hell hath no fury like the wrath of Ravens fans, royally pissed at anybody who had doubted their football team. Peyton Manning and the Broncos had not even retreated to the

Denver locker room when the e-mails of vengeance began pounding
my inbox:

> God is having His revenge. Ray Lewis is the messenger to John
> Elway and John Fox for cutting His player: Tim Tebow. And for
> Elway stiffing Baltimore in 1983. (Ravens fan Steve Murfin of
> Queenstown, Maryland)

Whew. The God to whom Murfin prays must really hold a grudge.

Elway left Stanford with an economics degree nearly 30 years before
Lewis beat Manning in the NFL playoffs. Wow, a young Elway must
have spurned Baltimore so ruthlessly it would take God three decades
to get even. In 1983, the young quarterback and his father decided it
would be bad for the Elway family business to play for Frank Kush, the
irascible coach of the Baltimore Colts at the time. The uncommon
leverage held by Elway had nothing to do with football.

The big stick Elway brought to the discussion was a nifty .361 batting
average as a college baseball player. It allowed Elway to issue a threat to
skip out on the NFL draft and join the New York Yankees rather than
suffer with Kush. "Even though the Colts thought I was bluffing, I was
not bluffing," Elway said. "My plan was to go play baseball for a year
and then go back in the NFL draft."

Well, Colts owner Robert Irsay was not going to get pushed around
by some snot-nosed college punk. On May 2, 1983, Irsay ordered the
team to send Elway packing in a trade with Denver for quarterback
Mark Herrmann, the rights to offensive lineman Chris Hinton, and a
future first-round draft choice.

Less than eight months after Elway had forced a controversial,
blockbuster trade, the Colts had played their last game in Baltimore.
Irsay moved the team to Indianapolis. The tough rust belt town in
Maryland cried in its beer. Years later, Manning would join the Colts
and win a championship for Indy. Farther on down the road, Elway
would forsake Tim Tebow and sign Manning.

In the twisted minds of bitter old Baltimore fans, the karmic dots all
finally connected when Ravens rookie kicker Justin Tucker drilled a

field goal through the heart of Elway's grand designs on returning to the Super Bowl with Manning as his quarterback.

But, even for those misguided souls who believe God loves Lewis more than Elway, it might be dangerous to predict the demise of Old No. 7 at any juncture. At age 36, Elway and the two-touchdown favorite Broncos suffered a stunning playoff defeat at home to the Jacksonville Jaguars.

At the time, Elway was an aging quarterback who had never won a championship. His legacy was in doubt. Would Elway ever win the big one? But, rather than sulk, the Broncos used the setback against Jacksonville as motivation. And, a season later, Elway was hoisting the Vince Lombardi trophy to celebrate what would become triumphant, back-to-back Super Bowl runs.

Was this mere coincidence or foreshadowing? The Denver quarterback who hugged Lewis on the field after throwing an interception that set up Baltimore's winning field goal was 36 years old. Is time running out on Manning? Or can Elway envision a storybook ending for Manning that will echo Old No. 7's own heroic finish as player in the late 1990s?

"It's all how we look at it . . . as people, as players, as coaches, as personnel people," said Elway, when conducting the postmortem on the 2012 season, determined not to allow one stunning setback be the death of a Super Bowl dream.

"If we get defensive as individuals and don't listen to the ideas of what happened and how we can learn from those, then, to me, we don't get better. But, if we listen to it, evaluate [the shortcomings], and then correct them, we have a chance."

Winners of the Super Bowl go to Disney World to hang with Mickey Mouse. Goats in the NFL tournament get thrown to the snarks. At the outset of his first season with the Broncos, the arm strength of Manning was questioned. At the end, in the immediate aftermath of losing a home playoff game, Manning endured something far worse. His strength of character was doubted.

"Manning chokes." (Tweeted at 6:48 PM on January 12, 2013, by
Mike Freeman of CBSSports.com)

"Papa Bear just told me he kicked his grill over." (Tweeted at 7:10
PM on January 12, 2013, by @PeytonsHead)

"Dear Peyton Manning: You can never be me—Signed, Tim Tebow." (Tweeted at 7:22 PM on January 12, 2013, by Jemele Hill of
ESPN)

The narrative of an MVP-worthy season had taken a cruel turn:
Manning is pure genius during the regular season. In the playoffs, he
thinks too much.

Fair or not, Manning got stuck between the 1 and the 8 of his
Broncos jersey with the reputation of a lightweight under pressure,
after his three turnovers against Baltimore led to 17 points by the Ravens. His postseason record dropped to a very ordinary 9-11. Worse,
from Indianapolis to Denver, a team with Manning as the starting quarterback has been one and done in the playoffs eight times.

The blitz came hard. Manning got buried with criticism. The allegations stung. His genius shrivels when left out in the cold of winter, when
the temperature at kickoff drops below 40 degrees. His performance in
the clutch stinks.

Do these statistics lie? In 224 regular-season games, Manning's
touchdown pass to interception ratio is a phenomenal 2 to 1. In 20
playoff games, however, his touchdown pass to interception ratio drops
to a pedestrian 1.5 to 1.

In the new media, opinions are formed as quickly as the refresh
button can be hit. Once a headline is repeated or retweeted a thousand
times, it becomes shouted as all-caps absolute truth: MANNING
CHOKES!

There is no denying that Baltimore quarterback Joe Flacco came up
big in the clutch, while Manning took a knee. But as Elway stood at the
entrance of the Broncos locker room fewer than 48 hours after the
abrupt end to Denver's season, he presented some meaningful context

regarding Manning and his hidden anxiety of playing for a new NFL team.

The truth was: Elway was genuinely surprised Manning performed as spectacularly as he did for the Broncos in 17 games, considering Manning had said good-bye to the Colts and uprooted his family after nearly 14 years in Indianapolis.

"Knowing Peyton now compared to how I knew him when he first got to Denver, I realize how much tougher this transition really was for him, because of the type of person he is," Elway said.

Elway and Manning are both Hall of Fame quarterbacks. But they are a football odd couple. Built for chaos, Elway trusts his impeccable instincts and comes out firing. With a red Sharpie and a checklist, Manning cannot rest until he assigns a place and a task to every atom in his universe.

"For him," Elway said of Manning, "the picture of playing quarterback is so much bigger. He looks at so many different things. Everybody's different, but as I look at Peyton now, I realize the transition to a new team had to be huge for him.

"I'm not saying it's wrong. Everybody's different. But he likes to know every detail. He doesn't like the building falling down around him. He wants to know every brick in the building. That's his personality. He wants to know everything that's going on. And, if he doesn't know it, he doesn't feel as comfortable and he's not as confident."

For Manning, the football unknown is the equivalent of the monster under a kindergartner's bed. It makes it hard for Manning to sleep at night. A member of the Broncos staff joked with me that Manning will not truly feel at home in Sports Authority Field at Mile High until he memorizes not only the full legal names of all 75,000 fans in the stadium, but also the make, model, and license-plate number of every car, truck, and minivan they all drive to the game.

Well, here is another theory: It is not fear of the cold that messed with Manning's ability to play quarterback against the Ravens. After spending the vast majority of his pro career playing home games in a dome, it was the lack of firsthand exposure to freezing weather that prevented Manning from calculating every variable to fine-tune his physical and psychological adjustments to adverse conditions. To the bitter end and in the bitter cold, Manning will always be a mad football scientist on a never-ending quest for data points that can give him an edge.

Sure, the loss to Baltimore churned in Manning's gut. But, within hours of the upsetting defeat, his road to recovery began with trying to make sense of it all, learn from it all, and grow from it all. Losing stunk. It also made the NFL's most unabashed brainiac quarterback even smarter.

"That was another good hurdle for me. Weather-wise, we had not had anything like it all season. There was some unknown going into that game, and you can't simulate it. I tried everything from putting my hand in a freezing tank, but you just can't simulate it," Manning confided to *Denver Post* reporter Mike Klis.

Obsessed with details even while stuck in the funk caused by defeat, Manning had already taken a peek at the 2013 NFL calendar, a season that would end, after the calendar flips to 2014, with a Super Bowl contested in the dead of winter in a stadium across the Hudson River from New York City.

Does Manning think too much to be clutch in the playoffs? Well, maybe, but it might be easier to halt the world from turning than to stop the mind of Manning from processing info.

On a day when Broncos Nation was grieving a squandered championship opportunity, the team's quarterback was already plotting and scheming how to win the next Super Bowl.

Eli Manning won a ring with the New York Giants to conclude the 2011 NFL season, when the final game was played in Indianapolis, on his big brother's home turf.

Have you checked the calendar? On February 2, 2014, the Super Bowl is scheduled for MetLife Stadium, the home field of the Giants and Peyton Manning's little brother.

Think maybe the football gods have already connected those karmic dots?

> This loss has such a stench of fix and pay-off and Black Sox, I can't keep any food down. I call for an audit of both Champ Bailey's and Rahim Moore's bank accounts. This is a league fix to have all these inexplicable plays happen, along with the most bush-league refs I have seen since "'The Replacements.'" The Broncos were told to lay down and not make it look too obvious. (e-mailed at 11:22 AM on January 13, 2013, by Bill Voor, NFL fan in Indiana)

Is it unreasonable to scream the fix was in after a Broncos loss? Totally.

Is it unusual to find a dark cloud hanging over one of the sunniest states in America when the Broncos get beat? Not at all.

Around here, NFL football does have the spooky ability to transform otherwise gainfully employed and mild-mannered people into stark-raving mad snarks. There must be a cable-network executive who can figure out how to profit from this stranger-than-fiction craziness. "Snark Week." Coming soon to Discovery Channel. Check your local listings.

In Broncos Country, there were crying baby boys, girls, and puppies named Peyton. In Broncos Country, the tears of this playoff loss to Baltimore were recorded for posterity by video camera–toting family members. In Broncos Country, defeats are bad for productivity and profits, from depressed workers calling in sick with the orange-and-blue flu to empty bar stools at watering holes in the LoDo entertainment district of downtown Denver.

"Growing up, I always wondered what it be like to be a Boston Red Sox fan and see your city endure a Bill Buckner moment. Or to be a Chicago Cubs fan and live through that Steve Bartman moment. For Denver, this was that moment. The Rahim Moore moment. It is a scar. It is a sports scar on the city," said Peter Burns, host of *The Press Box*, a sports talk show simulcast weekday mornings on 93.7 FM and 1510 AM.

On the afternoon after Flacco launched a desperation pass and the sky fell on the Broncos, the top-rated television station in Denver focused a camera on the team's empty stadium as the sun hid behind the Rocky Mountains in shame.

"It looks sad and empty, doesn't it?" said 9News anchor Mark Koebrich, looking at images of the deserted football venue.

"Oh, it does. I hate to see that," replied evening news cohost Cheryl Preheim, with the same empathy a mother uses to soothe an injured child.

Then, in a tone as somber as Edward R. Murrow reporting from the front, Koebrich declared: "A sad day for Colorado."

It could have qualified as parody, except in Denver, where football mourning is deemed absolutely necessary.

The team conducted its own postmortem, where Elway and Broncos coach John Fox were interrogated in the same theater at the team's training facility where the signing of Manning had been announced months earlier. The real peek behind the curtain of the Broncos' anguish, however, was offered after the formal press conference ended.

Out in the hallway, it was apparent Fox did not want to leave the building, as if he feared the sound of the door closing behind him would rattle his soul. His next assignment was to hop on a jet to Hawaii, coach the AFC all-stars at the Pro Bowl, and hang out for a week by the pool. "You think I'm looking forward to that? Hell no," Fox confessed. "Hawaii is the last place I want to go right now."

The coach's pain was real and to the bone. Before turning on his heels and getting on with life, Fox gently put a hand on my elbow and said: "I'm sorry. Tell everybody I'm sorry."

In Broncos Country, as miserable hours stretch into interminable days after an upsetting loss, there is No Plan B.

Love hurts.

Broncos Country needed something to mend broken hearts.

> You can post this where ever . . . Denver broncos will win the Super Bowl 2013 #4UJEREMIAH #IGUARANTEEIT58 if you are with us Retweet (Tweeted at 8:17AM on March 5, 2013, by Broncos linebacker Von Miller)

The moping ended with a tweet.

Von Miller, the top defender on the Broncos, guaranteed a Super Bowl victory.

He could have taken out a full-page newspaper ad. But that would have been so 1998. Instead, Miller shared his bold prediction with 784,711 followers on Twitter and mobilized his army of admirers to spread the word.

"I fully believe in the Broncos winning the Super Bowl and am fully committed to it," Miller said from New York City, during a telephone interview in early March. "If you go in the Denver Broncos locker room, I'm sure there are other players who have made the same guarantee to themselves."

It was a six-year-old car wreck victim that inspired Miller's quest.

When Denver won its first NFL championship by beating Green Bay in January of 1998, Broncos owner Pat Bowlen dedicated the victory to quarterback John Elway.

Miller vowed the next one will be won in the name of Jeremiah, whose emergence from a coma filled the linebacker with joy he felt compelled to share.

In late February of 2013, Jeremiah Clark-Martinez and two members of his family were hurt in a car accident near their West Texas home. Jeremiah's brother suffered a fracture in his back, while his mother broke her collarbone.

The accident shook Miller to the core. "That was the whole feeling behind this guarantee. It wasn't because I felt all cocky," Miller explained. "This is bigger than me. This is all about my little cousin coming back from a serious accident."

His spirits lifted by a child who dodged death, Miller stole a page from legendary New York Jets quarterback Joe Willie Namath, the original Super Bowl prognosticator in the house. So what if the early betting line established by Las Vegas oddsmakers had established the New England Patriots as the 5-to-1 favorite to win Super Bowl XLVII?

When Jeremiah opened his eyes from a coma, it allowed Miller to see the future so clearly it felt like destiny.

Long before the Broncos were scheduled to open training camp, much less win a game in the 2013 regular season, Miller put pressure on himself and his teammates with a singular goal: Super Bowl or bust.

"Being a pass rusher in the NFL is all about pressure. I'm no stranger to pressure. I embrace it," said Miller, plucked by the Broncos out of Texas A&M with the number two overall pick in the 2011 NFL draft. He has met, or exceeded, all expectations, recording 30 sacks and twice being named to the Pro Bowl.

His love for Jeremiah is too big to shrink from high expectations.

As Miller told the story, his six-year-old cousin lapsed into a coma that was medically monitored. Young Jeremiah was transferred from the site of the accident in the Midland-Odessa area to a hospital in Lubbock, then to another healthcare facility in metropolitan Dallas.

When Jeremiah finally awoke during the first weekend in March, medical personnel asked the young boy questions to test his brain functions.

Do you have a cousin who plays football?

"Yes," Jeremiah said.

Do you know his name?

"Von," Jeremiah said. "Von Miller. He's a linebacker for the Broncos."

Miller was touched. And fired up. The Denver linebacker who wears number 58 hopped on his Twitter account and declared his mission to nearly 800,000 followers.

Yes, the incredible comeback story of Manning jumped the snark. It was a sad turn of events.

Miller was the first member of the Broncos to fight back against that sad fate. The story of this team was not done, Miller insisted. It had only just begun.

Of course, Miller understood as well as anybody: Words do not count in the NFL. Touchdowns do. But pressed to reconsider, Miller refused to back down one inch from his pledge. "You're not going to have success in football or any other endeavor in life if you don't embrace pressure," Miller said.

On the night when all of Denver struggled to deal with the double-overtime loss to Baltimore, long after his teammates had departed the stadium, Miller slumped in a chair in front of his locker stall, still wearing his white uniform pants long after all his teammates had left the building. "Devastating," Miller repeated, as reporter after reporter sought his opinion of the loss.

Healing requires time. But inspired by a six-year-old cousin who relentlessly battled back from a serious injury, Miller sent a message to Denver:

The crying game was over.

17

DOOM 'N' BOOM

This is how a dream frames NFL stardom: The handsome young millionaire emerges from a Bentley with a brunette supermodel on his arm, then slips effortlessly past the velvet rope for bottle service at a club where the rhymes of Jay-Z thump deep into a sweet summer night.

The life seems almost too good to be true.

But know the trouble with dreams? Dreams are short. Reality bites. It bites long. It bites hard. It leaves a mark.

Ask Elvis Dumervil. During six seasons working for the Broncos, he sacked the quarterback more than 60 times. Despite coming up short in his quest to reach six feet tall, Dumervil earned Pro Bowl accolades in 2009, 2011, and 2012. His lucrative contract, richly deserved, paid Dumervil $61.5 million over the course of its six-year term.

Being Doom was better than a dream.

Then, he got kicked to the curb by the Broncos.

Dumervil loved the NFL team that made him a star. His identity was tied to the Broncos, with the same deep-rooted pride that Peyton Manning believed he would be the Colts quarterback for life.

The question is: Would you take a 35 percent pay cut to keep a job you loved?

It is an unfair question. But it is the question the Broncos asked of Dumervil.

Whether you drive a bus or rush the quarterback for a living, the question can challenge the core value of any man. In America, many of us keep score through our paycheck stubs.

In the NFL, the toughest part of taking a pay cut is never the reduction in dollars. The real pain for any athlete is in choking down his pride.

Dumervil did good work for the Broncos. Then, he was told by the boss that his labor was no longer good enough to merit his $12 million annual salary.

"It's not all about the dollars. But when it's way out of whack? Then it's so out of whack you've got to say: That [salary] can't be it, especially when you look at the market and what's out there now," said Broncos executive John Elway. He had a dilemma with a salary for Dumervil that the team had carefully analyzed and deemed extravagant.

"It's so far out of whack," Elway concluded. "Hopefully, he realizes that."

As a quarterback, Elway wrote his legend on save-the-day comebacks, as the scoreboard clock ticked toward disaster that could be averted only if he delivered a big play. Elway feasts on adrenaline. His heart beats slowly when chaos swirls around him. But even a football hero can have a soft underbelly. When Elway needs to make a tough call, his tummy growls.

As the hours and minutes slipped away toward 2 PM on March 15, 2013, the deadline pressure was treating Elway's stomach like a punching bag. It was a drop-dead deadline. At the moment the clock struck 2, the Broncos would have to guarantee a salary they were not willing to pay Dumervil.

It shaped up to be an uncomfortable staring contest. An old quarterback versus a young defensive end. In the beginning, this tiff was about money. Nothing can ruin a beautiful relationship in a happy home faster than financial squabbling. But, in the end, as negotiations drag on, the disagreement becomes a matter of ego. Machismo makes it hard for either side to back down.

After losing to Baltimore in the playoffs, Elway was determined to improve the talent level of his ballclub. He wasted no time getting down to business in free agency, signing reinforcements for the offensive line, the receiving corps, the big uglys in the defensive trenches and a secondary that had been torched by Baltimore quarterback Joe Flacco.

A major remodeling project is not cheap, especially if quality parts are used. Before negotiations with Dumervil approached the eleventh hour, the Broncos handed out the money they wanted Doom to sacrifice. That money was given to cornerback Dominique Rodgers-Cromartie, defensive tackle Terrence Knighton, perennial Pro Bowl receiver Wes Welker, middle linebacker Stewart Bradley, and right guard Louis Vasquez.

Those purchases alone were a commitment of more than $45 million from the wallet of franchise owner Pat Bowlen. And here was the rub. Every last dime went into the pockets of new players, athletes who had yet to give a bead of sweat or a drop of blood to the Broncos. Dumervil had worked hard for his money, and done his work with a smile since joining the team as an unheralded, underappreciated fourth-round draft choice from the University of Louisville in 2006.

With precious little wiggle room left to negotiate under the salary cap, the Broncos needed Dumervil to take a pay cut. A major haircut, with a shave of more than $4 million off the top. How did a salary in the neighborhood of $7.5 million sound?

The 29-year-old defensive end could take it, or leave town. The NFL calendar dictated the money on his old contract would be guaranteed at 2 PM on March 15, and Elway made it obvious the Broncos were not bluffing. They would rather do without Dumervil than pay him far above market value.

If the Colts could cut Manning, then Dumervil had to understand that Elway would not hesitate to fire him.

"These are the deals that wrench your gut," said Elway on the eve of a deadline. Elway pulled out his cell phone and gave it a glance for messages. He had Dumervil's fate in his hands. Elway stood in team headquarters, one floor above the Broncos locker room, in the executive offices where sentiment must be shoved aside and decisions are made that impact the life of an athlete.

Dumervil had benefited from the inexperience of former Broncos coach Josh McDaniels, who rewarded one of the league's fiercest pass-rushers with a hefty contract in 2010. But Doom's leverage was gone, because the deal was no longer worth much more than the paper on which that contract had been printed.

Fans love the fact that unlike the NBA, where a point guard gets paid whether he deserves the money or not, the NFL limits guaranteed money to its athletes. In practice, however, it allows pro football teams to make players pay for management's budgetary mistakes.

"As an ex-player, I hate to see that," Elway admitted. "I hated to see that happen to a teammate. And I hate having to do it in the position I'm in now. But I've got to do what's best for this football team."

The hammer in the tool belt of any builder of an NFL franchise is public opinion. For fans, football is a lifelong labor of love. For a player, football is a short career that could be ended by one fluke injury.

Players are blessed with a job many fans would do for free. But it is a job. And many fans do not get it. So what we have here is failure to communicate. Without a second thought of reflection, die-hard Broncomaniacs questioned Dumervil's loyalty to the city and dedication to a championship cause, all because Doom showed the temerity to put his personal financial welfare above what pleased Denver fans.

"It isn't just about the money. We also know what Elvis brings to the team and what his leadership means," Elway said. "But, at a certain point, you have to make a decision, one way or another. Is it worth doing X and losing Y?"

It was on Dumervil to capitulate. Was that fair? Hell, no. Is that life in the NFL? Lord, yes.

For years to come, the words "March 15th" might sound like a curse coming out of Elway's mouth. It was not among the brighter days in Broncos history, but it surely will be remembered as one of the more bizarre melodramas ever to play out at Dove Valley.

The Denver career of Dumervil ended not on the field, but at Kinko's in South Florida. A $30 million deal fell apart because of a $750 piece of office equipment.

Dumervil has beaten Pro Bowl offensive tackles to the quarterback. But his effort to get back on the Broncos roster after a messy contract squabble was blocked by a fax machine.

Yes, a fax machine.

At 2 PM on March 15, the Broncos cut Dumervil because he was unable to get his signature on a contract worth $30 million to the team's Dove Valley headquarters on time.

We are a nation of procrastinators. We are late with the rent, late to admit our mistakes, late for our own funerals.

But Dumervil took so long to make up his mind that by the time he hit the transmit button on a fax machine in Florida, it was too late and his procrastinating derriere was being sent out of Colorado forever.

When the Broncos finally received the signature page of Dumervil's contract, the clock flashed 2:06 PM. Six minutes and a second earlier, a fuming Elway had officially cut one of the team's best defensive players. The Broncos felt as if they had no other choice.

When the clock struck 2, NFL regulations would have required the terms of the defensive end's old, overpriced contract to take effect. Without a new document to ship to the league office, Denver saw cutting Dumervil as less unsavory than paying him a guaranteed salary of $12 million for 2013.

In a world where a smartphone can light the fireplace in your hearth from halfway across the country or issue the airline ticket to fly you home, Dumervil was done in by old, dumb technology. A fax fiasco spelled doom for him.

All week long, Elway had been whispering sweet nothings in Dumervil's ear: Stay in Denver. Chase a Super Bowl ring with the Broncos.

Better yet, those words of encouragement were backed with cold, hard cash.

In the end, the Broncos offered Dumervil a 2013 salary of $8 million. Sure, it was a 33 percent pay cut. But it was a nicer salary than prized defensive end Cliff Avril received when signing as a free agent with Seattle earlier in the same month, when players discovered it was a buyers' market.

Late on that fateful Friday morning in March, the Broncos issued Dumervil an ultimatum, in the friendliest way possible: Negotiating was done. The deal would get no sweeter. The team needed a final answer no later than 1 PM, in order for the paperwork to be filed with the league office ahead of the deadline.

Doom said no.

Through his agent, Marty Magid, the Broncos' last, best offer was rejected at 1 PM. The team began drawing up termination papers and discussing life after Dumervil.

Twenty-five minutes later, Doom changed his mind. It was a classic case of big-decision remorse. He instructed his agent to contact the team with the good news: Doom wanted back on the Broncos.

At 1:25 PM, team executives were surprised and delighted to hear Dumervil would sign the contract after all. But the game became beat the clock. All the paperwork needed to be filed within 35 minutes.

The complicating factor? Magid was in Philadelphia. Dumervil was in Miami. Elway was in Colorado.

Everybody got beat by logistics.

As hearts raced faster, the fax machine bonked. The contract stalled somewhere between South Beach and the Rocky Mountains. Dumervil tried to send the fax. His intentions were good. His transmission was bad.

At 1:55 PM, the Broncos pulled the plug on the deal. Putting it politely, the team was miffed.

Within the next testy 24 hours, Dumervil fired Magid, leaving little doubt where blame for the fax fiasco was dumped. The shaken football star hired Tom Condon, whose list of NFL clients reads like a Who's Who list of players.

But any technology-literate fifth grader could have given Dumervil all the advice he really needed for free: Never fax. Scan and e-mail. It is faster. And less expensive. About $30 million less expensive.

It is a tribute to both Dumervil and Elway that a fax machine did not shred their relationship. After cooling down and recovering from the shock, the team and the player both approached the league office to inquire if the fax faux pas could be forgiven, so the agreement between the two parties could be honored. It sounded like a reasonable solution. But the NFL decided against giving the Broncos special consideration. The answer was no.

From the instant the appeal was denied, try as Elway and Dumervil might to patch things up, it was a losing proposition.

While the Broncos had saved considerable out-of-pocket expenses by cutting Dumervil, the action also forced the team to take a $4.89 million hit against the salary cap for 2013. And perhaps that was the worst damage done by the fax machine. The fax fiasco put a major ding in Denver's ability to acquire more talent for another Super Bowl run. Trust was broken. If I wrecked your car yesterday, you might forgive me today. But are you going to let me take it for another spin tomorrow? Only if you are a saint. Or a fool.

So, in the end, it came as zero surprise that Dumervil and the Broncos were unable to repair their fractured relationship. The only slap-in-the-face shocker was where Dumervil landed on the NFL map.

For the second time in barely more than two months, Baltimore beat Denver in the end. Dumervil signed with the Ravens, agreeing to a five-year, $35 million contract on March 24. But the devilish detail was his salary for 2013 of $8.5 million. That was $500,000 more than the Broncos' best offer. Guess everything has a price, including a man's pride.

Keeping with his nature, Dumervil did his very best to be gracious as he glanced back at Colorado in his rearview mirror. When introduced by Baltimore, Dumervil said: "At the end of the day, there was no ill will or hard feelings. I just felt it was a time to change scenery."

Pro football players might be rich and famous, but they are not really so different from you or me. Everybody needs to feel wanted. The same as Manning before him, Dumervil was stupefied and mortified that the Broncos actually cut him. The same as Manning before him, Dumervil sought refuge in an NFL city that felt comfortable. The linebacker

coach of the Ravens is Don "Wink" Martindale, who not so coinciden-
tally worked for the Broncos in 2009, when Dumervil switched posi-
tions from defensive end to outside linebacker in a 3-4 scheme and
recorded 17 sacks during the breakout season of his pro career.

Bitterness converted to positive energy can propel a jilted football
player toward redemption. When Doom joined the Ravens, the honesty
leaked from the corners of his smile. "I never intended to leave Denver,
but things happen," Dumervil said, before delivering his real farewell
shot at the Broncos: "I have a chip on my shoulder. I may have a brick
wall now."

No act of loyalty goes unpunished in the NFL.

In New England, the connection between Tom Brady and Wes
Welker was far stronger than the more than 500 throws and receptions
between them. They were best friends forever. When Welker teased
Brady for his lack of running ability, the tall, dark, and handsome quarterback cursed and the feisty 5-foot, 9-inch slot receiver laughed. When
Brady vacationed with wife Gisele Bündchen in Costa Rica, his little
buddy was invited along to hang out on the beach.

"When you think of dependability, you think of Wes," Brady told the
Boston Globe.

Welker was a quarterback's best friend. And New England coach
Bill Belichick treated Welker like a dog.

The Patriots Way is sustained excellence built on disposable parts.
Whenever Welker hinted at his desire for a contract commensurate to
his production, Belichick shot him the evil eye, and Brady's BFF
backed down. In 2011, when Welker should have made a stink with a
holdout, he instead made peace by accepting a franchise tag worth $9.5
million. He was New England's patsy. The team seemed to believe
Welker did not have the stones to leave.

Well, the Patriots were wrong. Welker busted coverage, and
grabbed a two-year, $12 million offer to join the Broncos on March 13,
two days before Dumervil was cut. Elway might be 52 years old and
walk on an artificial left knee, but with one bold move, Old No. 7
proved he can still beat the snot out of Brady.

A month earlier, Brady had agreed to a contract extension with New England with the specific goal of allowing the Pats to maintain a strong supporting cast in return for the veteran quarterback's charitable act of taking less than market value for his services during the waning years of a Hall of Fame career. When the team let Welker walk over what amounted to chump change by NFL standards, Brady felt as if he had been "pierced in the heart," according to Michael Silver of Yahoo! Sports.

"That was definitely the hardest part, leaving Tom," Welker admitted, as he was being fitted for a Broncos jersey at age 31.

Working the middle of the field as a slot receiver should qualify for hazardous duty pay in the NFL. For six seasons in New England, when Welker removed his uniform at the end of games, his back often resembled one giant ink-blot test, black and blue from the bruises. So I asked Welker: To be a slot receiver, do you need to be tough, or crazy? "Both," he replied. "I think you have to have a little something about you."

That tough little bastard had worn out his welcome in New England. It is toughness the Broncos needed, to such an extent that when Welker was introduced to the Denver media, coach John Fox stood at the side of the room and applauded.

While pounding his palms together, Fox caught my eye and I laughed, tickled by the coach's spontaneous, genuine, childlike enthusiasm. "Hey, Kiz," Foxy said later. "Why were you killing me when I clapped for Welker? I didn't know you were supposed to be quiet at a press conference. So I applauded. Heck, I'm happy to see him. I'm happy we've got him."

In the NFL, they always applaud on your way in the door.

But, in the NFL, even stardom fails to provide sanctuary.

Loyalty is often a one-way street.

Manning gave Indianapolis 11 seasons of quarterback played with Pro Bowl excellence. The Broncos got three Pro Bowl seasons from Dumervil. Every year from 2008 to 2012, Welker did not stop running precision routes until he got to Pro Bowl.

Three players. And those three stars have 20 appearances at the Pro Bowl among them. Yet, at the end of the day, what Manning, Dumervil, and Welker did for their NFL employers was deemed not quite good enough to merit their big salaries.

Remind me: Who has the commitment issues in this league?

Whether your name is Manning, Dumervil, or Welker, somebody's career gets blown up every day in the Not For Long.

Boom.

18

NEVER TAKE A KNEE

The words were not only barked with authority at the line of scrimmage as Peyton Manning awaited the snap of the football, they also definitively described his first year in Denver:

"Hurry! Hurry!"

Stop and smell the roses? At times, Manning was so obsessed with giving the team its $18 million worth, you wondered if the quarterback even noticed the snowcapped majesty of the Rocky Mountains that overlook the team's practice facility. Early in his debut campaign with the Broncos, Manning was asked which of Colorado's many splendid tourist attractions he had crossed off his do-list. Garden of the Gods? The Denver Mint? "Sorry," Manning said, "I can't help you there." His whole world was the playbook, the film room, and the huddle.

In fact, after leading the Broncos on 78 scoring drives in 17 games, Manning sheepishly admitted a Pro Bowl quarterback can be lost and utterly without a clue when he is behind the wheel while running errands in Denver, even after more than 12 months as a Colorado resident.

"I'm still capable of getting lost on my way to the barber shop, because I've never really had a good sense of direction. So I still might have to call my wife from the car to find my way around town," said Manning, shaking his head with bemusement at his chronic inability to differentiate north from south unless he is on a football field.

Hurry? Hurry? Well, want to know the real secret of Manning's success with the Broncos after a tumultuous year when both the game he loved and the only job he ever wanted were taken away from him in Indianapolis?

The secret was slowing down. Manning, the riddler with an insatiable desire to know it all and know it all now, managed to take it one step at a time, while rebuilding his quarterback skills from scratch and learning to heed his body's advice on new physical limitations. The physical constraints of a banged-up, aging body required adjustments as obvious as that bright orange glove he wore on his throwing hand when winter arrived in Colorado. Recognition is an invaluable football skill. But recognition is only the first step. Nobody in the NFL adjusts better than Manning.

"Getting to know the fans of Denver has added to my comfort level. When I came in here a year ago, I really didn't have time to get to know Colorado very well, because I really had to immerse myself in learning everything I could about playing football for the Broncos," Manning said.

In the five-year period from 2008 through 2012, more than three million net jobs were lost in the United States. Manning fell prey to those grim statistics, another good American worker kicked to the curb. Of course, being an NFL quarterback does have its privileges. Manning never had to worry about putting food on the table. But as he sat and helplessly watched the Colts prepare for a future that did not include him, Manning did worry a job he loved might be gone forever.

When a proud man gets knocked down, what can he do?

The options are: (1) hide beneath the covers and wallow in the pain, or (2) get your sorry butt out of bed and move on to Plan B.

Manning was John Elway's first and only choice to return the franchise to championship glory.

But truth be told: The Broncos were Manning's Plan B.

There is no Plan B? Without it, Manning would have never made Broncos Country his home.

For an unabashed perfectionist, the plan all went perfectly for Manning until the final minute of the fourth quarter against Baltimore. On that day, you could smell trouble coming.

In that stunning playoff loss, as the game grew older and the evening grew colder, it appeared the Broncos had lost their appetite for the fight. They began playing the odds rather than finishing off the Ravens. Safety Rahim Moore recognized the deep pass coming. But he adjusted too late. And the contest was over as soon as Manning took a knee with the score tied and 31 seconds remaining in the fourth quarter.

No más.

The look of surrender in players' eyes was a sad sight Broncomaniacs never want to see again.

"Just because you've watched a fight," said Broncos coach John Fox, responding to my howls against his conservative fourth-quarter strategy, "doesn't mean you know what it's like to get hit."

Well, I know this: The battle goes on, even if you do not. There's no safe place to hide in the NFL.

From here on out, so long as Manning is the emcee rapping the audibles in Denver, there should only be one circumstance in which it is acceptable to take a knee: in a victory formation, when the crowd is counting down the seconds to the final gun. "We want our offense to dictate what the defense does and not react to what any other team is doing," brilliant young Broncos assistant coach Adam Gase said.

The Broncos found reasons to play angry in 2013.

The Colts told Manning thanks for the memories, but get lost. Fox was fired in 2010 by the Carolina Panthers when ownership dismantled the roster and blamed a 2-14 record on the coach. After being burned for two long touchdowns by Baltimore receiver Torrey Smith in the loss to the Ravens, perennial Pro Bowl cornerback Champ Bailey heard disrespectful grousing from the cheap seats that it was time for him to move to safety, or maybe to a rocking chair on the porch.

This was a team with a bag full of chips on its shoulders. Having failed once to win the Super Bowl with Manning, maybe what Denver discovered is that it does need a Plan B. Under the harsh light of self-evaluation, perhaps the Broncos found a new motto in the relentless pursuit of a championship: Never take a knee.

"I know that John Elway wants to set kind of an attitude and an edge around here, maybe a little bit of an uncomfortable atmosphere, which I believe in," Manning said.

Never be satisfied. Never slow down. Never take a knee.

In his first season as quarterback in Denver, Manning and the Broncos led the league in scoring, at 30 points per game. Impressive? Sure. But is it good enough? Not in the NFL of 2013, when defenses often appear defenseless.

Pro football has entered a cycle where it is all crazy video-game numbers. During the quarterfinal round of the Super Bowl tournament, the Broncos scored 35 points. How could that not be good enough? The four winners who advanced to the conference finals did so by averaging in excess of 38 points.

Any quarterback can throw for 300 yards in an afternoon. The new standard of excellence is 400 yards in a game. The NFL requires a new metric for measuring offensive success. The traditional charting of time of possession is as quaint as the old ticktock of a grandfather clock.

What might be a more meaningful statistic for the NFL's brave, new, wired world? Points per possession. During Manning's first year in Denver, the Broncos scored 49 offensive touchdowns and 26 field goals on 190 regular-season drives. That averaged to 2.22 points per possession. Should Denver find a way to average 2.50 points per possession, defensive coordinators throughout the league would turn into grumpy insomniacs.

But was it realistic to expect that Manning could somehow improve on his passer rating of 105.8, a number that suggested his debut with the Broncos was the second-best season of his brilliant career?

"I think Peyton can keep getting better," Elway said. "There's no question."

Anything less than a championship is not good enough. Never take a knee.

Although he wears clothes on the sideline that look as if they were retrieved from the bottom of the hamper, New England coach Bill Belichick marches one step ahead of the fashion curve. From 2010 to 2012, the go-go Patriots averaged 529 points per season. This is no time for the Broncos to slow down.

"We're going to try to play faster," said Gase, promoted to offensive coordinator less than a week after the Broncos were eliminated from the playoffs. The Denver offense took 1,090 snaps in 2012. He sought to find a way to give Manning 100 more snaps a season.

"We're looking to go pedal to the metal and play as fast as possible and score as many points as possible every game," said Gase, who thinks so fast there's often no room for a comma, much less a breath, when he speaks.

"I know this: We want as many plays on offense as we can possibly create. Because you know those guys on the other side of the field don't want to see the football in the hands of Peyton Manning upwards of 80 plays a game, especially in Denver, at altitude. That's the last thing a defense wants to see. As a defense, that will get in your gourd, man."

Take a knee? Never again.

"I think we averaged 68 plays per game. And New England was number one with 75 plays per game," said Manning, who knows the exact number of snaps he took in 2012, without having to peek at the stat sheet. "We can play faster. Any time you can put different types of pressure on the defense, that's what you want to do. I think we have shown that we can play super fast or we can slow it down with a check audible at the line of scrimmage. Our offense plays better the faster we go. I think that's clear-cut."

Welcome to the revolution. Entering his 16th NFL season, the last thing Manning wanted to do is pump the brakes. With the addition of Pro Bowl receiver Wes Welker to the offense, the football would be flying fast and furious in an offense directed by Manning. "I don't think it can ever be maxed out," Gase said.

Hurry! Hurry!

On the road to the Super Bowl, there is no speed limit.

As a player, Elway lost the Super Bowl three times, by an aggregate score of 136–40, before finally putting a big, happy squeeze on the Vince Lombardi Trophy at age 37. On the way to the Hall of Fame, even a quarterback on his A game gets sacked again and again and again.

More telling, Elway lost his marriage to divorce, his sister to cancer, and his father to a heart attack before meeting a new wife and discovering a new purpose as the Broncos executive vice president of football operations. It inevitably happens to almost every man after his 40th birthday. Things you love begin to die. Going a little middle-age crazy is normal. Coming out the other side is tougher. It requires adjustment. It requires a Plan B.

"As a player, all I wanted was the hope instilled by the people at the top of the organization. I wanted the hope they were going to give me the very best chance to compete and win a world championship," Elway said.

"When you have the genuine hope of competing for the Super Bowl, the level of play by everybody increases. It doesn't guarantee we are going to win the Super Bowl. But if you have that hope, you play better, you enjoy the job more, the nicks and pains seem to heal quicker, and the hard work is not as hard."

As a quarterback, Elway only required a handful of seconds on the scoreboard clock to produce a miracle. As an executive, what Elway gives the Broncos is more than a prayer of winning a championship. He has issued an order: No dream will be deferred. When linebacker Von Miller was the first to guarantee Denver would win the Super Bowl in February 2014, it was all part of the plan, and it was in step with the swagger Elway gave back to the Broncos.

The souvenirs from the 13-3 regular season that renewed this cocksure strain of hope in Denver could fill a trophy room. "When you take a year off from football, you come back for all the enjoyable moments," Manning told Mike Klis of the *Denver Post*. In the quarterback's photo album, here were the snapshots that jumped off the page:

There was that river of orange, born before dawn from an outpour-
ing of affection for a new football hero in town, as fathers, sons, and
sisters lined up outside the gates of Dove Valley on the first day of
training camp, many of them wearing a number 18 uniform.

There was the laughter of the Transplant Club, a Friday-evening
ritual on team road trips, when the grizzled veterans brought in by
Elway sat down at the dinner table, broke bread, and swapped stories
with Manning. The regular lineup was receiver Brandon Stokley, linebacker Keith Brooking, safety Jim Leonhard, and tight end Joe Dree-
sen. Five NFL vets, with 59 combined years of professional football
scars among them. All the QB's men.

There was the roar of a city rising off the sofa in unison, in homes
from Northglenn to Highlands Ranch, with a full-throat cheer for every
step of the 65 yards Tony Carter traveled with a fumble recovery at San
Diego, during the remarkable comeback against the Chargers that empowered this Denver team with the belief anything was possible.

The were those giant, white, cutout letters—one M, one V and one
P—that offered a salute to Manning, as he trotted into the huddle on a
field where he slowly began to feel at home.

"You can't squeeze 14 years of memories and comfort of living in
one place into three, four, five or however many years I'm going to be
here in Colorado. But you try to do the best you can with the adjustment," Manning told me before his first workout at the outset of his
second season in Denver.

"Now, I still want to keep that uncomfortable edge at work, because
I think that helps you win. But there's no question the upheaval of
moving to a new town should not be as much of a burden as when I first
got here. I'm more at home now. The fans of the Broncos have been
great to me. Anything that can lighten the load and help me do my job
better? It's a real positive, and I'm grateful for that."

Not 48 hours after the sky fell on the Broncos in the playoffs and the
city was reluctantly relearning how to smile, my cell phone began blowing up, buzzing with texts, all from the same person: John Hessler,

former University of Colorado quarterback. Hess demanded we have lunch. He even offered to let me buy.

At a burger joint in a strip mall on the north end of Denver, Hessler pulled his well-preserved 1997 edition of the *Sporting News* college football preview issue from its protective wrapper, to brag on his recently obtained autograph from Manning.

"Have I shown you this yet?" Hessler asked.

"Yes," I replied, chuckling, "only about three times in the past month alone."

But the cherished signature from Manning was not the primary reason Hessler had excitedly fired off a half dozen text messages to set up this summit meeting.

"Can you keep a secret?" said Hessler, after the restaurant proprietor slid our platters of food across the booth.

He took a big, sloppy bite of his burger, and allowed me to chew on the question.

After grabbing a fistful of sweet potato fries and letting the suspense build, Hessler finally spilled the beans.

"I'm going to be a dad again!" announced Hessler, his voice so loud and proud that other customers turned toward him and grinned.

A star CU player who fell so hard after his playing career was over that there once was a do-not-resuscitate notice taped to his fridge now had a whole new life to celebrate. "Can you believe it?" Hessler said. "After my car accident, the doctors told me I would never be able to have kids again, because of the medical procedures to put me back together."

Remember? Hessler was left for dead in the road, the victim of a hit-and-run accident in October 2003. Who would have thought that 10 years later, during the same week in August of his 39th birthday, Hessler could be pacing in the maternity ward, waiting for his wife, Sarah, to deliver a child?

There was time when the last person who would have believed in that little miracle was Hessler himself.

No Plan B?

"Sooner or later, buddy, you're going to need a Plan B," Hessler said. "The trick is figuring out what you're going to do after getting knocked on your ass."

Losing is not defeat. Defeat is surrendering the opportunity at a second chance. Never take a knee.

"Being out of football for the 2011 season and not really knowing what the future held, and whether I was going to be able to play again, I certainly had a great appreciation for 2012 and being back on the field playing with my new teammates," Manning said. "It was a new atmosphere for me, a totally different culture and a huge transition. But I did not take it for granted one single moment."

Anybody can love sports from the backseat of a convertible during the victory parade. But can you love the game when a team cuts you, or the playoffs end with a bitter loss in the bitter cold? Can you love football when it hurts, when it breaks your body or spits on your pride?

What his 37 passing touchdowns and 4,659 throwing yards for the Broncos proved about Manning was not so much about what was left in his arm, but what always resided in his heart. As a quarterback who obsessively tries to calculate and control every variable on the football field, Manning understands the truth about his sport. It is not always pretty. But he loves the truth anyway. In football, nothing is guaranteed. For even the best team in the league, the chance of winning the Super Bowl in any given season is no better than a coin flip.

Do not, however, tell Manning the odds are stacked against him. He plays to win. But that is not why he plays.

"I know I like being in the arena. I like knocking on the door every year. The closer you get, the harder it is sometimes, when it doesn't happen. I know what it feels like to win one, like John Elway has, and how it feels to lose one," Manning told me way back in March 2012, on the afternoon he turned the page from Indianapolis, joined the Broncos, and began chapter 2 of his NFL life.

Looking philosophical, the veteran quarterback reached for the personal meaning of this second chance in Denver. He caught me leaning in for something profound, then knocked me out with a sucker punch line.

It was absolutely perfect. And perfectly Manning.

Picking an underappreciated quote from a beloved sports movie, Manning dryly noted, "It's kind of like Ebby Calvin 'Nuke' LaLoosh said in *Bull Durham*: 'I love winning. . . . It's like, uh, you know, better than losing.'"

Losing stinks. Life hurts. But quit? No way. The strong laugh in the face of failure.

The real game begins with Plan B.

And every great comeback starts with only one absolute rule:

Never take a knee.

19

UNFINISHED BUSINESS

The Broncos had yet to make a tackle, throw a block, or sweat a drop in training camp for the 2013 NFL season. But it appeared their shot at winning the Super Bowl had gone up in smoke. Linebacker Von Miller, the team's best defensive player, was in trouble with the league's substance-abuse program.

It was a sticky situation for Miller. Marijuana was big news in Colorado. The state's citizens had passed Amendment 64 in a paradigm-breaking, headline-making vote that legalized personal use of the drug by adults throughout Colorado. My neighbor began smoking weed on the front porch. Wacky tabacky jokes flown in from across the country echoed in the Rocky Mountains. "In Colorado . . . voters approved a tax on marijuana to fund the building of schools," Conan O'Brien explained to his television audience. "In other words, kids: Don't do drugs, but stay in the schools funded by them."

Fair or not, who became the new poster child for this new Rocky Mountain high? Miller.

George Atallah of the NFL players association wanted everybody to know that Miller's case did not involve steroids. The *Denver Post*, however, received documentation that indicated Miller had multiple positive tests for marijuana and an undisclosed amphetamine dating back to his rookie season in 2011.

Cheba Hut Toasted Subs, a chain of sandwich shops in Colorado that proudly advertises itself as "Home of the Blunts," offered Miller free subs for life. You know, like, in case he got the munchies, man. "We got some great response on that one," shop owner Matt Clark-Johnson told the *Post*. "We're getting from, 'Why would you give a millionaire free sandwiches for life?' to 'Who cares?'"

Should the NFL care if players smoke marijuana? More than one retired NFL player has told me weed is more of a healthy choice than potentially addictive painkillers often prescribed to athletes dealing with chronic injury in a violent game.

Miller joined the ranks of fellow Americans from Barack Obama to swimmer Michael Phelps and singer Willie Nelson alleged to enjoy a puff of marijuana. If you ask me, it should be none of the league's business who smokes weed, which has never been mistaken for a performance-enhancing drug. All football fans really care about is: Will the gridiron warrior make big plays on Sunday?

An annual Denver tradition on the eve of training camp is a barbecue. Reporters munch on sandwiches and coleslaw in a big tent at the team's Dove Valley headquarters. The Broncos whet everyone's appetite for the season ahead, as coach John Fox and star players meet the well-fed press and talk a little football before the serious blocking and tackling begin.

At the luncheon, everybody on the team is usually loose and full of optimism. Not this year. The tent was filled with tension as soon as Miller walked in. The media was there to barbecue his butt. It did not take long for the heat to be turned up on Miller.

"Is marijuana part of your life?" asked Darren McKee, co-host of "The Drive," the popular afternoon sports talk show on 104.3 FM in Denver.

"Absolutely not," Miller replied.

The all-star linebacker was full of bravado and seemed supremely confident that a looming four-game suspension would be reduced or thrown out on appeal. Miller proved to be dead wrong. As the league gathered more evidence, things only got worse for the Broncos. In the end, Miller's suspension was increased to six games.

So here was the tough question: Entering the season with a hefty salary of $2.28 million, would Miller be worth a nickel to the team's championship chase?

Absolutely not. After guaranteeing the Broncos would win the Super Bowl, Miller proved to be nearly worthless in the quest.

In late August, I asked Miller if he had damaged his relationship with Denver fans.

"True Bronco fans, they have been great, coming out to practice, still believing in the guy that I am. The media, they'll do some crazy stuff to you and paint a different picture," Miller replied. "But the fans know me for laying it out on the field, being a great teammate. . . ."

That was a big, stinking pile of denial. Miller is beloved by team-mates, but he acted like a dope. When any player, whether he's an All-Pro linebacker or a special-teams scrub, gets kicked out of the league for six games, it's the opposite of being a great teammate. The absence of Miller from the Denver lineup would be a one-point detriment in every game he missed, according to Las Vegas sports analyst Todd Fuhrman.

The Broncos, however, opened the season with six straight victories without Miller. He played in nine games, recording a disappointing five sacks, before suffering the bad luck of ripping up his knee during a game against Houston in December, which forced Miller to watch the team's playoff run from the sideline.

"Next man up!" became the unending mantra, the rallying cry and the answered prayer of the Broncos. While lauded for the twinkle-toed, high-scoring talent that allowed Denver to sweep its two-game, regular-season series against Kansas City to finish first in the AFC West, the raw courage this team displayed in gutting through tough times was overlooked.

"This whole business is coming up with a Plan B and sometimes a Plan C," Fox said. As Fox often liked to quip, his Broncos went through a lot more "stuff" than the typical championship contender.

Pro Bowl tackle Ryan Clady never played a down in 2013. He was lost to a Lisfranc injury to his left foot, yet a patchwork orange offensive line somehow kept quarterback Peyton Manning from being sacked no more than 18 times during the regular season.

Rahim Moore rewarded the faith coaches kept in him after his playoff blunder against Baltimore, playing well at safety until he awoke in the middle of a November night, only hours after a rousing 27–17 victory against Kansas City. Moore was stricken by what alert doctors quickly diagnosed as lateral compartment syndrome, a rare blood disorder that could have cost him a limb in addition to the remainder of a promising season after emergency leg-saving surgery.

Denver's defensive line was blown apart by Kevin Vickerson's dislocated hip and mysterious seizures that plagued Derek Wolfe. Heck, it seemed as if the run of bad luck never took a day off, even when the Broncos were supposed to be relaxing.

Knocked to his knees and unable to breathe on the 14th hole, Fox forgot about his par putt or the Super Bowl and began to wonder if November 2, 2013, was going to be the day he died.

Was his heart failing? How could he have been so stupid to delay a surgery needed for months? Would Fox see his wife or kids again? Was this any way for a coach's life to end—during the NFL bye week, playing golf with buddies, crumpled on the ground barely 200 yards from his vacation home in North Carolina?

"When I was on my knees on the golf course, I remember praying to God: 'You get me out of this and I'll get it fixed.' That's how scary it was. . . . It was like being smothered. I couldn't breathe," said Fox, recalling those agonizingly anxious minutes when it was uncertain if he would live to see his 59th birthday, watch his young daughter grow up to be married, or take one more ski run in the Rocky Mountains.

In broad daylight, his world was fading to black. His playing partners screamed at him to stay strong. With every fiber in his body, Fox struggled to remain conscious.

"I knew I was in trouble," said Fox, whose grotesquely purple lips signaled to friends at the scene in Charlotte, N.C., that his physical distress was severe.

As he reconstructed the frightening scene, Fox looked me in the eye and spoke the nitty-gritty truth: "Luckily, I was able to fight it off. Because, if I passed out, I wasn't sure I was coming back."

Fox told his story in the hallway of the Broncos' facility at Dove Valley, with a smile plastered on his face, a coach delighted to be back at work with his first-place football team only four weeks after open-heart surgery on November 4 to repair a faulty aortic valve.

"It definitely scared my family, because they're not ready to lose me," Fox said. "My sons are all older. But I haven't watched any weddings yet. I have a 13-year-old daughter. My wife is younger than me by eight years. Nobody was ready for me to not be here. So this was eye-opening for our family, just because it was a little touch-and-go there for a minute."

But nightmares that can be induced by manipulative life-insurance commercials have not turned Fox into a worrying insomniac, and a joke told by the coach at his own expense was proof.

Waiting in the hospital for doctors to crack open his chest, Fox filled part of his final night prior to heart surgery by taking a peek at a Sunday night NFL game, when Houston Texans coach Gary Kubiak collapsed on the sideline at halftime, suffering from what would quickly be diagnosed as a TIA (transient ischemic attack), more commonly referred to as a mini-stroke.

"I'll tell you what was bizarre," Fox said, in a raspy voice crunchier than car wheels on a gravel road. "I was sitting there watching TV, and I watched Gary Kubiak. The combination of me, then him, I thought: 'Aw, we're killing this profession.'"

His heart defect was diagnosed more than a decade ago, during a routine physical while he was working as an assistant coach with the New York Giants. But the blood flow had deteriorated to the point where Fox could no longer ski more than 40 yards without stopping to rest, and he had vowed to finally fix the problem with elective surgery within days after Denver concluded the 2013 season.

"I put off the surgery because I figured this was a big year for the Broncos, and I didn't want to be coming to training camp at less than 100 percent," Fox explained. "Yeah, it was dumb. But that's what I chose to do."

Fox has stuck his nose in the NFL coaching grind for 25 years. Prior to this health scare, it was my suspicion he might ride off into the sunset on the day after he finally won a Super Bowl ring.

Fox, however, now insists this heart surgery might actually lengthen his coaching career. "This is like getting a knee replaced, something that will increase my quality of life. . . . I'm going to be more active, I going to have more energy," he said.

"My approach to coaching has been: 'I'm not going to do this for 30 more years.' But I haven't said: 'I'm going to do this for one more contract.' . . . I'm past the point of doing this for the money. It's hard to say how long I will coach, because I'm very competitive and I love [football]. I've seen too many of my coaching friends say: 'If I'm doing this at age 70, punch me in the face.' Well, I would have punched a lot of those friends in the face."

Maybe it's because he was raised in a military family, but for Fox, it matters far more that the mission is accomplished than who gets the credit in victory. He didn't want a medal for returning to work with a scar across his chest. He doesn't like fuss. But Fox does know what it's like to stare at death and not blink. That experience probably would not hurt, if the Broncos are down by three points in the fourth quarter of the championship game.

Football is only fun in the NFL if you win. Laughter, however, comes naturally to Fox. Not long after collapsing on the golf course, he made a little confession to one of the friends who pulled him through the frightening episode:

"Hey," Fox told his buddy, "after I get my heart fixed, I'm good. But I think I might also need surgery on this left eardrum from you screaming at me in the golf cart: 'Breathe!'"

Moral of the story: What's the joy in living if a football coach can't give good-natured grief to the guys who helped save his life?

Without a doubt, Fox entered the season with immense pressure to deliver a Super Bowl victory. The oddsmakers in Las Vegas had listed the Broncos as prohibitive favorites.

"I want to make something perfectly clear: My situation had nothing to do with the stress of coaching," Fox said. "In today's world, there's a lot of pressure jobs. . . . There's a degree of pressure in every profession."

Want to know the truth? When Fox returned to the Denver sideline barely a month after open-heart surgery, he looked like a man playing with house money.

Guess that makes sense.

After cheating death, every new series of downs is a bonus.

But the team that greeted Fox's return had serious issues nobody wanted to mention. The Broncos were running on fumes. This had been a better team back in October. Injuries had taken their toll. As they entered the playoffs, the Broncos were far from dead men walking. But they definitely were walking wounded. Denver needed help. Could an old pro help save them?

Cornerback Champ Bailey heard the dirt that was talked behind his back. People muttered he was washed up, broken down, and a step slow. A 12-time Pro Bowler reduced to a defensive liability.

"I've listened to the radio. I've read the newspaper. And I heard all these things: 'He's done. He's lost a step. Yada, yada, yada,'" Bailey told me on a warm December afternoon. "It's funny. Because those people don't know me, they don't understand me, and they don't know what it takes to play in the NFL. So I took it all in stride. But it's all motivation. I used everything little thing I heard as motivation. Did I ever think I was done? Hell, no."

For 14 NFL seasons, Bailey was the league's premier shut-down corner. He threw a blanket on the best receivers in football with the flair of a matador and made his artistry look effortless.

Then something funny happened to Bailey in 2013. The bull got him. His body betrayed him. And it hurt.

Check that. For Bailey, his 15th NFL season was a royal pain.

"I'm not going to cry about it. It was bad. But I feel good now, and I'm ready to go [play]," Bailey said. "A lot of my motivation for getting back to playing had nothing to do with anybody around me. It was just me. It's just the way I am. You're not going to tell me I can't do something."

At age 35, Bailey got torched deep by Father Time. During the team's second game of the preseason, the turf in Seattle bit Bailey in the foot. It was a Lisfranc sprain, which can cause agony in a man's arch with his every step. It's an injury that has been cursed for centuries, all the way back to a time when cavalrymen in Napoleon's army suffered the curse of Lisfranc; the prescribed remedy was amputation.

"I had a million thoughts go through my head with this injury. And I've never had to deal with something like this. This was definitely my toughest challenge of my career. I wanted to see if I could overcome it," Bailey said.

In the most obvious of ways, this was the worst football season in Bailey's brilliant NFL career. He couldn't get on the field. During 16 regular-season games, Bailey made only 14 tackles. Reduced to a footnote on Denver's 13-3 record, he lost his starting job at outside cornerback, a position built on equal parts swagger and skill.

In a more subtle way, however, the season revealed why Canton, Ohio, anxiously awaits the pleasure of swinging wide the front door for Bailey's entrance into the Pro Football Hall of Fame.

From fighting the betrayal of an aching body to suffering the indignity of standing on the sideline in his uniform at Kansas City as the Denver defense hung on for a 35–28 victory against the Chiefs, there were ample reasons for Bailey to cry tears of self-pity. The best defensive player in franchise history, however, refused to let any of us see him sweat.

The grace with which Bailey has stared down his athletic mortality was the very definition of mental toughness and a testament to his professionalism.

"It hasn't been easy," Bailey said. "I was ticked. I was frustrated. But I live with it. So I'm going to make the best of it."

To the credit of the coaches and the veteran cornerback, the Broncos figured out a way to do right by Bailey and improve the team's maligned defense at the same time. He moved inside to nickel back, reducing the number of snaps he played in a game, while leaving the task of running stride-for-stride with receivers to younger cornerbacks on the Denver roster.

"I've always been a mainstay out there on the field, but it's not like that now. I accept it," Bailey said. "I'm not going to sit here and predict what's going to happen. But I expect to start every year."

Early in 2011, shortly after John Elway returned to the Broncos as vice president of football operations, Bailey could have left the Broncos as a free agent. He decided to stay. Loyalty in pro sport? It's rare. But it still exists.

"I could have run out of here. I was a free agent," Bailey said. "But I wanted to be here in Denver. And Elway wanted me to be here. I wanted to be a part of what Elway started with this team. I didn't see this guy touching anything and being a loser. He hasn't lost in football."

When it would have been easy to give up hope and surrender to the pain, Bailey refused. All he wanted his entire career was one good crack at winning the Super Bowl.

Unfinished business.

After the Broncos trounced Oakland 34–14 on the final Sunday of the regular season to clinch the AFC's No. 1 seed for the playoff tournament, Fox wanted to send a message to his players before they hit the showers.

"Great regular season, men. But that ain't what we came for," said Fox, summoning the Broncos to huddle up. The real hard work had not yet begun. Men caked in dirt and sweat, the survivors of a team beat up by the season's heavy physical toll, formed a tight circle and raised their hands as one.

"We have a season to finish, men," shouted Fox, his words so anxious they bumped into each other while racing out of his mouth. Three victories in the playoffs, and the Broncos would win the franchise's first championship in 15 years.

"That's three games, one at a time," Fox exclaimed. "Let's finish this thing on three. One, two, three: Finish!"

Together, Broncos repeated their vow and shouted it out loud, with one voice and a single purpose: "Finish!"

20

SHOVE IT WHERE THE SUN DON'T SHINE

When a quarterback old enough to know better sat down for a television interview and was ambushed by Ron Burgundy, the biggest buffoon in the history of broadcasting, Peyton Manning rolled with the punches. Comedian Will Ferrell had a new movie to promote. With Manning as his foil on a split-screen shot videotaped by ESPN cameras, Ferrell effortlessly slipped into his role as America's favorite bungling anchorman. Madcap hilarity ensued. Manning can play that game.

Burgundy gave Manning unsolicited advice: Grow a moustache. Football heroes are supposed to look tough. And, as the face of the franchise, Manning had a big problem. The clean-shaven mug of Manning, declared Burgundy, appears as soft as a "succulent baby lamb."

What makes any joke funny is the hard kernel of truth wrapped in the laughter.

There was unfinished business for Manning during his second season with the Broncos. Among the issues to tackle: Stop the snickering behind his back. He does look like the quarterback from next door. But in the 16th year of his brilliant NFL career, the veteran QB wanted to put a halt to any suggestion he is as soft as a succulent baby lamb. He was a Manning on a mission, out to prove he does not fold in the cold; he does not wilt under pressure; he does not suck in the playoffs.

Exactly 12 months to the day after the sky fell on the Broncos during the most upsetting playoff defeat in franchise history, Denver beat San

Diego 24–17 on January 12, 2014, to open a playoff run destined for an appearance in Super Bowl XLVIII.

It was an afternoon for killing ghosts and burying bad memories. In the eyes of Broncomaniacs who wear the scars of tough setbacks for life, this was a must-win for coach John Fox, who could at long last be forgiven for taking a knee during the fourth quarter of that dreadful loss against Baltimore that abruptly ended the team's Super Bowl dreams a year earlier, on the 12th day of 2013.

After hearing ad nauseam about how he had suffered elimination in the opening game of the postseason eight freaking times, Manning put in solid, blue-collar work against the Chargers, with a performance that should have been toasted with a beer and a shot rather than the popping of champagne corks.

There was zero glitz in the veteran quarterback's 230 yards passing against San Diego. It was a friendly reminder that a "W" in the postseason never needs to be delivered in fancy wrapping paper. Asked about his legacy for the umpteenth time after the victory, Manning dryly replied: "What's weighing on my mind is how soon I can get a Bud Light in my mouth."

But the story of this victory was more than a sigh of relief. The most lasting sound from a day that made all of Colorado happy was the unbridled joy of a single two-year-old boy.

"Daddy! Daddy!" Marshall Manning screamed excitedly to the quarterback standing at the podium for his postgame press conference. The kid was wrapped in the arms of another famous quarterback, his grandpa Archie Manning.

A slow grin spread across the face of Peyton Manning. The maestro who controls everything at the line of scrimmage could not control this interruption in his formal discussion with dozens of media members, all in a hurry to file reports about Denver moving on down the road to the Super Bowl.

Here is what was so beautiful about the unscripted moment: Marshall Manning was too young to remember anything about that loss to Baltimore a year earlier. How could he? Marshall and his twin sister,

Mosley, were born in March 2011. Toddlers do not keep a record of which NFL quarterback has the most championship rings on his fingers or the most MVP awards on the mantel. In the eyes of his children, Peyton Manning is just plain Daddy. Win or lose, being Daddy is all that is required to qualify him as their hero.

With a hint of regret and a trace of bitterness, Indianapolis Colts owner Jim Irsay had mouthed off during 2013 that the statistics produced by Manning are jaw-dropping *Star Wars* numbers. Irsay, however, added a bummer of a caveat: All the offensive fireworks, with the inherent dependency on a highly paid quarterback, make it harder to win championships in the salary-cap era, when roster payrolls are strictly regulated by the league's financial rules.

But know what? Maybe Irsay has a valid point.

The mind-boggling numbers Manning posted during his second season in Denver boldly explored a dazzling new universe where no quarterback had ever gone before. While leading the Broncos to a 13-3 record and first place in the AFC West division, Manning threw for 5,447 yards and a league-record 55 touchdowns.

On the eve of the Super Bowl, he would be named Most Valuable Player for the fifth time in his brilliant career by near unanimous vote, finishing first on all except one of 50 ballots cast by a nationwide panel of 49 experts and a single knucklehead either too blind or too stubborn to recognize Manning's greatness. Wayne Gretzky was named MVP nine times in hockey. The seven MVP awards of Barry Bonds sit under a cloud of suspicion from alleged use of performance-enhancing drugs. The NBA saluted Kareem Abdul-Jabbar six times as the most valuable player in basketball.

In football, Manning is king. He is MVPeyton. When Fox broadcaster Joe Buck was asked where Manning ranked on a list of the most impressive athletes he has had the pleasure of covering, Buck replied: "Number one."

Manning showed the NFL something else beyond football greatness in 2013, something far more enduring and endearing. He peeled back the mask of his famously stern and serious Peyton Manning Face to show how vulnerable and soft the ultimate field general can be.

Yes, PFM cries. He allows himself a little smirk when taking vengeance. Dare we say it? The dude is human.

"I am not a robot," Manning said.

Not a robot? Those might be the most revealing, myth-debunking words Manning has ever told me.

For years, the legend of Manning was carefully built by all of us in the media. He was an Iron Giant in shoulder pads. He was robotic in his film study. He brought X-ray vision to the line of scrimmage and unlimited storage of files containing every tiny weakness in a defense. And much of the myth was based in truth. Almost always, in public, Manning is as measured and as polished as a presidential candidate on the campaign trail.

But now we are supposed to believe there's more on this brainiac's mind than football? Behind the serious, demanding frown of Manning Face, there is really a regular guy who drinks beer and never misses an episode of *Boardwalk Empire*? We are supposed to believe PFM 2.0 is made of flesh and blood rather than computer circuitry?

Believe it.

A natural-born grinder whose infinite curiosity caused Archie Manning to long ago dub him The Riddler, the veteran Broncos quarterback did go home after games during Sundays in 2013 to watch video.

But the subject matter of the video that so engrossed Manning he could not take his eyes from the screen? It was not what you might think.

On Sunday nights in 2013, Manning turned off football and tuned in Enoch "Nucky" Thompson.

To chill out, the quarterback is an unabashed, can't-get-enough fan of *Boardwalk Empire*, the HBO drama set during the Prohibition era that stars Steve Buscemi as the kingpin of Atlantic City, N.J.

"I was a *Sopranos* guy. I loved *The Sopranos*. I was devastated when that screen went blank (during the series' last episode). I liked the ending, personally. But it was a tough moment, because I knew the series was over," said Manning, who likes to veg in front of the television as much as any red-blooded American. "Sunday night is my night to watch a show. . . . So when *Boardwalk* came out, that was big for me."

When Manning came to Denver after being fired by the Colts, there was no guarantee he would play in the Super Bowl again. All he wanted was the opportunity.

Well, to quote "Nucky" Thompson: "This is America, ain't it? Who the fuck is stopping you?"

This might sound odd: When we celebrate Manning's fifth MVP award, a toast should be raised to "Nucky."

Why? It was a pain in the neck, but Manning finally learned to get out of his own way late in his brilliant NFL career. Yes, Manning still pounds away more relentlessly than a hammer and burns brighter than the sun. But he has also learned to relax. PFM can be a couch potato, without feeling guilty. And that's a good thing.

We tend to draw our legendary athletes with the biggest, boldest colors in the crayon box to make it easy to distinguish heroes from villains.

The quick sketch of Manning is: Quarterback as automaton. You've read the comic book version. PFM is harder to solve than Chinese algebra during the regular season, only to see Mr. Smartypants blow a fuse with hyperactive over-analysis during the playoffs. He's obsessive, compulsive, and maybe too uptight for his own good.

Manning acknowledges: That's the robot he used to be.

"There was a time when I would come home from practice and I would stay up until 1 to 1:30 in the morning, because I had to watch all four of [an upcoming foe's] preseason games that night. I thought that if I didn't watch all four of those games, the world might come to an end the next day. I felt like I had to do it. I didn't need to sleep as much, and I was a younger player," Manning said. "My preparation has changed. I come home after practice, and I love spending time with the kids and putting them to bed. I don't stay up as late. I need to get my rest more.

Maybe I was a robot early on. I think now maybe I am a little more human."

As long as he had to relearn how to throw a spiral again before joining the Broncos, Manning figured: Why let the reinvention end with his playing style? Manning dialed back the intensity and dialed up the goofiness in his personality. It wasn't a big stretch. The teacher's pet always had a mischievous alter ego; teammates well know PFM is an unrepentant practical joker.

"No one's more intense than Peyton when we're in a team meeting or at practice. But nobody's more of a prankster when we're done working," Denver tight end Jacob Tamme said. "I shouldn't tell you this, because Peyton will get mad at me if I let the word get out. But I will give you a clue: If he offers you sunscreen on the golf course, don't take it. When you put it on your body, it will not protect you from the sun. It will actually make you feel as if your body is on fire."

That's not sunscreen, it's icy-hot muscle balm that Manning carefully and deviously injected into the tube.

Maybe the real kick of watching Manning at age 37 was observing a very buttoned-down quarterback let down his hair a little, before male pattern baldness begins in earnest.

"I think you get better at everything, hopefully, with age. Even in college, there was always misinformation. They used to say that I would stay up after the college game on Saturday night to watch the film of the game. The truth was that the replay of the game on TV would come on about 2 a.m., just as I was coming in with my teammates after a post-game celebration. I thought I was a normal college football player, a college student-athlete, who, after a game, went out and enjoyed it. I was lucky enough that the broadcast was on, and I got to stay up and watch it. I wasn't studying the game film on Saturday night," Manning told me, as he sat on a cruise ship docked in the Hudson River during the final week of January 2014. It was an absurd location to conduct an interview, but it somehow fit perfectly with the crazy hype of press coverage during Super Bowl week. Manning was relaxed, quick with a joke, at peace. His body language shouted: Man, this has been one strange and wonderful trip.

"At 37 years old, and in my 16th season . . . I think it's healthy to take some time to reflect and smell the roses. The legacy question keeps popping up, and I guess I had a little more time to think about it. If I had my choice what my legacy would be, it would be I played my butt off for every team I ever played on, I was a really good teammate, and I did everything I could to win. Whatever else comes along in that time is fine with me."

A great paradox of the human condition is how a man's strength can also be his weakness.

If anything, maybe the young and earnest Manning cared too much about football.

Long ago, he mastered the quarterback's art.

But the real secret of being Manning is his insatiable desire to expand his knowledge.

At age 37, before his legs give out and he is finally forced to surrender to the gravity that slows down every guy in middle age, Manning has learned to dance as if nobody is watching.

The NFL has never seen Manning play quarterback more precisely than he did during his 16th professional season. But here is what might have been more remarkable: The NFL has never seen Manning play quarterback with so much emotion.

Manning had begun The Unfinished Business Tour by dubstepping all over the Baltimore Ravens on September 5, 2013. As a writer with a freshly printed hardcover book on Manning and the Broncos to promote, I did radio interviews nonstop around the clock in the days leading up to the NFL season-opener.

On airwaves across the country, from Washington, D.C., to the state of Washington, I uttered the same bold prediction with a sound bite that could certainly come back to bite me. Why did I do it? I believed John Elway's promise that Manning would be a better quarterback in his second year with the Broncos, and I knew the plan of new offensive coordinator Adam Gase to crank up the pace of the team's snap count.

So I made talk-show hosts from coast to coast scoff by predicting: "You know the record of 50 touchdown passes that New England quarterback Tom Brady set in 2007? That record is going down. Manning is going to break it."

The tone for the most spectacular statistical season of Manning's career was set on opening night. The Baltimore Ravens never knew what hit them. During a resounding 49–27 Denver victory, Manning slammed the defending Super Bowl champions with seven—count 'em, seven—touchdown passes. "It didn't seem like that many," said Wes Welker, who caught took two of Manning's throws to the end zone. "You were just sitting there like, 'That was really seven?' because he's so nonchalant about it."

From Day 1 of the season, the Broncos put the league on notice of the two working themes for this team: (1) Never take a knee, and (2) Pedal to the metal.

With almost ruthless efficiency, Manning relentlessly drove Denver until the Broncos became the first NFL offense to score 600 points in a season. But he also showed a little piece of his heart when returning to Indianapolis to play a game in Lucas Oil Stadium, the house he built.

On October 20, as thousands of longtime fans dressed in his old blue-and-white Colts jerseys stood and cheered before kickoff, Manning removed his helmet, peered into the crowd and tapped his chest. It was a messy divorce with the Colts. But time heals. The quarterback wanted fans to know the love from Indianapolis will always be a part of him. He let the applause echo in his heart. "It will be something I always remember," Manning said.

When the forecast for Colorado on December 8 called for frigid temperatures only a polar bear could love, the narrative that Manning suffers from brain freeze and a squeaky arm in the cold got the Broncos hot and bothered. "The thing that pisses me off the most [about the criticism] is that I don't want anyone else as my quarterback," said Gase, the assistant coach who works closest with Manning when installing the offensive game plan.

Manning conducts himself with class. But doubt him, and he does a slow burn. Manning does not get mad. He gets even. As the thermometer struggled to stay above 15 degrees, Manning torched the Tennessee Titans, completing 39 of 59 passes for 397 yards and four touchdowns in a 51–28 victory. The quarterback then poured a little bile and served it cold to critics who suggested he cannot operate in the cold. "Whoever wrote that narrative," Manning said in an exclusive interview with KOA radio, "can shove that one where the sun don't shine."

Manning loves the history of sports in America. He memorizes names and years and records with the same enthusiasm he brings to learning the game plan. Maybe that explains why Manning especially cherished one award in 2013, even if that award has grown a little old and creaky, kind of like the quarterback himself.

During the age of cable television and the Internet, the diminished influence of *Sports Illustrated* is as obvious as the shrinking number of pages in the weekly magazine. But Manning knows track star Roger Bannister was the magazine's first Sportsman of the Year, way back in 1954. So the quarterback was genuinely humbled to be honored in December, during the 60th anniversary of an award that has gone to legends as varied as Muhammad Ali and Billie Jean King.

At a dinner in Denver to celebrate his selection, Manning cracked wise, with self-deprecating jokes about career triumphs and failures chronicled by *Sports Illustrated*. Then, he told the story about being asked to pose for the cover when he was the quarterback for the University of Tennessee in 1996. The clever photographer asked young Manning to lean against a giant cardboard replica of an *SI* cover from 36 years earlier, featuring a Mississippi quarterback named Archie Manning cocking his arm to fire a pass.

"For a moment in time, my Dad and I got to be college football players together," a suddenly sentimental Manning confessed to the hand-picked audience of special friends invited to the ceremony in the team's locker room. "I think only *Sports Illustrated* could have accomplished something like that. It was something very special. . . ."

The voice of Manning cracked. The quarterback dropped his head, fighting back tears.

Even robots cry.

No NFL player has ever been more dominant at 37 years old than Peyton Manning was in 2013. So how much longer can he beat everybody, including Father Time? As winter melts into spring during the rest of his career, Manning will take a medical exam and carefully listen to what doctors might discover about the structural integrity of his surgically repaired neck, then decide if he will play another year for the Broncos.

"My brother Cooper dealt with neck surgeries and injuries as a high school and college player, and he had to give up football. That made a big impact on my life," Manning said.

"I remember at the time, when Cooper got injured, they did a test on me and Eli. I would have been a junior in high school and Eli would have been a sixth grader. They said our necks weren't picture perfect and didn't look ideal, but they're stable enough to keep playing football. Cooper had to give up playing football. In some ways, when I had my neck problems [with Indianapolis], I thought maybe I had been on borrowed time this entire time. I was fortunate to have 20 years of health to play football. If that was going to be the end of it because of a neck injury, I really—believe it or not—had a peace about it."

Written in orange and blue, chapter 2 of his NFL career has often read like a fairy tale. Manning could walk away at any point wearing a big smile, carrying not a single ounce of regret into retirement.

But here's a guess why Denver's franchise player is in no hurry to leave the huddle and go sit on the porch: At two years old, Marshall Manning has yet to develop any clear picture or sustainable memory of his Daddy as a quarterback.

His five-year contract with the Broncos runs through the 2016 season. By late 2016, Marshall and Mosley Manning will be old enough to read Daddy's name in the newspaper after he has lit up the scoreboard with touchdown passes on Sunday.

Think that could be a powerful motivation for Manning to keep playing football? A man's real legacy is the memories and dreams he instills in his children.

After everything one of the most accomplished players in NFL history has achieved, there is at least one more important and true thing No. 18 can do in football: Daddy can walk off the field, hand-in-hand with his kids, framed by a photograph guaranteed never to fade in the memory, a lasting image that defines three generations in America's first family of quarterbacks.

21

THE HUNGRY HEART

Gone, gone, gone. The Super Bowl dream was gone in 12 seconds. The Broncos' determined, yearlong quest to finish the job was gone in 12 lousy seconds. Has the NFL championship ever been lost in one play?

Seattle beat the Broncos 43–8. Yes, it was ugly. For old Broncomaniacs, it caused flashbacks to Super Bowl indignities suffered early in John Elway's playing career. You want analysis of what went wrong against the Seahawks? Can you handle the truth?

From their first snap of Super Bowl XLVIII, the Broncos appeared lost, undermanned, and poorly prepared. The first NFL team in league history to score more than 600 points in a season messed up the opening play in the biggest game of the season, and Denver never recovered.

With a raucous Super Bowl crowd of 82,529 fans shaking MetLife Stadium in East Rutherford, New Jersey, Peyton Manning and the Broncos got rattled by the din. With first down at their own 14-yard line, Manning stood in the shotgun, barked signals for the first play from scrimmage, surveyed the Seattle defense, and did what the best quarterback in the league had done all season. He gesticulated, he orchestrated, and he instructed Denver teammates as the play clock ticked down before the snap.

There was one problem: "Nobody could hear me," Manning said.

As the quarterback walked toward center Manny Ramirez to fix the communication breakdown, the trusted center snapped the ball, launching it far over Manning's head.

How did that happen?

"There's no explanation," said Ramirez, taking full responsibility. He added that Manning had expected the snap three seconds before it was hiked. Without realizing his quarterback was out of position to catch the football, the 6-foot-3, 320-pound center who had contributed so well all season long to a patchwork Denver offensive line made one regrettable blunder. Ramirez did not even know exactly what went wrong until he trotted to the sideline, and the mistake was explained to him.

"It was a cadence issue. We were using the snap count on the play and, due to the noise, no one could hear me. So, really, I was walking up to the line of scrimmage to make a change and get us on the same page, and the ball was snapped," Manning said. "Nobody's fault. Not [Ramirez's] fault. Just a noise issue that caused the play to happen."

In a scene as slow and agonizing as your worst sports nightmare, the football bounced into the end zone. Running back Knowshon Moreno turned in hot pursuit, chased down the errant snap, and fell on it in the back of the end zone, conceding a safety to Seattle. The score was 2–0 in favor of the Seahawks before Denver could exhale.

Blame Manning for his failure to be an agent of calm amid the chaos of the opening snap. Blame coach John Fox for underestimating the stadium noise. Blame the Broncos for wilting under the pressure.

"That's the way the start of any Super Bowl is going to be. It's going to be loud," said Denver receiver Wes Welker, who learned the mania that accompanies the craziest sporting event on the American calendar while playing for New England. "Fans are going to be yelling. I don't think they even know why they're yelling. It's just the start of the Super Bowl. We didn't prepare very well for that, and it showed."

In fairness, the biggest problem in the game for Denver proved to be far bigger than one botched snap. The Seahawks won with the No. 1 rule of the playground: They were the stronger, faster, and meaner kids. On offense. On defense. On special teams. Seattle dominated every phase of the championship game. Denver never stood a chance. It was depressing.

"We were on a national stage, in the biggest game in America. And to come out and play like that?" said Denver receiver Eric Decker, as shell-shocked and disappointed as any man, woman, or child who bleeds orange in Broncos Country.

But do not suggest to Manning the blowout loss was embarrassing. At the podium during the postgame press conference, with the weight of defeat heavy on his shoulders, Manning was peppered with questions about the meltdown of his team, which finished with a 15-4 record.

"A lot of people will put the blame on Peyton Manning. . . . But this is a team loss. It's not Peyton Manning's loss. It shouldn't be a knock on his legacy," Broncos defensive tackle Terrance Knighton insisted. But did anybody listen to Knighton's impeccable logic? In the media world where opinions are formed as fast as any TV personality, newspaper curmudgeon, or New Age blogger can hit the send button on a cell phone, loud, instant outrage is far more common than studied, in-depth analysis.

The Super Bowl was a rout by halftime, when the Seahawks took a 22–0 lead to the locker room. The Broncos' quick-strike offense did not register a point on the scoreboard until the final play of the third quarter, when Manning tossed a 14-yard touchdown pass to Demaryius Thomas. Against Seattle, the league's most valuable player suffered through his worst performance of an otherwise remarkable year, completing 34 of 49 attempts for 280 yards, and for the only time in 19 starts during the 2013 season threw more interceptions (two) than touchdowns (one) in a game.

Although teammates came to the defense of Manning, it was the quarterback who got smacked with the toughest question: Was this defeat an embarrassment to a proud team?

"It's not embarrassing at all. I would never use that word," replied Manning, keeping his cool and choosing his words carefully as he shot a stern look at the reporter.

"There's a lot of professional football players in that room, that lock-er room, that put in a lot of hard work and effort into being here and into playing in that game. The word embarrassing is an insulting word, to tell you the truth."

On the way out of the Super Bowl press conference, however, Man-ning quietly shook the hand of more than one Denver journalist and earnestly said: "I'm sorry." How often does a superstar apologize for a loss? It was an amazing display of how seriously Manning takes his responsibility to the Broncos and Denver fans.

At Tokya, a midtown Manhattan sushi lounge and nightclub where a Denver victory party had been organized, the corks on the bottles of Ace of Spades Champagne were never popped.

Taking his cue from the Broncos, Old Man Winter showed up late for the Super Bowl, then dumped eight inches of snow that began falling shortly after the loss. It made for a mess that added insult to already miserable Denver fans, as more than 1,000 flights from major airports throughout the New York area were delayed or canceled on Monday.

In the aftermath of the 35-point thumping, Denver coach John Fox reviewed the loss and made a vow. What would Fox do differently in game preparation if the Broncos got back to the Super Bowl? "Probably everything," Fox told Mike Klis of the *Denver Post*.

All the team's best-laid plans went wrong. And Fox caught grief for it all, from every direction. On the eve of the championship game, Fox moved players away from family distractions in the Jersey City hotel where they had stayed all week to lodging near the Newark Airport. Fox chuckled through the pain of defeat: "Even my kids were getting on me: 'Getaway hotel? Dad, that's 80 percent bad.'"

While a Super Bowl victory would have started a happy discussion about Manning being the greatest quarterback of all time, the loss gave critics new ammunition to fire at a 37-year-old player who finished the 2013 regular season with a QB rating of 115.1, a grade so sterling it was never matched by the legendary Joe Montana during his 14 full seasons as a starter for San Francisco and Kansas City. "For years Manning has dragged around the criticism, like tin cans tied to the back of a high-end car, that he produces more great statistics than great victories, and the noise just got louder," respected sports columnist Sally Jenkins wrote in the *Washington Post*.

After losing his second Super Bowl in three appearances as a player, Manning said: "It's not an easy pill to swallow, but we have to. I don't know if you ever really get over it. You have to find a way to deal with it and process it."

Amid the dark clouds of depression after the lopsided defeat, however, the love and appreciation for Manning came shining through like the sun after a Colorado winter storm. NFL fans across the country view Manning fondly, as the quarterback next door. America loves Peyton like a brother.

Sick and tired of hearing football analysts poke sticks in the rubble of this Super Bowl loss to determine how it might affect Manning's legacy, a college professor in South Carolina wrote a thank-you note to the Broncos quarterback on her blog. Laurie Lattimore-Volkmann is a Colorado native and mother who once named her dog in honor of Broncos linebacker John Mobley. She is now a professor at the College of Charleston. The heartfelt words she sent Manning went viral with football fans from coast to coast.

"I actually understand—on the most basic level—what legacy truly means. Legacy is something handed down that matters. It is something that matters to young players and athletes and kids looking for mentors to help them find their way. You don't hand down Super Bowl trophies. You don't hand down NFL MVP titles or franchise records. And you don't hand down touchdowns, statistics or win-loss records," Lattimore-Volkmann wrote on a blog post that became an overnight Internet sensation.

"You hand down an example of work ethic, or courage to come back after a career-threatening injury, of humility in victory and graciousness in defeat, and of perspective in one's own accomplishments. That legacy matters, and that's why yours is untarnished even—and especially—after last Sunday's Super Bowl XLVIII loss."

In defeat, Manning received a beautiful sympathy card.

In defeat, 12-time Pro Bowler Champ Bailey got cut.

In case anybody has forgotten: NFL = Not For Long.

At the conclusion of a season-recap press conference, Elway fixed the reporters gathered at the team's Dove Valley headquarters with eyes that stung from defeat but burned with passion.

"I want to say one thing. I kind of get the sense that these questions are 'How the hell are we going to overcome this?' Right? . . . But I will tell you this: Right now the focus is on what happened, instead of how we got there, and what we did this year and what we went through as a team. And the farther you get away from this, the less you concentrate on just that one game, and the more you look at the full season and really what we did as a football team and as an organization. And I tell you what: I'm very proud of that," said Elway, the Broncos vice president of football operations.

"There are some changes we've got to make and we'll make those. But the thing is, we can use that game as a game that, OK, we now know what it's like to be there. Now we're going to use that as the experience of we've been there, but we've got to start with step 1 again."

Get back to the championship? The Broncos' mission is not impossible, but the team would be advised to avoid reading NFL history. Among 47 previous losers of the Super Bowl, the teams that failed to make the playoffs the following season outnumber the teams that returned to the championship game by a 2:1 margin.

Even more daunting: It has been more than four decades since the last Super Bowl loser recovered and won the Super Bowl within 12 months. The Miami Dolphins last pulled off the feat in 1972. "One of the reasons it's so hard is what makes our league so great. You have teams going from the outhouse to the penthouse and the penthouse to the outhouse every year," Fox said. "In football, you don't have a team that's a dynasty because it spends 30 times more than everybody else."

After getting their clock cleaned by Seattle, the Broncos cleaned house. The Super Bowl loss left a lot of emotional scar tissue in the

Denver locker room. Elway purged it. Before the Broncos could begin at step 1 on the long climb back to the championship game, the team needed to reshape its locker room and put new boots on the ground.

Moreno, who led the Broncos with 1,038 yards rushing, was allowed to walk out of town and sign as a free agent with the Miami Dolphins. Linebacker Wesley Woodyard, a captain made a scapegoat for the team's defensive struggles, departed for the Tennessee Titans, where he was joined by defensive end Shaun Phillips, deemed expendable despite the 10 sacks he recorded during his lone season in Denver.

Although Zane Beadles had made the Pro Bowl as a guard for the Broncos, he found a $30 million contract with Jacksonville too rich to ignore. Popular wide receiver Eric Decker? Gone to the Jets, where he and country music singer Jessie James could give their reality TV marriage a sexy new locale and provide the New York City tabloids sensatinal new headline material. When Dominique Rodgers-Cromartie hesitated for a hiccup at the team's contract offer, Elway instead showed the steady cornerback the door.

The point amid the flurry of activity was clear. The Broncos do not let players they deem essential to success get away. To move forward, Denver had to move on without popular players who had done the uniform proud.

The change in personnel that cut deepest was the release of Bailey. The Broncos gave up on the 35-year-old cornerback, believing his best football was behind him. "It sucks, but at the same time, I have to move on," Bailey told Lindsay H. Jones of *USA Today*. "I have to move on. I can't dwell on it. I know they're not dwelling on it."

On a sunny morning in March 2014, Fox sat in his office, reflecting on all the good players and good people that the Broncos were forced to tell goodbye. On his head, the 59-year-old coach wore a ball cap stitched with the words: "It is what it is." In his heart, Fox knew Bailey was correct on one point: The harsh financial realities of the NFL really do suck.

"If you lose your last game, it's always devastating. . . . The loss of the Super Bowl sticks with you, but when you make decisions in personnel, you do it only to improve your football team," Fox said. "It's the business side of football. For most of us, it's not the most enjoyable part. But it's a necessary evil, and you make hard decisions."

It did not take long for Elway to decide: Denver will not win a championship with a defense that allowed 24.9 points per game, as it did in 2013. "When you need a push, you hear somebody say '35,'" said defensive end Malik Jackson, whose teammates embraced the ugly point differential in the Super Bowl as an inspirational tool. In free agency, the Broncos spent aggressively, allocating more than $32 million for the 2014 season on highly decorated Dallas Cowboys defensive end DeMarcus Ware; cornerback Aqib Talib, stolen from the roster of AFC rival New England; and young, hard-hitting Cleveland Browns safety T.J. Ward.

"We want to hoist the Lombardi Trophy. That's our ultimate goal. That's our goal this year," said Fox, given a strong vote of confidence by Elway in the wake of the Super Bowl rout when the Broncos empowered their coach with a new, three-year contract worth a reported $16.5 million.

At 6:30 on an April morning, Manning strolled through the Pepsi Center, dressed in a suit and orange tie, as caterers filled plates for the 38th annual sports breakfast benefiting the Boy Scouts of Denver. Speaking publicly for the first time since the night of the Super Bowl loss, Manning looked out at the faces of businessmen and scouts huddled around tables on the arena floor and earnestly said: "Before anyone can become a game-changer, they first have to thrive on discomfort."

The magic of 2013, when Manning joined Brett Favre and Dan Marino as the only players in NFL history to throw for 60,000 career yards, cannot be re-created. The challenge for the Broncos will be to establish a new identity and never waver in their commitment to winning the franchise's first Super Bowl since the 1998 NFL season.

"Just because you were there last year in the game, it doesn't guarantee you anything," Manning said. "It does take a lot of hard work and sacrifice. I think forming that chemistry takes time."

Manning is guaranteed a spot in the Pro Football Hall of Fame. He has won a championship ring with the Indianapolis Colts and been awarded too many trophies to count. He could retire from football today and go be governor of Tennessee or sit on the beach. After hanging up his cleats, he could tackle a brave new world or relax and count his money. So I asked Manning: Are you hungrier than ever to win the Super Bowl?

"Yeah, absolutely I am. That's what I want to do. That's what the Denver Broncos want to do," said Manning, looking me square in the eye. "I'm glad to be a part of a team where that's what they want to do. I want to try to do my best to do my part."

Although Ware, whose NFL resume includes 117 career sacks and seven selections to the Pro Bowl, was signed to lead the defense, and Fox takes most of the heat when the team loses, everyone knows that there is one man who makes Denver a championship contender. This is Elway's town. But the Broncos are Manning's team.

"I feel that I have a responsibility to the team to be on top of my game. And that's what I think about every day when I go over there to work and lift weights and throw with my receivers: Doing my job to help the Denver Broncos. That's what I've tried to do since I've been here [in Denver], and that's what I'll keep doing until . . ."

Manning paused for a heartbeat, searching for the precisely the right words to complete the thought, stopping just long enough so a listener could hear the NFL's most beautiful mind at work.

According to rankings compiled by ESPN, Manning is the 16th best-paid athlete in the world, at a salary of $25 million. What makes Manning so much like any one of us who has ever stared at the ceiling at night, wrestling with doubt and regret, is that he has known the pain of getting fired. He will keep playing football until somebody takes away his playbook and tells him to go sit on the porch.

In his moment of hesitation, a heartfelt emotion flashed in Manning's eyes. His right arm is not the magnificent carving tool that it once was. Every year, doctors will examine his neck and offer advice on the risks football presents a father of twins. There's nothing sweeter than

NFL Sunday for a 38-year-old quarterback, but the other six days ache a little louder with every passing week.

What Denver has given Manning might not be as shiny as a Super Bowl ring, but it is far more valuable. The Broncos kept what Manning loves alive. In one essential way, a five-time league MVP is no different than a kid catching a pass in the backyard with the sun sinking behind the Rocky Mountains in the fading light of an October afternoon. Manning will keep playing football until somebody calls him home for dinner.

While quarterbacks are paid to throw touchdown passes, the image that defines Manning shows a man reveling in all the little details of his job: With a scar on his neck peeking out the backside of a Denver helmet, Manning stands in the shotgun, giving a rapid-fire lecture on football theory to teammates. He surveys the defense for weakness and calls an audible, then shouts: "Hurry! Hurry!"

But, truth be known, Manning is in no hurry. No hurry to leave this job. No hurry at all. As the play clock winds down, he loves and cherishes every second of being a quarterback.

"That's what I'll keep doing until . . ." Manning said, ". . . until I stop playing."

The beautiful mind is what makes him Peyton Manning.

A heart hungry for one more snap, one more perfect spiral, and one more shot at the Super Bowl is what makes him America's most beloved quarterback.

22

KICKING AND SCREAMING

John Elway was ticked. Do we really have to explain why he was so mad?

After all the sweat Denver put in the 2014 NFL regular season to win 12 games and earn a No. 2 seed in the Super Bowl tournament, the last thing anybody in Broncos Country expected to see was the home team get rudely bounced by Indianapolis in the playoffs and, even worse, go down without a whimper during an embarrassing 24–13 loss. Are you kidding me? This was not part of Elway's master plan to return championship football to Colorado.

There is an unwritten, but well-documented rule at the team's Dove Valley headquarters: Piss off the boss at your own peril. When there's trouble, Elway does not dance. He swings the hammer of Thor. Problems do not linger. Elway pounds them to smithereens.

When Denver exited meekly from the playoffs, somebody was going to pay. So it was no surprise when Elway promptly said goodbye to coach John Fox after Denver was eliminated from championship contention. But the defeat would also cost Manning dearly.

How Elway operates as general manager is informed by pain he endured while playing quarterback for the Broncos from 1983–98. There are football scars on his soul, etched by a rusty blade with the numbers 39–20, 42–10 and 55–10. Three times early in his playing career, Elway was embarrassed on the NFL's biggest stage, and he remains tender about those Super Bowl losses after all these years.

When working for Elway, it's a bad idea to take a knee of surrender. And, let's be honest. It appeared the Broncos quit against the Colts. "To go out this way, I feel like we let a lot of people down, including ourselves," defensive lineman Malik Jackson said. "We let down our families. Our friends. Denver, Colorado. We expected more." Yes, John Fox fashioned a sterling 46-18 regular-season record and won the AFC West all four seasons he coached in Denver. In the end, maybe the real surprise is that Elway didn't tell Fox to leave town sooner.

"At least in the last game you want to feel like you go out kicking and screaming. When you're right there . . ." said Elway, disappointed the Broncos exhibited so little fight during that 43–8 loss to Seattle at Super Bowl XLVIII, then disgusted when his team showed so little fire as Indianapolis dominated a playoff game in Colorado fewer than 12 months later. "Two years in a row, it didn't feel like we went out kicking and screaming."

In the aftermath of getting trounced by Andrew Luck, the quarterback who took his job in Indianapolis, Manning dropped a bombshell: Plagued by poor health and poor play down the stretch of this disappointing season, he was having second thoughts about returning to the Broncos in 2015. "I guess I can't just give that simple answer. I'm processing it. So I can't say that," said Manning, whose strained quadriceps robbed him of the strength to connect on deep sideline routes against the Colts.

A few minutes later, Manning left the auditorium where he had stunned reporters with the admission that his retirement could be on the horizon. After gathering his belongings in the locker room, Manning walked down a hallway in the stadium, only to be confronted with two more unsettling shocks to his system. It broke the quarterback's heart when Marshall and Mosley, his 3-year-old twin children, approached him with tears in their young eyes, distraught because their Daddy suffered such a tough day at the office against the Colts.

What's more, Manning expressed genuine dismay when informed by two reporters from the *Denver Post* that prior to kickoff against Indianapolis, there was a televised report by NFL insider Jay Glazer, a close friend of Denver's head coach, that suggested if the Broncos lost in opening round, Fox could lose his job and immediately become a top candidate for league rivals with coaching vacancies.

"Is that true?" said Manning, a creature of habit who hates change. Was Fox looking for a new job when he should have been concentrating on beating the Colts? If Denver dumped Fox, might the quarterback be less likely to return for another season with the team?

Fewer than 24 hours later, the worst fears of Manning were proven to be 100 percent correct. Elway and Fox mutually agreed to part ways on January 12, 2015. "In any relationship, you're always going to have bumpy patches. I think the main thing between (Fox) and I was we disagreed how to get to that next step," Elway said.

But it was my strong feeling that Fox abandoned ship before he was forced to walk the plank, and my opinion was strongly reinforced when Fox was hired by the Chicago Bears within four days of his sudden departure from Denver. Why did Fox want out? Although he received a two-year contract extension after losing to Seattle in the Super Bowl, it seemed the Broncos almost immediately had buyer's remorse after giving him a raise to $5.5 million. In addition, it was an open secret Fox sought more input in player personnel decisions, while Elway was irritated when Fox's coaching staff was slow to develop draft picks Michael Schofield and Cody Latimer into contributors on the field.

The signs of trouble for the Broncos were hidden in plain sight long before the loss to Indianapolis caused Elway to blow a gasket. The team did not have its head in the game. The musty stench of distraction had infiltrated the Denver locker room. Too many key members of the organization had their sights set on the exit door when the situation demanded they keep their eyes on the prize.

Prior the playoffs, defensive coordinator Jack Del Rio was being wooed by Oakland to take over on the Raiders sideline, while offensive coordinator Adam Gase engaged in what proved to be a futile pursuit of the head coaching vacancy with San Francisco. Tight end Julius Thomas, who had been Manning's favorite target in the red zone, was being not-so-quietly trashed behind his back for refusing to play through a chronic ankle injury. Star receiver Demaryius Thomas was perplexed by teammates who seemed fearful the road to the Super Bowl might well force the Broncos back to play the AFC championship game in New England, where they had been trounced 43–21 during the regular season.

With the skills of Manning in irrevocable decline and Fox, Del Rio and Gase all released from the coaching staff as Elway cleaned house, it seemed as if the Broncos might require a major overall before they could make another serious attempt at climbing to the top of the NFL heap. Rather than admit flaws in his football philosophy, however, Elway doubled-down on his bet that the talent on Denver's roster was on the verge of the franchise's greatest success since he retired as quarterback way back in the spring of 1999.

"There still is no Plan B," Elway insisted. "Plan A is still the same. And that is to win the world championship."

In a jam, Elway knew exactly what to do. He called an old friend. Gary Kubiak was the obvious choice to be the new coach in Denver, if what Elway wanted was a wingman to play Cougar to his Maverick.

From the time they joined the Broncos as rookie quarterbacks in 1983, they bled orange together. Elway wore No. 7; Kubiak was No. 8. They quickly grew as close as the numbers on the back of their jerseys.

They hung out at the Smiling Moose Bar after long, hot summer practices at training camp in Greeley, Colorado. Elway called his little buddy Kubes. While the rest of Broncos Country crowned Elway as the Duke of Denver, he was known simply as Woody to Kubiak. They could be friends because they were never rivals. Elway won the most valuable player award in 1987, and made regular appearances on the cover of Sports Illustrated. The biggest moment of Kubiak's playing career might have been a windy November night in 1989, when Elway came down with food poisoning and his backup stepped in, leading Denver to a road victory against Washington.

So of course it was a no-brainer for Kubiak to accept the job when Elway asked for his help. "The contract took about five minutes," Kubiak said. He signed a four-year deal and was formally introduced as the 15th coach in team history on January 20, 2015. "Coach Kubiak knows how to win," said Broncos president Joe Ellis, citing the championship rings the team's new hire had earned during previous stints as assistant in San Francisco (1994) and Denver (1997 and '98).

When Kubiak went to work for Elway, they had been friends for nearly 32 years. The NFL was a much different place way back in 1983, when players knocked the slobber out each other during brutal full-contact practices and even a superstar never complained about sharing a hotel room with a teammate during road trips. So it might seem old-timey quaint to football fans of today, but let me tell you how Elway and Kubiak become football brothers for life. Their bond started with a television flickering deep into the night.

"The Andy Griffith Show," Elway recalled.

When bunking together, two young NFL quarterbacks discovered they shared an affinity for the classic sitcoms that were at the height of their first-run popularity during the 1960s, when Elway and Kubiak were kids in elementary school.

"John couldn't fall asleep unless the TV was on in the room. And I couldn't stand the noise, so I'd get up in the middle of the night and cut it off," Kubiak said. "But he'd wake up at 3 a.m. and tell me, 'Hey, turn it back on!' The compromise was we both liked all those sitcoms from the days when shows were in black and white. We must have seen every episode of *The Andy Giffith Show* at least five times."

Elway and Kubiak nodded off to sleep laughing to the wackiness of rural America, whether it was the Andy Griffith Show episode when townsfolk were worried Mayberry might blow sky high after a stray goat ate sticks of dynamite for lunch, or it was a Deputy Barney Fife going on one of his trademark rants, explaining why he gave a septic tank as an anniversary gift to his parents. ("Well, they're really hard to buy for. Besides, it was something they could use.")

So I had to ask: If Elway developed his leadership style by watching the unflappable calm of Sheriff Andy Taylor in a crisis, then which citizen of Mayberry helped prepare Kubiak for the patience required to deal with the craziness of being a football coach? Floyd the Barber? Aunt Bee?

"Oh hell, I don't know," said Kubiak, chuckling as he dismissed my silly question with a wave of his hand. He had more important things to do, because 24 hours seems inadequate for the tasks an NFL coach must complete each day.

Kubiak does have serious coaching chops. In Denver, where the sun rises and sets with Elway, Kubes has the gift to steer his famous friend's thinking without stepping on the toes of a legend. What made Kubiak a quarterback whisperer is the ability to criticize without grating on the ego of a star player. He mastered the skill during 12 years as an NFL assistant, while coaching Steve Young in San Francisco, Elway in Denver and later serving as the buffer in an often volatile relationship between Mike Shanahan and Jake Plummer.

But perhaps Kubiak's most spectacular work was on display when he landed his first NFL head coaching gig with the Houston Texans in 2006. He not only made the playoffs twice with journeyman Matt Schaub taking the majority of the team's offensive snaps at quarterback, Kubiak also made the thoroughly unremarkable Schaub look good enough to be rewarded with two trips to the Pro Bowl.

In November 2013, however, stuck in a rut of losing 11 of 13 games, a bad streak that would get Kubiak fired in his seventh season leading the Texans, he collapsed on the sideline at Reliant Stadium and was rushed to the hospital. Doctors diagnosed a transient ischemic attack, which occurs when a clot in an artery briefly shuts down blood flow to the brain. Stressed out by losing, Kubiak suffered a mini-stroke.

Before Elway tossed his buddy back in the pressure cooker of working for a franchise where every year is Super Bowl or bust, he made certain Kubiak had learned not to let all the blame regularly heaped on a coach ruin his health.

"I remind him all the time about it, and say, 'Listen, we want you here in Denver for a long, long time, so let's make sure you take care of yourself,'" Elway told Andrea Kremer in an interview with NFL Network.

Talk about stress: All Kubiak had to do in order to justify Elway's faith in him was exceed the gaudy 71.9 winning percentage achieved by Fox and not only return the Broncos to the Super Bowl, but win it.

To make things even tougher, Kubiak had to figure out a way to implement his run-heavy, play-action-pass offense with a veteran quarterback that didn't like operating under center, and whose old, heavy legs were not equipped to roll out of the pocket. "This was a major challenge and it was not easy," Manning admitted.

Even worse, the Hall of Fame skills of Manning had eroded so badly he could no longer consistently perform at a Hall of Fame level. Need proof? In 2013, Manning turned a tough-as-barbed wire Baltimore defense into papier-mâché, shredding the Ravens for seven touchdown passes in the season-opening game. During the entire month of September in 2015, which included dates against Baltimore, Detroit and Minnesota, Manning threw a grand total of three touchdown passes.

Guess who shouldered the blame when the Broncos offense encountered difficulty reaching the end zone? Kubiak.

"He didn't sign up for this," Manning said.

Oh, yes Kubiak did. In fact, he was signed to mold a football team that would no longer be defined by Manning.

After being far too dependent on Manning bringing his "A" game for far too long, Elway had decided to seriously revamp his approach to winning a championship, even before Kubiak was hired. The watershed moment was November 16, 2014, when the Broncos were thumped 22–7 in St. Louis. Manning flinched in the face of the Rams' fierce pass rush. He was asked to throw 54 times, and that was a mistake, especially when a deep pass in the third quarter to Emmanuel Sanders fluttered weakly in the air for so long that it allowed safety Rodney McLeod to load up on a vicious tackle that knocked Sanders from the game with a concussion. "Any time a player gets injured on the end of one your passes, my heart drops," Manning admitted.

Manning would never again throw 50 times in a game during the remainder of his career with the Broncos. In the wake of that ugly loss to the Rams, team management made the tough decision to emphasize running the football, which took it out of Manning's hands. It was not a popular move with Manning or Broncos fans in the beginning. But credit Elway with having the nerve to boldly shift the focus away from a 14-time Pro Bowl quarterback, and gamble that Denver could build a defense that would intimidate foes and dominate games.

The "D" in Denver has always stood for defense. The first chapter of pro football glory in Colorado was written by the Orange Crush. In basketball, Nuggets center Dikembe Mutombo wrote his ticket to the Hall of Fame with a wagging finger he used to admonish foes after blocking a shot. And the steely blue eyes of goalie Patrick Roy were the force behind two Stanley Cup championships by the Avalanche.

But son of a Bum, the man who created a defense to beat them all was Wade Phillips, a 68-year-old football lifer pulled off the unemployment line by Kubiak. Football is fun with Phillips, a defensive coordinator who would rather his players attack aggressively than worry about mistakes. To keep the vibe loose, it was not unusual to see Phillips dancing in the locker room or find him talking smack in his Twitter posts. The Broncos loved every minute of it. "I was surprised because he told us he liked Drake," defensive end Malik Jackson told Troy Renck of the *Denver Post*. "We asked him why and he said: 'I started from the bottom and now I'm here.'"

How to describe the attitude Phillips instilled in the Broncos' defense, from the opening kickoff to the final snap? All inside linebacker Brandon Marshall needed was two tiny syllables.

"Nuh-uh," he told me.

Nuh-uh means no way, no how, not in tour house.

"That's the attitude we have. Every play. Every down," said Marshall, who made 101 tackles for the Broncos during the 2015 regular season.

What defined this Denver defense was fiercer than the pass rush of outside linebacker Von Miller and nastier than the disposition of cornerback Aqib Talib, known to poke a foe in the eye just to make a point that you don't mess with Denver. The real, core strength of the defense was based in the brotherhood, which Marshall described as a deep trust and genuine affection rarely found in NFL teams during the salary-cap era, when financial realities cause constant roster churn.

"I love these guys, man. "And I love going to war with them, because when it looks all lost, we find a way," Marshall said. "We have the best defense in the league. This is the best defense I've ever been around in my life. Our players are so headstrong. And we're the brothers, man. We're all brothers."

Crunch the numbers, and there's no denying how Denver's defense brought the pain in 2015: The Broncos ranked No. 1 in the league in total defense, allowing a stingy 283 yards per game. They were No. 1 in sacks, recording 52 takedowns of the quarterback. They scored five defensive touchdowns, including a fumble recovery for a score by cornerback Bradley Roby that allowed to Denver to escape Kansas City with a victory in the final minute of the fourth quarter and a 74-yard interception return for a touchdown by Chris Harris Jr. that proved to be the difference in a road win at Oakland.

But maybe this was the most amazing statistic of all: During a championship season that saw the Broncos win a dozen times during the regular season and three more times during the playoffs, their record in games decided by seven points or less was 11-3. In the history of the NFL, no team had ever won 11 games decided by no more than a touchdown during a single season until this Denver defense, which stood tallest with its back to the wall.

Maybe Manning said it best: "I'm glad I am on the same team as that defense and don't have to play against them."

23

FROM ZERO TO HERO

The date was November 15, 2015, and it will forever live in infamy for Peyton Manning. It was a day when football mocked him and foes began to feel sorry for him. At one point during a disheartening 29–13 loss to the Kansas City Chiefs, I felt so embarrassed and hurt for the helpless, 39-year-old quarterback that I stood up in the press box, turned my head and whispered a prayer after Manning threw yet another interception: "Please, get him out of there."

The impossible had happened. On the stat sheet, next to Manning's name, was his quarterback rating. It read: 0.0. One of the greatest players in NFL history had been transformed into the football equivalent of Bluto Blutarsky, pencils stuck up his nose, earning a grade so low it even shamed Animal House.

November 15 was the first time football shouted at Manning it was time for him to get the hell out. It was his 265th regular-season start as an NFL quarterback, and it proved to be his most humiliating game as a pro. The crowd booed his team as he trotted off to the locker room at halftime. He was benched in the third quarter by coach Gary Kubiak, who made a stunning admission after the shockingly lopsided defeat. "I am disappointed in myself. This one is on me," Kubiak said. "I should have probably made the decision not to play Manning."

And that was the stinking truth. With a painfully injured left foot and a dead right arm, Manning looked washed up, after completing only five of 20 passes for a pitiful 35 yards against the Chiefs.

This was not how a Hall of Fame career was supposed to end. At age 39, Manning found himself trapped in a Kevin Costner sports movie. You know the plot: Lovable old player, hanging on, defiantly spitting in the eye of Father Time. The only trouble is it often works better in a Hollywood script than on a football field.

November 15 had been circled in on the calendar as a day of celebration in Broncos Country. With the sky a carefree shade of blue and the temperature of 64 degrees tailor-made for orange T-shirts, it was a perfect football Sunday in Colorado. What could possibly go wrong?

A giddy buzz filled the stadium, with Broncomaniacs certain a victory against Kansas City would all but clinch the AFC West title, making a postseason berth for Denver a foregone conclusion nearly two weeks prior to Thanksgiving. Among the crowd of 76,973 in Sports Authority Field at Mile High was Joe Horrigan, dispatched from Canton, Ohio, on a happy mission from the Pro Football Hall of Fame. "We have enough items for a whole Peyton Manning wing in the building," he said. But Horrigan, the affable Hall monitor, was back in Denver to collect one more souvenir from the quarterback's brilliant career.

With his first completion against the Chiefs, Manning would break Brett Favre's record of 71,838 passing yards, and Horrigan wanted the game ball. It would be one more way to measure greatness. Think of it this way: The ground covered by Manning's throws had stretched nearly 41 miles, greater than the distance, as the crow flies, from downtown Denver to the peak of 14,271 feet tall Mount Evans.

November 15, however, turned out to be a celebration cursed from the start. From his first pass, intercepted by Kansas City cornerback Marcus Peters to set up an easy touchdown for the Chiefs, something was terribly amiss with Manning, who appeared afraid to throw. He did bag the career-yardage record in the opening quarter, on a 4-yard catch by running back Ronnie Hillman. The game was halted briefly to salute Manning's accomplishment. He waved to the crowd with a smile that looked more like a grimace. It was an awkward moment, about to turn into unmitigated agony.

"I didn't play well, I had a bad game. Not much else you can say about that," said Manning, after being benched with Denver trailing 22–0. "Whether it was because of my injuries or my poor-decision making, I tend to lean on the poor decision-making and some bad throws."

His worst decision? Choosing to play hurt. By doing so, Manning hurt any chance Denver had of beating the Chiefs.

The date was November 15, and it's no exaggeration to suggest it could have been the day the Denver dream of a championship died. As stunned players trudged off the field after the 16-point loss to Kansas City, they clung to the solace of still being in first place of the AFC West standings. But momentum in the NFL can flip in a heartbeat, and the Broncos not only had lost two games in a row, nobody knew when— or if—Manning, hobbled by a partially torn plantar fascia near his left heel, could return to the lineup again. The starting quarterback job fell on the unproven shoulders of Brock Osweiler, who had started zero times and thrown only 30 passes since being drafted in 2012.

In back-to-back defeats, that cocksure attitude of Denver's outstanding defense was also rocked by surrendering a total of 56 points. The swagger in the locker room had vanished. The Broncos were suddenly tip-toeing toward an uncertain future, peeking with trepidation around the corner. "You can't panic. You can't say, 'Oh, this is the end of our season.' No way," Denver defensive end Antonio Smith said. "But I've seen that one loss give you three or four more, before you can say 'Wait a minute!' and hit the restart button."

As the sun set on November 15, the Broncos were a team in crisis. Despite a 7-2 record, Denver appeared to be more of a threat to miss the playoffs than make a serious run at the Super Bowl.

In the end, football can be cruel to its legends. Rather than a blaze of glory, Hall of Fame quarterback Dan Marino went down in the flames of a 62–7 playoff defeat during his final NFL game, while New York Jets icon Joe Namath limped away on gimpy knees, throwing four interceptions as quarterback for the Los Angeles Rams during his farewell performance. Rather than chasing a championship, would Manning's time in Denver end with him plopping his broken-down body on the Broncos bench? Those who loved him lost sleep, worried sick that he would hobble into retirement on an injured foot.

"I wasn't sure he was going to play again," admitted Archie Manning, the famous quarterback's famous father. "I even talked to my wife about it. Told her: 'Peyton might be done. . . . He might not play football again.' That thing, that foot, was killing him."

On his final snap before being yanked from the Kansas City game, Manning threw his fourth interception on an embarrassing afternoon. The last pick was nabbed by Chiefs safety Ron Parker, who damned Manning with faint praise. "That's him. He's getting pretty old," Parker said. "He's still a good quarterback. He tried hard."

He tried hard? In the view of Parker, a Hall of Fame quarterback had been reduced to three lousy, condescending words, and those patronizing words read like an obituary for Manning's brilliant 18-year NFL career.

But, as doubters threw dirt on Manning, there was this ray of optimism offered by his coach. "Peyton is our quarterback," Kubiak insisted after the loss to Kansas City. "If he's healthy and ready to go, Peyton's our quarterback."

At the time, it sounded to me like a dreaded, hollow vote of confidence for Manning, suffering through by far the worst season as a pro. But, in reality, it was an expression of faith more valuable than all the money in the Denver Mint. When the league was ready to bury its five-time MVP, Manning had a friend in Kubiak.

And what happened next was the most amazing comeback ever staged by Manning. What happened next is the story of an old quarterback, his skills diminished by injury and eroded by age, uncertain if he had anything left in his throwing arm, defiantly pushing the sun back up in the sky one more time, just long enough to get back in the Denver huddle, because, for the love of the game, there's no quit in Manning.

Damn, it was a Costner movie.

"We were nine weeks into the season, we were 7-2, we had a rough day against Kansas City," Kubiak said. "I knew (Manning) wasn't feeling good. I knew his foot was hurting. We went in my office and I said, 'You're going to get well.'"

Hand me a chisel and ask for my Mount Rushmore of quarterbacks, and I will gladly carve out a larger-than-life tribute to Joe Montana, Otto Graham, Johnny Unitas and Manning. But Kubiak had the stones to tell one of the greatest quarterbacks who ever lived to stay away from the Denver huddle until he was healthy enough to help the Broncos.

"He was not real happy with that, not real happy," Kubiak said.

During Manning's final NFL season, the Broncos scored 422 points in 19 games from a narrow victory against Baltimore in September through the Super Bowl upset of Carolina in February. But nothing counted more toward the championship than that difficult conversation behind closed doors between an injured quarterback and a coach scrambling to prevent his team from falling apart. In times of big trouble, it's the shared vulnerability of two proud men that can pull them through a crisis.

What did Kubiak tell Manning at the most crucial juncture of Denver's season?

"He told me: 'I got you,'" Manning said. "And I trusted him."

Coaches defined by X's and O's can draw up fantastic plays, but only a coach with the guts and heart to administer tough love can draw the best out of his players.

While the Broncos got down to business of nailing down their fifth-straight division championship, Manning began a tedious slog to beat the clock, with each hour of rehabilitation passing slowly, while at the same time, the weeks remaining on the regular-season schedule flew by way too fast for a quarterback anxious to get back in the huddle.

So not to be a distraction, Manning practiced on his own, away from teammates, on the artificial turf in the Pat Bowlen Fieldhouse with a motley crew that included practice squad receiver Jordan "Sunshine" Taylor, equipment managers Chris Valenti and Mike Harrington, plus injured rookie tight end Jeff Heuerman, shelved for the season after tearing the anterior cruciate ligament in his left knee in May. Like a rat in a scientific study, every step of Manning's recovery was recorded by a camera for analysis by Kubiak.

"I'd be lying if I sat here and told you it was not a frustrating time," Manning admitted. Then, with humor as distinctive as the Tennessee whiskey that made Jack Daniel's famous for smoothness and its mule-kick finish, Manning described being an outcast at Broncos headquarters for more than a month, when the injured quarterback was barely seen and rarely heard outside of the one team meeting each morning.

As Demaryius Thomas and Von Miller gathered with position coaches and went off to practice, "I go over in a little quarantined sandbox in the far corner," said Manning, with a heavy pour of 90 proof sarcasm. "It was nice of them to give me a practice-squad receiver, an equipment guy and a guy on injured reserve to throw to. That really helped. I really appreciated it."

In Manning's absence, the Broncos won three straight games, including a 30–24 overtime victory against New England, which saw Osweiler became an instant folk hero in Colorado during his second NFL start, by sending Tom Brady and the Patriots to their first loss of the season. It seemed too good to be true. And it was. Osweiler proved to be very human; his inexperience under center began to show. Oh, there was no shame and little real surprise in consecutive setbacks against the young, improving Oakland Raiders and the offensively explosive Pittsburgh Steelers in December. But, with a 10-4 record, Denver suddenly found itself in real danger of becoming the first team in NFL history to miss the playoffs after winning 10 of its opening dozen games.

In Pittsburgh, Osweiler and his teammates blew a 14-point lead at halftime, went scoreless during the final 30 minutes and lost 34–27. In the visiting locker room at Heinz Field, the disheartened Broncos were reeling. "Gary called the team together and bared his soul. He said: 'Guys, are you in with me or not?' It was part anger, part emotion, part frustration, but a huge part passion," said team president Joe Ellis, who witnessed the coach's post-game speech. "He was putting everything he had into this (season) and he wanted his players to join him."

Desperate to halt the team's slide, it was understandable why Kubiak had renewed urgency to gauge Manning's progress as the quarterback threw to his motley crew on Christmas Eve.

"During the workout, he sent me a signal on the film," Kubiak said.

As anybody who has watched Manning conduct his business at the line of scrimmage knows, he can communicate an encyclopedia of football knowledge with a simple wave of his hand. So what not-so-subtle message was Manning trying to convey to his coach with one extension of a single finger?

"'Hey, we're No. 1.' You could take it that way," said Kubiak, suppressing the urge to laugh at the memory of Manning flipping him the bird. "I took it as, 'I'm ready to play, Coach.'"

With one profanely defiant gesture, Manning revealed more about himself than the guy America thinks it knows from him singing endearingly off-key about chicken parm tasting so good in television commercials for Nationwide Insurance. Yes, Manning is a good guy. He does write thank-you notes to players when they retire from the NFL and his foundation has helped at-risk youth through grants in excess of $10 million. Those random acts of kindness are real and genuine.

The Manning I came to know during his four years in Denver, however, was also a ruthless competitor. If there's one shared trait among transcendent athletes, from Michael Jordan to Serena Williams, it's a relentlessly unhealthy obsession with not only beating any person or thing standing in the way, but crushing the obstacle. The magic of Manning is in hiding this addiction to winning with charm and grace.

The rap on Manning has always been he was a prisoner of his statistics and a choke artist in the clutch. I don't buy it. Manning would not have persevered through the chronic pain in his foot and the embarrassment of being the 34th ranked quarterback in a 32-team league during his final season without a deep-seeded need to succeed. He swallowed his pride after getting benched and finally embraced the idea of being a game manager of Kubiak's run-heavy offensive system for the singular purpose of earning that Super Bowl ring he came to Denver for in the first place.

During the final week of December 2015, Kubiak instructed Manning to assemble with his tiny practice crew at the team's indoor facility for a 9 o'clock workout, so the coach could have a firsthand inspection of how far his quarterback had progressed in rehabilitation. By the time Kubiak arrived, however, the passing drills were done and Manning was ready to send his training partners to the showers.

In a small act of insubordination, Manning had intentionally started 60 minutes early. After 18 years in the NFL, he was done auditioning for the role of quarterback. When Kubiak demanded an explanation, Manning cut off his boss with a direct statement: "I'm ready to play."

A control freak might have freaked out in response to Manning's outburst. Instead of going berserk, Kubiak patiently listened for 25 minutes as Manning stated his case for being issued a uniform on game day for the first time since he was benched against Kansas City.

All Manning wanted for Christmas was a chance. Call it luck. Call it fate. But don't forget to call re-write for a comeback story that grew juicier after Osweiler and the Broncos escaped with a 20–17 victory against Cincinnati on December 28, when Brandon McManus atoned for a field goal he badly hooked at the end of regulation with a 37-yard kick that split the uprights to win the game in overtime. The wildly changing, unpredictable trajectory of Denver's fortunes was about to get so weird it could make Stephen Hawking quit looking for a logical explanation and order a pizza.

On the first Sunday of the New Year, the Patriots inexplicably attempted to win their final regular-season game in Miami without really trying to do anything on offense except to keep Brady healthy for the playoffs, and lost 20–10 to the Dolphins during a totally unforeseen meltdown in Florida. Thanks, Flipper. It was a gift that kept on giving. All the Broncos had to do in order to secure the No. 1 seed in the AFC and home-field advantage in the playoffs was beat San Diego, which entered Sports Authority Field at Mile High with a 4-11 record and no real motivation to put up much of a fight.

Can you say quarterback controversy? Despite the 4-2 record compiled by Osweiler as the emergency starter at quarterback, he was victimized by five Denver turnovers that left him fussing with the coaching staff early in the San Diego game. His ineffectiveness moving the ball against the Chargers incited a nervous home crowd to beg for something, anything that could give the Broncos a spark.

At precisely 4:27 p.m. on a chilly afternoon, with Denver trailing 13–7 in the third quarter, Manning discarded his parka and entered the Broncos huddle to a standing ovation that instantly chased all the darkness from the stadium. Maybe the old quarterback still had the strength in his arm to push the sun back up in the sky.

"I heard the crowd go wild. I turned around, and that's when I saw Peyton running on the field," said Smith, who was sitting on the Denver bench with his defensive teammates. "That energy was exactly what we needed, exactly when we needed it. People don't like to talk about stuff like that, because there ain't no way to gauge it, ain't no way to prove it to be true. But it is what it is. You could just feel the energy change, the shift. And the rest was history."

Manning, often accused of being a robot fully loaded with artificial intelligence but devoid of blood and guts, led a comeback by stirring every soul in the stadium. His arm was not particularly impressive, as he passed for only nine times for 69 yards against the Chargers. But his spirit was the stuff that ignited four scoring drives, including a 23-yard scamper to the end zone by Ronnie Hillman that proved to be the difference in a 27–20 victory.

Archie Manning and his wife Olivia watched the game from their home in New Orleans as nervous parents. Although delighted Peyton was back in uniform on the Denver sideline after a lengthy absence, "He told me beforehand, 'I'm not going to play,'" Archie recalled.

Shortly after halftime, Olivia peered at the television and could not believe what she saw, then exclaimed to her husband: "Peyton's warming up!"

"Aw," replied Archie, "he's probably just doing a little throwing, just in case."

"No!" insisted Olivia. "He's warming up to go in the game."

This comeback was dedicated to every father and mother who have ever sat in the stands and prayed a silly game would not break their kid's heart.

Archie Manning is the proud father of three boys. Ask him the favorite performance in his middle son's pro football career, and the surprise is it's not a Super Bowl victory. No. 1 on Dad's list was when Indianapolis rallied from a 21–3 deficit against New England during a much-hyped AFC championship showdown in January 2007, when Peyton overcame a pick-six interception during the second quarter to lead the game-winning drive in the final minutes of the fourth quarter.

"But the second most important game that Peyton has ever been a part of might be his only bullpen game," added Archie, the patriarch of America's first family of quarterbacks.

After 186 career victories as a starting NFL quarterback, Peyton came off the bench and got credited with a huge save against the Chargers.

In the span of seven weeks, he went from zero to hero. He saved his best for last. In the end, with time running out, Manning saved the Broncos' season.

24

THE LAST RODEO

Peyton Manning won back his job as the starting quarterback. And there was gratitude in his heart. But it did not take away the hurt.

On a chilly January morning, coach Gary Kubiak ended any possibility of a prolonged quarterback controversy. In the playoffs, which began with a home date against Pittsburgh, the Broncos were going with the legend over the kid. Brock Osweiler would watch. Manning would play.

As Manning strapped in for another wild ride, I had one question for him:

Could this be your Last Rodeo?

"I'd be lying if I said I'm not thinking about that," Manning replied.

It was a startling admission from a quarterback who sets the agenda with the media as deftly as he directs traffic at the line of scrimmage. If Manning was thinking this was his last, best chance to win a championship with the Broncos, then it was the first strong indication he had begun to make peace with the idea of retiring from football.

Controlling the chaos is Manning's thing. A blitzing linebacker? No problem. But showing any sign of vulnerability to the public? That scares him. In those rare moments when Manning reveals a little of what makes him tick, the tell is how his voice of authority is reduced to a soft stammer, as if he is working out uncertain emotions as the words tumble slowly out of his mouth. On January 7, 2016, shortly after Manning was given his job back as starting quarterback, the veteran quarter-

back pulled me away from the crush of television cameras around his
locker. Manning needed to share some unfiltered truth: The previous
12 months had been brutal on him, with humbling changes to his role
with the team and unexpected attacks on his character from far and
wide. It had been a tough year that forced him to grow in uncomfortable ways.

"There were a lot of firsts . . . a lot of firsts for me this year. It's weird
in your 18th season to have so many firsts," Manning said. "But when
you sign up to play, you sign up for anything."

Then, Manning looked me in the eye and made a confession: Nothing in his long and brilliant career had prepared him for the adversity
that blindsided him in so many ways that he could never saw it all
coming. His favored offensive scheme was junked. His touchdown-to-
interception ration stunk. His foot hurt and his coach benched him. He
was accused of being a malcontent, a drug cheat. . . .

"You learn about yourself and how you handle it," Manning said.
"That's been my theme all year: Just keep being a pro. I've been
through a lot of stuff. . . . But that's what I drew on during this time: Be
a pro. Handle it. And keep the faith."

Long before he threw the first of his 17 interceptions, 2015 got off to
a rocky start during the chilly winter months that followed a bad playoff
loss to Indianapolis. The Broncos slashed Manning's salary, initially asking him for a 50 percent cut, then reached a compromise that paid the
quarterback $15 million plus incentives. Money talks in pro sports, and
what general manager John Elway told Manning by reducing his base
salary by $4 million was unmistakable: You ain't what you used to be.
Money drove a wedge between Elway and Manning, creating a frosty
relationship between the team's general manager and quarterback.

After Manning was benched in favor of Osweiler nine games into the
2015 season, NFL Network insider Ian Rapoport reported it created "a
very uncomfortable and difficut situation in Denver" because Manning
"really does not want to be a backup." Being characterized as a malcontent infuriated Manning. He derided the story in the strongest terms,

angrily telling me after a December loss to the Pittsburgh Steelers: "It's a flat-out lie. It's insulting. That's 100 percent bullshit."

Al Jazeera, a news organization based in the Middle East, attacked Manning's integrity during its telecast of "The Dark Side: Secrets of the Sports Dopers," which was released at the end of 2015. The documentary claimed to have knowledge human growth hormone had been shipped in the name of Manning's wife to their home while the quarterback recovered from neck surgeries in 2007. He denounced the story that tried to link his name to performance-enhancing drugs, and welcomed an NFL investigation.

On top of everything, it often hurt to watch when the 39-year-old quarterback was physically able to play. During more games than not, he wasn't Peyton Freakin' Manning any longer, but an imposter wearing No. 18 for the Broncos, trying to fool opponents into believing it was still the Hall of Fame player he used to be.

During training camp in August, Manning finally confirmed to Peter King of Sports Illustrated what had been obvious to me for years: The most crucial fallout from the four neck surgeries during his final months in Indianapolis was not weakened arm strength but nerve damage in his throwing hand that made it difficult to spin the ball with precision: "I can't feel anything in my fingertips. It's crazy," Manning said. "I've talked to a doctor recently who said: 'Don't count on the feeling coming back.'"

Even legends grow old. The mind trick is not to be defeated by that bummer of a realization. There were Sundays when the Broncos won in spite of Manning. A pathetic 67.9 quarterback rating, as well as his 224.9 yards passing per game, were the worst statistical markers of his career. It was not easy for Manning to accept the betrayal by his body. Weakened by age, he could no longer produce Hall of Fame results when he dropped back to pass. But it did not stop Manning from winning. He won seven of nine starts as a starter, and led Denver to its crucial comeback victory against San Diego during a relief appearance.

From the negotiating table to the rumor mill to the Denver huddle, there was never-ending bad news on his doorstep. "A drama," Manning said. "I've always told you all I'll never write a book. I could probably write a pretty good short story, though, on the past offseason and season."

Recalling that Manning took a mental break from the pressures of football during his early years in Denver by plopping in front on the television to watch the travails of Enoch "Nucky" Thompson in *Boardwalk Empire*, I suggested all this melodrama might be material for a future soap opera on HBO.

"Now that," Manning said, "would be an insult to *Boardwalk Empire*."

Denver extracted revenge for a regular-season loss to the Steelers with a 23–16 to open the NFL playoffs. There was nothing subtle about how the Broncos won. The defense took a sledgehammer to Pittsburgh quarterback Ben Roethlisberger. After jump-starting a sputtering Denver offense in the nick of time for a comeback victory, Manning admitted he did just enough to survive and advance. Up next was an even bigger challenge for linebacker Von Miller and the No-Fly Zone secondary: Tom Brady and the New England Patriots.

In the AFC championship game, Manning connected with tight end Owen Daniels for two touchdown passes that staked Denver to an early 17–9 advantage over the Pats. But down the stretch, Manning was a game manager, conservatively throwing only a dozen times for a mere 48 yards in the second half. He again leaned leaning heavily on the Denver defense, which halted a furious rally by Brady when Broncos cornerback Bradley Roby intercepted a pass in the end zone that could have tied the score on a two-point conversion with a scant 12 seconds remaining in the fourth quarter.

After the city of Denver could exhale, a tense 20–18 victory against New England complete, I crossed paths with Archie Manning, who pulled two leather gloves from his coat pocket. "On January first, I made a resolution not to bite my fingernails. So I wore these gloves the whole game," said Archie, proudly curling his fingers so I could inspect his pristine nails, fully intact. "Still got 'em. So I guess the gloves worked."

While I was chatting with Archie, his son was out on the field, shaking hands with New England coach Bill Belichick. It was a brief, but revealing private conversation between two longtime foes that was caught on tape by an eavesdropping camera from NFL Network. "Hey listen," said Peyton, speaking in the ear of Belichick, "this might be my last rodeo. So it sure has been a pleasure."

Manning got the best of Brady in the 17th showdown between the two QBs who defined football excellence in the opening quarter of the 21st century. Reviewing the great escape against his longtime nemesis, there was a twinkle in the eye of an old quarterback playing with house money.

"Never a doubt, right?" said Manning, stepping in a stadium elevator. As the doors closed behind him, a red arrow pointed straight up, toward Super Bowl 50.

Everybody wanted to know: Was the championship game to be the final chapter in one of the greatest quarterback stories ever told?

"Daddy," 4-year-old Mosley Manning asked at the outset of Super Bowl week, "is this the last game of the season?"

"Yes," replied the Broncos quarterback.

Mosley: "I sure do want you to win that trophy."

Daddy: "I do, too, Mosley. And that's what we're going to try to do."

Then, as kids often do, Mosley got down to the real nitty gritty: "Daddy, is this the last game ever?"

NFL Nation was antsy, with loyal fans in New Orleans, Knoxville, Tenn., and Indianapolis all hoping and praying Manning could retire on top. We're all suckers for a fairy-tale ending, aren't we?

Super Bowl 50, however, was billed as another heartache waiting to happen for Broncos Country. Carolina had won the NFC championship by routing Arizona 49–15. The oddsmakers in Las Vegas established the Panthers as 5½-point favorites. When Broncos president Joe Ellis was asked what he it would be like watching Manning take the field with his teammates at Levi's Stadium in Santa Clara, Calif., his blunt answer came straight from the gut. "Any way you chalk it up, it's 3½ hours of unmitigated misery," Ellis said. "It's all fire in the belly."

It was the Last Rodeo.

In a sport where quarterbacks rule, Manning figured to have no shot against Cam Newton of Carolina, who would be awarded the first MVP trophy of his pro career on the eve of Super Bowl 50. If Manning was the grizzled old face of the NFL's glorious past, then the 26-year-old Newton was certainly the league's future.

Manning is affectionately called the Sheriff. But Newton? He is Superman, known for a celebratory dance dubbed the Dab and an ego as large as his 6-foot-5, 245-pound frame.

"Everybody sees the super hero in how I play," Newton boasted in September, then backed his boast by throwing 35 touchdown passes for the league's highest-scoring team. "I've gotten the nickname Superman, Super Cam, ever since I can remember."

But here's the one secret of Super Bowl 50 you need to know: In the days prior to kickoff, members of the NFL's top-ranked defense grew sick and tired of hearing about Superman. "Cam, Cam, Cam. It got old listening to all the talk about him all week," Broncos defensive end Malik Jackson said.

What's more, as the game on Sunday drew closer, word slowly began to leak that defensive coordinator Wade Phillips had installed a game plan to use Newton's own arrogance against the Carolina quarterback and his teammates. "They're front-runners," safety T.J. Ward told me fewer than 36 hours prior to kickoff. When cornerback Chris Harris Jr. also confided it would be the Denver defense that dictated how Newton would play, I knew: There might not be a money-back guaranteed the Broncos would win the game, but that definitely was the smart way to bet.

Rather than react to Newton with a spying linebacker assigned to mirror the quarterback's moves, the Broncos decided to attack Newton with blitz packages. The conservative blocking scheme of the Panthers, which regularly employed a tight end and sometimes also a fullback to protect Newton in the pocket, allowed Phillips to aggressively rush Brandon Marshall or another defender unburdened by pass-coverage responsibility against Carolina's easy-to-read offensive tendencies.

Denver dared to do more than tug on Superman's cape. Phillips's ballsy idea was to hit Newton hard, physically and emotionally. The Broncos wanted to knock doubt into the head of Carolina's quarterback. Maybe Superman would be stunned to learn he was not bigger and badder than every other football player on the field. The Broncos intended to gobsmack Newton and see if Super Cam cracked.

The plan worked to perfection. On a clear, 76-degree February afternoon of which California dreams are born, Lady Gaga sang a rendition of the "Star-Spangled Banner" that raised goose bumps on 71,088 spectators who had paid top dollar to attend the Super Bowl. Denver took a 3-0 lead on its opening drive, which ended with a 34-yard field goal by Brandon McManus. The teams traded punts. Then, with 6 minutes, 34 seconds remaining in the first quarter, Broncos linebacker Von Miller and the defense dropped the full force of its shock and awe on Newton.

As Newton retreated to pass in the shadow of his goal line, Miller blew by Panthers offensive tackle Mike Remmers and promptly introduced Superman to the player affectionately known in Denver as the Vonster. Pouncing on Newton without warning, Miller ripped the football from the quarterback's hands. Jackson fell on the turnover in the end zone for a touchdown. Orange pandemonium rocked the stadium. Denver was ahead 10–0. The tone for Super Bowl 50 was set in stone.

Superman blinked. Pounded by the Broncos with the same disdain they showed for Roethlisberger and Brady earlier in the playoffs, the arrogance of Newton turned to panic. He could not run. He could not hide. He would only complete 18 of 41 passes for 265 yards against the Broncos.

"I don't care who we're playing. There's 100 percent confidence," said Ward, who dissed the Panthers as poseurs who were wannabe rappers and dancers. "It doesn't matter if we're playing Johnny Unitas. If he came out there, we'd shut him down."

Manning is the Sheriff. But it was Miller, the most valuable player of this game, who laid down the law. It did not matter that the 194 yards in total offense were fewer than the production of any of the previous 49

Super Bowl winners. It did not matter that while clinging to the lead in the second half, the Broncos ended four consecutive possessions with three meek punts and one awkward fumble. It did not matter, because with 4 minutes, 16 seconds remaining in the fourth quarter, with Denver up 16–10, Miller stripped Newton of the football one more time, forcing a turnover that set up an insurance touchdown, scored on a 2-yard run by C.J. Anderson.

For the third time in franchise history, the Broncos were Super Bowl champions. There was no arguing the primary reason why this 24–10 upset victory happened: "The best defense in Broncos history. We can say that now, without reservation," declared Alfred Williams, a fierce pass-rusher for the Broncos when the team won back-to-back championship in the late 1990s.

The Last Rodeo was a grind for Manning. He hung on more than he stood out. His body took a pounding and it hurt to look at his stats: 13 completions for 141 yards, five sacks, one interception. But do you think he cared? Of course not. And, as far as he was concerned, the inevitable trip to Disneyland for the Super Bowl winning quarterback could wait. His first stop was going to be the fridge. "I'm going to drink a whole lot of beer," Manning said.

As gold confetti fluttered in the air and Elway raised the Lombardi Trophy while shouting "This one's for Pat!" in tribute to 71-year-old franchise owner Pat Bowlen, confined to care in Colorado fighting the ravages of Alzheimer's disease, there was a little scene off to the side of the raucous celebration maybe only a mother could appreciate.

On the field, Olivia Manning exhaled with relief. She had wished so earnestly for her son to beat the Panthers it hurt. "I would like for him to retire. I would," Olivia confided to Sam Farmer, an excellent reporter from the *Los Angeles Times*. "Physically, I just don't think it's worth going on. He won a Super Bowl. It's the best way to go out."

Her son was on the podium, standing front and center of the football universe. Commissioner Roger Goodell turned to Manning, and spoke for everybody from trombone players in the University of Tennessee marching band the QB had led in renditions of "Rocky Top" to waiters that served his steak dinner at St. Elmo's after dozens of Colts victories in Indianapolis.

"Peyton, I don't know if this is your Last Rodeo," Goodell told America's favorite quarterback. "But it was one heck of a ride. And we thank you for the ride."

The weeks that followed the Super Bowl included a parade through the streets of downtown Denver lined with an estimated one million admirers and a happy, little chat with Jimmy Falion on "The Tonight Show." But when the party hit the pause button, it was not an easy time for Manning.

His reputation was dragged through the mud, when the *New York Daily News* instigated a nationwide debate with its deep and splashy dive into a 20-year-old story. While in college, Manning was alleged to have sexually harassed a female athletic trainer by exposing his buttocks and genitals as she examined him for a foot injury. "I did not do what has been alleged. And I'm not interested in re-litigating something that happened when I was 19 years old," Manning said.

Although one year remained on Manning's contract with Denver, at the tidy sum of $19 million, the team did not want him back in 2016, so he seriously explored if there was a possibility to join the Rams, newly relocated to Los Angeles, or another franchise in desperate need of help at quarterback. But the harsh reality was there were no good options for continuing his football career. The game was telling Manning it was time to go home.

On March 7, 2016, exactly one month after winning the Super Bowl, Manning entered Broncos headquarters, walking hand-in-hand with 4-year-old son Marshall, then faced a big room crammed with friends, family and a live television audience to announce he was retiring from football. It was one of the most eloquent valedictions ever heard from an athlete.

"I've learned a lot through my mistakes, stumbles and losses in football. I've also learned this game is a mighty platform that has given me a voice that can echo well beyond the game," Manning said. "Football has taught me not to be led by obstructions but instead be led by dreams."

Fired by Indianapolis in 2012, Manning followed a dream to Denver, and four years later, walked away from his Last Rodeo as a champion.

Out of necessity born from heartache, a legendary Colt grew into something more. As a Bronco, Manning broke records: most touchdown passes in a season, most passing yards in a career. But most of all, at the end of four seasons in Denver, with his body wearing out, Manning won with something more powerful than the beautiful mind that let us know the perfect play was on the way when he shouted the magic word: "Omaha!"

In the end, Manning had the heart to accept his physical limitations while still dreaming big, kept the faith he could lead with more than his passing arm and loved every little aspect of football until his final snap at Super Bowl 50. Heart proved to be enough.

So here is a heart-felt thank-you to Manning for the privilege of watching the greatest second act any quarterback has ever written in the NFL. Thanks for the 17,112 yards passing, the 140 touchdowns and the four AFC West division titles that he won in Denver. Thanks for the humility in victory and the grace in defeat. Thanks for everything. But more than anything, thanks for reminding us a quarterback who relentlessly pursues perfection might be a little crazy obsessive, but nothing can uplift a team or a town like crazy optimism.

"Well, I have fought the good fight, I have finished the football race and after 18 years it is time," Manning told fans on the day he retired from the game. "God bless you and God bless football."

What's next? He could run an NFL franchise. Or run for governor of Tennessee. No dream is too big for Manning to tackle.

During Manning's retirement speech, I chuckled at a moment when everybody else in the room was reverently quiet with rapt attention. Please forgive me, but I could not help but smile. There was Manning, being true to his reputation as a brainiac to the very end. Proving one more time he is no dumb jock, Manning managed to apply the wisdom of Johann Wolfgang von Goethe, a German poet, scientist and philosopher born in 1749, to playing quarterback in the NFL.

Manning told the crowd that had come to say goodbye to America's quarterback: "There's an old saying that goes, 'Treat a man as he is, and he will remain as he is. Treat a man as he could be and he will become what he should be.'"

Hey, we all want to be somebody. But how many of us are willing to sign up for the hard-earned growth required to become somebody?

Hanging around Manning, you learn some stuff. During his four years in Denver, the most important stuff I learned was: No Plan B? A bold mantra, but in practice, it seldom works for long as an effective way to deal with life. Even a football star can get blind-sided by change too fast to see coming and too big to stop.

Manning is done playing football. While retirement is also a convenient excuse to quit growing, he refuses to play by those rules.

Manning is not perfect. Never will be. Never can be. And here's the beauty: Walking away from the NFL as a champion might look, feel and taste like going out on top. But Manning has the audacity to hope for more. Looking for a way to define tomorrow as a chance to get better, this old quarterback is just getting warmed up.

Game on.

SOURCES

My sincere thanks to the following magazines, newspapers, and websites that proved to be valuable resources during my research for this book.

Chapter 1

The specifics of neck-fusion surgery as it relates to the health of an NFL quarterback were detailed by Seth Wickersham of *ESPN the Magazine* on October 7, 2011.

The anecdote of Peyton Manning getting lost on a trip to the barber shop shortly after moving to Colorado can be found in a feature by *Los Angeles Times* sportswriter Sam Farmer, published November 21, 2012.

Chapter 2

Patrik Jonsson reported and wrote "Top 5 Tim Tebow Eye Black Biblical Verses," a list that appeared in the *Christian Science Monitor* on February 3, 2010.

Chapter 3

Mike Klis, "Peyton Manning–Led Denver Broncos the Toast of NFL," *Denver Post*, March 27, 2012.

Tam O'Neill, "Albert Bierstadt, Great Art, True Love!" posted February 14, 2013, on tamoneillfinearts.com.

The anecdote of Peyton Manning assigning backup quarterback Brock Osweiler movies to watch was prompted by a Dave Krieger question during *The Dave Logan Show*, which aired April 17, 2013.

Chapter 4

Peter King, *Sports Illustrated* senior staff writer, asked University of Southern California quarterback Matt Barkley what he learned from Peyton Manning in the "Monday Morning QB" column, posted February 25, 2013, on SI.com.

Chapter 5

The critique of Peyton Manning and the accusation that ESPN was hiding the truth about a washed-up quarterback appeared in a Foxsports.com column by Jason Whitlock, posted September 19, 2012.

The details of Peyton Manning's use of a glove on his throwing hand during games were reported by Mike Klis in the January 8, 2013, edition of the *Denver Post*.

Chapter 6

Dr. Pat Robertson made his comments about the Broncos treating Tim Tebow "shabbily" during a broadcast of *The 700 Club* on the Christian Broadcasting Network, March 22, 2012.

Lindsay H. Jones of *USA Today* learned NFL front-office executive John Elway believed Tim Tebow fans and Broncos fans did not always root for the same outcome in "John Elway: Peyton Manning Was a Risk Worth Taking," published November 14, 2012.

Chapter 7

Sally Ruth Bourrie and Patrick Sullivan, "Elway's Empire," *Colorado Business Magazine*, September 1, 1994, detailed off-field success in the automobile business by the Broncos' star player.

Woody Paige, *Denver Post* columnist, sat down with the quarterback to write "Ol' No. 7, Denver's Legendary Quarterback, John Elway, Reflects on Reaching 50," published June 27, 2010.

The anecdote of young John Elway's smashing debut as a peewee football player has appeared in numerous publications, including *In the Huddle with . . . John Elway*, written by Matt Christopher, Hachette Book Group, copyright 1999.

Chapter 8

Dan Patrick, employed by ESPN at the time, conducted the lengthy interview in which Peyton Manning described his first game as quarterback at the University of Tennessee. A condensed version of the interview appeared in the September 3, 2001, edition of *ESPN the Magazine*, while more expansive outtakes of the conversation were posted at ESPN.com on December 6 of the same year.

Eddie Pells, national writer for the Associated Press, interviewed Archie Manning for the details of a cross-country hunting trip by his son after the Broncos season. The story was published January 19, 2013.

Chapter 9

Peter King, "Peyton Manning's Long Game," in the April 2, 2012, edition of *Sports Illustrated*, was the source of the anecdote regarding the anniversary well wishes sent Mr. and Mrs. Manning during the Broncos' recruitment of the veteran quarterback.

Gary Dulac reported on John Fox's NFL roots in a story published December 23, 2010: "Panthers' Fox learned from Steelers' Noll" in the *Pittsburgh Post-Gazette*.

Mike Klis, "Denver Broncos Coach John Fox Has Different Way Motivating Players," noted the coach's fondness for military literature in a feature published November 11, 2012, by the *Denver Post*.

Chapter 10

David Climer wrote a profile of Peyton Manning at the University of Tennessee, "Just One of the Guys," *Sporting News*, August 18, 1997.

Cover story "Colorado Is No. 1" described quarterback John Hessler's relationship with coach Rick Neuheisel, by Terry Frei, *Sporting News*, August 18, 1997.

Chapter 12

Mark Alesia reported live from New York, as an eyewitness to Peyton Manning's shot as guest host of *Saturday Night Live* in stories written for the *Indianapolis Star* and published March 27, 2007.

Ryan McGee recounted the anecdote of Peyton Manning schooling rookie tight end Dallas Clark in "Help Me Help You," published August 25, 2012, by *ESPN the Magazine*.

Gray Caldwell, "Prater-Beadles Not Quite Montana-Rice," September 30, 2012, denverbroncos.com.

Andy Fenelon, "Peyton Manning Roasts Players in Pro Bowl Address," January 23, 2013, NFL.com.

Chapter 13

Arnie Stapleton, "Read Option Is Back in NFL and Better Than Ever," Associated Press, December 4, 2012.

Mike Klis interviewed NFL historian Gil Brandt for "NFL's Read-Option Offense Has Become Super Bowl Relevant," published February 3, 2013, in the *Denver Post*.

Dan Graziano, "Tomlin Not a Believer in Read Option," posted March 20, 2013, on ESPN.com.

Chapter 14

Colin Shattuck, "This Whole Manning Thing Doesn't Feel Right," posted August 15, 2012, by southstandsdenver.com.

Stefan Fatsis, "Peyton Manning Is a Genius. He's Also a Pain in the Ass," February 4, 2010, *Slate* magazine.

Chapter 15

Ryan Parker reported on Michael Hancock's playoff wager with the city of Baltimore, "Injured Denver Mayor Puts Off Ray Lewis Dance to Pay Off Broncos Bet," in the *Denver Post*, January 15, 2013.

Mike Burrows, a copy editor at the *Denver Post*, compiled the weird similarities in two playoff defeats, which were detailed in "Amazing Comparisons between Broncos Stunning Losses to Jacksonville & Baltimore," a blog posted by Mike Klis on January 13, 2013.

Chapter 17

Jeff Zrebiec and Aaron Wilson reported the introduction of Elvis Dumervil as a Baltimore Ravens player in "Dumervil on Joining Ravens: 'It Was Time to Change the Scenery,'" published March 26, 2013, in the *Baltimore Sun*.

New England quarterback Tom Brady's quote of appreciation for Wes Welker appeared in "5 Memories from Wes Welker's Patriots Tenure," compiled by the *Boston Globe* staff and published March 13, 2013.

Christopher L. Gasper described the falling-out between New England and its star receiver in "Patriots to Blame for Loss of Wes Welker," *Boston Globe*, March 14, 2013.

Michael Silver reported the disappointment of New England's quarterback about the departure of Welker in "Tom Brady Should Feel Burned by Patriots Passing on Wes Welker for Danny Amendola," Yahoo! Sports, March 13, 2013.

Chapter 18

Mike Klis, "Peyton Manning Talks Broncos Upset, Looks toward New York Super Bowl," posted January 13, 2013, on denverpost.com.

Chapter 19

Mike Klis reported documentation of multiple positive tests for marijuana in "Broncos Von Miller Suspended by NFL Due to Drug Policy," published July 23, 2013, in the *Denver Post*.

Caitlin Swieca interviewed a Denver sandwich shop owner in "Colorado Marijuana Proponents Dismiss Von Miller Uproar," published July 28, 2013, in the *Denver Post*.

Chapter 20

The video of Peyton Manning's acceptance speech as *Sports Illustrated* magazine's 2013 Sportsman of the Year was posted December 16, 2013, by denverbroncos.com.

Chapter 21

"John Fox would do 'everything' differently if Broncos return to Super Bowl," published March 25, 2014, revealed the mistake of changing hotels on the eve of the NFL championship game during an interview with *Denver Post* reporter Mike Klis.

Sally Jenkins of the *Washington Post* examined what the Super Bowl loss meant to a decorated quarterback's legacy in "Peyton Manning Fails to Improve the Only Record That Matters," published February 3, 2014.

College of Charleston professor Laurie Lattimore-Volkmann wrote "Open Letter to Peyton Manning" as a blog originally posted February 4, 2014; it was reprinted by media outlets in Colorado.

Cornerback Champ Bailey's comments shortly after his release from the Broncos were made to Lindsay H. Jones of *USA Today* in "Done in Denver, Champ Bailey Has No Plans to Retire," posted March 6, 2014.

Chapter 22

Dialogue by actor Don Knotts as Deputy Barney Fife appeared in "Barney's First Car," which was Episode 27 of the third season on *The Andy Griffith Show*, written by Jim Fritzell and Everett Greenbaum.

John Elway expressed his concern for Gary Kubiak's health during interview with NFL Network correspondent Andrea Kremer that aired on *NFL Game Day*, telecast February 7, 2016.

Denver Post sportswriter Troy Renck reported the interaction between Wade Phillips and Malik Jackson about rap music lyrics in "Wade Phillips, with Texan Touch, Revamped Broncos as Defensive Coordinator," posted February 2, 2016.

Chapter 23

Denver Post sportswriter Nick Groke reported the critique of Denver's veteran quarterback by Kansas City safety Ron Parker in "He's Getting Old, Chiefs Say, After Bouncing Peyton Manning on 4 INTs," posted November 15, 2015, at denverpost.com.

The locker-room speech to the Broncos after a 34–27 loss at Pittsburgh was described by Troy Renck of the *Denver Post* in "Joe Ellis Saw John Elway's Vision Come to Life in Gary Kubiak's Message," posted March 25, 2016.

Chapter 24

NFL insider Ian Rapoport broke the news of Peyton Manning's discomfort with being a backup quarterback during an NFL Network telecast on December 20, 2015.

A possible link between Peyton Manning and human growth hormone was the subject of speculation in Al Jazeera documentary *The Dark Side: Secrets of the Sports Dopers*, released December 26, 2015.

Sports Illustrated senior staff writer Peter King reported the nerve damage in Peyton Manning's throwing hand during an interview for "Fallout, Fall Guys and Fingertips: A Week in the NFL," his Monday Morning Quarterback blog that appeared August 24, 2015, at SI.com.

The "last rodeo" conversation between Peyton Manning and New England coach Bill Belichick was recorded by an NFL Films camera and broadcast January 25, 2016, by *NFL Total Access* on the NFL Network.

Carolina quarterback Cam Newton referring to himself as Superman was reported by Steve Reed of the Associated Press in "Panthers' Cam Newton to Host Nickelodeon TV Show," posted September 23, 2015.

The irritation of the Denver players with the media attention given Cam Newton was reported by Troy Renck in "Von Miller, Defense Carry Broncos to Super Bowl 50 Victory," posted February 7, 2016, at denverpost.com.

The wish of Olivia Manning for her son to quit playing football was reported by *Los Angeles Times* sportswriter Sam Farmer in "Peyton Manning Caps His Career with Second Super Bowl Title, and His Mom Says It's Time to Retire," posted February 7, 2016.

The allegations against Peyton Manning while a student at the University of Tennessee were documented in a column by Shaun King of the *New York Daily News* in "Peyton Manning's Squeaky-Clean Image Was Built on Lies, as Detailed in Explosive Court Documents Showing Ugly Smear Campaign against His Alleged Sex Assault Victim," posted February 13, 2016.

SCOREBOARDS FOR THE DENVER BRONCOS

THE 2012 SEASON

Score: Broncos 31, Pittsburgh 19
Date: Sunday, September 9, 2012
Location: Sports Authority Field at Mile High
***Denver Post* headline:** MANNING UP
The Manning stat line: 19-26, 253 yards, 2 TDs, 0 interceptions
Highlight: Cornerback Tracy Porter's interception return seals victory

Score: Atlanta 27, Broncos 21
Date: Monday, September 17, 2012
Location: Georgia Dome, Atlanta
***Denver Post* headline:** GOING SOUTH
The Manning stat line: 24-37, 241 yards, 1 TD, 3 interceptions
Highlight: Broncos unable to clean up mess of early turnovers

Score: Houston 31, Broncos 25
Date: Sunday, September 23, 2012
Location: Sports Authority Field at Mile High
***Denver Post* headline:** OFF THE MARK

The Manning stat line: 26-52, 330 yards, 2 TDs, 0 interceptions
Highlight: Broncos can't block Texans defensive lineman J. J. Watt

Score: Broncos 37, Oakland 6
Date: Sunday, September 30, 2012
Location: Sports Authority Field at Mile High
Denver Post **headline:** UNLEASHED
The Manning stat line: 30-38, 338 yards, 3 TDs, 0 interceptions
Highlight: Running back Willis McGahee leads 165-yard rushing
attack

Score: New England 31, Broncos 21
Date: Sunday, October 7, 2012
Location: Gillette Stadium, Foxboro, MA
Denver Post **headline:** SPEED BUMP
The Manning stat line: 31-44, 337 yards, 3 TDs, 0 interceptions
Highlight: Tom Brady's record vs. Peyton Manning improves to 9-4

Score: Broncos 35, San Diego 24
Date: Monday, October 15, 2012
Location: Qualcomm Stadium, San Diego
Denver Post **headline:** ALL THE WAY!
The Manning stat line: 24-30, 309 yards, 3 TDs, 1 interception
Highlight: Denver storms back from 24-0 halftime deficit on the
road

Score: Broncos 34, New Orleans 14
Date: Sunday, October 28, 2012
Location: Sports Authority Field at Mile High
Denver Post **headline:** EASY BREEZY
The Manning stat line: 22-30, 305 yards, 3 TDs, 0 interceptions
Highlight: Denver steamrolls Saints with 530 yards of offense

Score: Broncos 31, Cincinnati 23

Date: Sunday, November 4, 2012

Location: Paul Brown Stadium, Cincinnati

***Denver Post* headline:** COOL CUSTOMERS

The Manning stat line: 27-35, 291 yards, 3 TDs, 2 interceptions

Highlight: Linebacker Von Miller sacks QB Andy Dalton three
  times

Score: Broncos 36, Carolina 14

Date: Sunday, November 11, 2012

Location: Bank of America Stadium, Charlotte, NC

***Denver Post* headline:** CAM SLAM

The Manning stat line: 27-38, 301 yards, 1 TD, 0 interceptions

Highlight: Real "Superman" in house is Von Miller, not QB Cam
  Newton

Score: Broncos 30, San Diego 23

Date: Sunday, November 18, 2012

Location: Sports Authority Field at Mile High

***Denver Post* headline:** RUNAWAY

The Manning stat line: 25-42, 270 yards, 3 TDs, 1 interception

Highlight: Denver opens daunting three-game lead in AFC West

Score: Broncos 17, Kansas City 9

Date: Sunday, November 25, 2012

Location: Arrowhead Stadium, Kansas City, MO

***Denver Post* headline:** PRETTY UGLY

The Manning stat line: 22-37, 285 yards, 2 TDs, 1 interception

Highlight: Quarterback Peyton Manning takes a licking, keeps on
  ticking

Score: Broncos 31, Tampa Bay 23

Date: Sunday, December 2, 2012

Location: Sports Authority Field at Mile High

Denver Post **headline:** WEST'S BEST
The Manning stat line: 27-38, 242 yards, 3 TDs, 1 interception
Highlight: Denver clinches AFC West division title, playoff berth

Score: Broncos 26, Oakland 13
Date: Thursday, December 6, 2012
Location: O.co Coliseum, Oakland, CA.
Denver Post **headline:** STAR POWER
The Manning stat line: 26-36, 310 yards, 1 TD, 1 interception
Highlight: Cornerback Champ Bailey records 52nd career interception

Score: Broncos 34, Baltimore 17
Date: Sunday, December 16, 2012
Location: M&T Bank Stadium, Baltimore
Denver Post **headline:** SPRINT TO FINISH
The Manning stat line: 17-28, 204 yards, 1 TD, 0 interceptions
Highlight: 98-yard interception return by cornerback Chris Harris ignites rout

Score: Broncos 34, Cleveland 12
Date: Sunday, December 23, 2012
Location: Sports Authority Field at Mile High
Denver Post **headline:** HO, HO, HO-HUM
The Manning stat line: 30-43, 339 yards, 3 TDs, 1 interception
Highlight: Linebacker Von Miller breaks franchise record for most sacks in season

Score: Broncos 38, Kansas City 3
Date: Sunday, December 30, 2012
Location: Sports Authority Field at Mile High
Denver Post **headline:** SUPER SETUP
The Manning stat line: 23-29, 304 yards, 3 TDs, 0 interceptions

Highlight: Denver takes 11-game winning streak, top AFC seed into playoffs

Score: Baltimore 38, Broncos 35, 2OT
Date: Sunday, January 12, 2012
Location: Sports Authority Field at Mile High
Denver Post **headline:** DEEP FREEZE
The Manning stat line: 28-43, 290 yards, 3 TDs, 2 interceptions
Highlight: Super Bowl dream ends after three Peyton Manning turnovers

THE 2013 SEASON

Score: Broncos 49, Baltimore 27
Date: Thursday, September 5, 2013
Location: Sports Authority Field at Mile High
Denver Post **headline:** RAVENOUS
The Manning stat line: 27-42, 462 yards, 7 TDs, 0 interceptions
Highlight: Road to Super Bowl begins with revenge for playoff loss

Score: Broncos 41, New York Giants 23
Date: Sunday, September 15, 2013
Location: MetLife Stadium, East Rutherford, NJ
Denver Post **headline:** EYES ON PRIZE
The Manning stat line: 30-43, 307 yards, 2 TDs, 0 interceptions
Highlight: In the Manning Bowl, big brother picks on Eli

Score: Broncos 37, Oakland 21
Date: Monday, September 23, 2013
Location: Sports Authority Field at Mile High
Denver Post **headline:** PEYTON'S PLACE
The Manning stat line: 32-37, 374 yards, 3 TDs, 0 interceptions

Highlight: Who needs suspended Von Miller? Raiders rush for only 49 yards

Score: Broncos 52, Philadelphia 20
Date: Sunday, September 29, 2013
Location: Sports Authority Field at Mile High
***Denver Post* headline:** RELENTLESS
The Manning stat line: 28-34, 327 yards, 4 TDs, 0 interceptions
Highlight: Never in 54-year history have Broncos scored more points in game

Score: Broncos 51, Dallas 48
Date: Sunday, October 6, 2013
Location: Cowboys Stadium, Arlington, TX
***Denver Post* headline:** HE'S THE MAN!
The Manning stat line: 33-42, 414 yards, 4 TDs, 1 interception
Highlight: Linebacker Danny Trevathan's interception biggest play in shootout

Score: Broncos 35, Jacksonville 19
Date: Sunday, October 13, 2013
Location: Sports Authority Field at Mile High
***Denver Post* headline:** NOT SO FAST
The Manning stat line: 28-42, 295 yards, 2 TDs, 1 interception
Highlight: "Nobody's a cakewalk," Champ Bailey says after beating winless Jags

Score: Indianapolis 39, Broncos 33
Date: Sunday, October 20, 2013
Location: Lucas Oil Stadium, Indianapolis
***Denver Post* headline:** OUT OF LUCK
The Manning stat line: 29-49 386 yards, 3 TDs, 1 interception
Highlight: Misty-eyed Peyton loses in return to House That Manning Built

Score: Broncos 45, Washington 21
Date: Sunday, October 27, 2013
Location: Sports Authority Field at Mile High
Denver Post **headline:** SMACKDOWN
The Manning stat line: 30-44, 354 yards, 4 TDs, 3 interceptions
Highlight: Down 14 points to former coach Mike Shanahan, Broncos rally

Score: Broncos 28, San Diego 20
Date: Sunday, November 10, 2013
Location: Qualcomm Stadium, San Diego
Denver Post **headline:** SCHOOLED
The Manning stat line: 25-36, 330 yards, 4 TDs, 0 interceptions
Highlight: A get-well card for coach John Fox after heart surgery

Score: Broncos 27, Kansas City 17
Date: Sunday, November 17, 2013
Location: Sports Authority Field at Mile High
Denver Post **headline:** BACK IN FIRST
The Manning stat line: 24-40, 323 yards, 1 TD, 0 interceptions
Highlight: Broncos expose previously undefeated Chiefs as frauds

Score: New England 34, Broncos 31 (OT)
Date: Sunday, November 24, 2013
Location: Gillette Stadium, Foxboro, MA
Denver Post **headline:** COLLAPSE
The Manning stat line: 19-36, 150 yards, 2 TDs, 1 interception
Highlight: Denver blows 24-point halftime lead in chilling loss

Score: Broncos 35, Kansas City 28
Date: Sunday, December 1, 2013
Location: Arrowhead Stadium, Kansas City
Denver Post **headline:** DRIVER'S SEAT
The Manning stat line: 22-35, 403 yards, 5 TDs, 2 interceptions

Highlight: "Gritty win on road," says interim coach Jack Del Rio

Score: Broncos 51, Tennessee 28
Date: Sunday, December 8, 2013
Location: Sports Authority Field at Mile High
***Denver Post* headline:** ICY HOT QB
The Manning stat line: 39-59, 397 yards, 4 TDs, 0 interceptions
Highlight: Manning debunks notion he cannot play well in cold

Score: San Diego 27, Broncos 20
Date: Thursday, December 12, 2013
Location: Sports Authority Field at Mile High
***Denver Post* headline:** STRUCK DOWN
The Manning stat line: 27-42, 289 yards, 2 TDs, 1 interception
Highlight: With only four days to prepare, Broncos look tired

Score: Broncos 37, Houston 13
Date: Sunday, December 22, 2013
Location: Reliant Stadium, Houston
***Denver Post* headline:** PEYTON'S PACE
The Manning stat line: 32-51, 400 yards, 4 TDs, 0 interceptions
Highlight: Manning breaks single-season record for TD passes

Score: Broncos 34, Oakland 14
Date: Sunday, December 29, 2013
Location: O.co Coliseum, Oakland, CA
***Denver Post* headline:** BOWL OR BUST
The Manning stat line: 25-28, 266 yards, 4 TDs, 0 interceptions
Highlight: Broncos first NFL team to score 600 points in season

Score: Broncos 24, San Diego 17
Date: Sunday, January 12, 2014
Location: Sports Authority Field at Mile High
***Denver Post* headline:** WHEW!
The Manning stat line: 25-36, 230 yards, 2 TDs, 1 interception

Highlight: Broncos bury ghosts by withstanding fourth-quarter scare

Score: Broncos 26, New England 16
Date: Sunday, January 19, 2014
Location: Sports Authority Field at Mile High
***Denver Post* headline:** SUPERB!
The Manning stat line: 32-43, 400 yards, 2 TDs, 0 interceptions
Highlight: Manning beats Tom Brady to earn third Super Bowl trip of career

Score: Seattle 43, Broncos 8
Date: Sunday, February 2, 2014
Location: MetLife Stadium, East Rutherford, NJ
***Denver Post* headline:** SEASICK
The Manning stat line: 34-49, 280 yards, 1 TD, 2 interceptions
Highlight: With one bad snap, championship dream gone in 12 seconds

THE 2014 SEASON

Score: Broncos 31, Indianapolis 24
Date: Sunday, September 7, 2014
Location: Sports Authority Field at Mile High
***Denver Post* headline:** HANGING ON
The Manning stat line: 22-36, 269 yards, 3 TDs, 0 interceptions
Highlight: Significance of beating all 32 NFL teams? "Means I'm old," Manning jokes

Score: Broncos 24, Kansas City 17
Date: Sunday, September 14, 2014
Location: Sports Authority Stadium at Mile High
***Denver Post* headline:** WHEW PART 2

The Manning stat line: 21-26, 242 yards, 3 TDs, 0 interceptions
Highlight: Defense stops Chiefs at 2-yard line in final seconds to preserve victory

Score: Seattle 26, Broncos 20 (OT)
Date: Sunday, September 21, 2014
Location: Century Link Field, Seattle
***Denver Post* headline:** ALMOST …
The Manning stat line: 31-49, 303 yards, 2 TDs, 1 interception
Highlight: Seattle QB Russell Wilson never lets Manning touch football in overtime

Score: Broncos 41, Arizona 20
Date: Sunday, October 5, 2014
Location: Sports Authority Field at Mile High
***Denver Post* headline:** HIS STORY
The Manning stat line: 31-47, 479 yards, 4 TDs, 2 interceptions
Highlight: Wide receiver Demaryius Thomas makes eight receptions for 226 yards

Score: Broncos 31, New York Jets 17
Date: Sunday, October 12, 2014
Location: MetLife Stadium, East Rutherford, NJ
***Denver Post* headline:** HISTORY CHASE
The Manning stat line: 22-33, 237 yards, 3 TDs, 0 interceptions
Highlight: Eight months after Super Bowl, Broncos finally leave stadium with a win

Score: Broncos 42, San Francisco 17
Date: Sunday, October 19, 2014
Location: Sports Authority Field at Mile High
***Denver Post* headline:** OF ALL TIME
The Manning stat line: 22-26, 318 yards, 4 TDs, 0 interceptions

Highlight: Manning breaks Brett Favre's record for career TD passes

Score: Broncos 35, San Diego 21
Date: Thursday, October 23, 2014
Location: Sports Authority Field at Mile High
***Denver Post* headline:** IN CONTROL
The Manning stat line: 25-35, 286 yards, 3 TDs, 0 interceptions
Highlight: Denver takes big step toward fourth straight AFC West title

Score: New England 43, Broncos 21
Date: Sunday, November 2, 2014
Location: Gillette Stadium, Foxboro, MA
***Denver Post* headline:** CRUSHED
The Manning stat line: 34-57, 438 yards, 2 TDs, 2 interceptions
Highlight: Blowout loss so scary bad it haunts Broncos for remainder of season

Score: Broncos 41, Oakland 17
Date: Sunday, November 9, 2014
Location: Sports Authority Field at Mile High
***Denver Post* headline:** EASY PICKINGS
The Manning stat line: 31-44, 340 yards, 5 TDs, 2 interceptions
Highlight: Trailing winless Raiders late in first half, 51-yard TD by C.J. Anderson ignites rout

Score: St. Louis 22, Broncos 7
Date: Sunday, November 16, 2014
Location: Edward Jones Dome, St. Louis
***Denver Post* headline:** BIG HURT
The Manning stat line: 34-54, 389 yards, 1 TD, 2 interceptions
Highlight: After this defeat, Broncos begin to reduce Manning's role in the offense

Score: Broncos 39, Miami 36
Date: Sunday, November 23, 2014
Location: Sports Authority Field at Mile High
Denver Post **headline:** WHAT A RUSH
The Manning stat line: 28-35, 257 yards, 4 TDs, 0 interceptions
Highlight: Maligned offensive line finds groove with 35 running
plays for 210 yards

Score: Broncos 29, Kansas City 16
Date: Sunday, November 30, 2014
Location: Arrowhead Stadium, Kansas City
Denver Post **headline:** SMACKDOWN
The Manning stat line: 17-34, 179 yards, 2 TDs, 0 interceptions
Highlight: Freshly signed kicker Connor Barth makes five field
goals

Score: Broncos 24, Buffalo 17
Date: Sunday, December 7, 2014
Location: Sports Authority Field at Mile High
Denver Post **headline:** PHYSICALITY
The Manning stat line: 14-20, 173 yards, 0 TDs, 2 interceptions
Highlight: Manning's streak of 51 games with at least one TD pass
is broken

Score: Broncos 22, San Diego 10
Date: Sunday, December 14, 2014
Location: Qualcomm Stadium, San Diego
Denver Post **headline:** CHAMPIONS
The Manning stat line: 14-20, 233 yards, 1 TD, 0 interceptions
Highlight: Dehydrated by flu, Manning suffers thigh injury while
scrambling

Score: Cincinnati 37, Broncos 28
Date: Monday, December 22, 2014

Location: Paul Brown Stadium, Cincinnati

Denver Post **headline:** BUNGLED

The Manning stat line: 28-44, 311 yards, 2 TDs, 4 interceptions

Highlight: Manning loses for first time in nine career starts versus Bengals

Score: Broncos 47, Oakland 14

Date: Sunday, December 28, 2014

Location: Sports Authority Field at Mile High

Denver Post **headline:** HELLO, BYE

The Manning stat line: 21-37, 273 yards, 0 TDs, 0 interceptions

Highlight: Beat-up Broncos earn opening-round bye in NFL playoffs

Score: Indianapolis 24, Broncos 13

Date: Sunday, January 11, 2015

Location: Sports Authority Field at Mile High

Denver Post **headline:** BUSTED

The Manning stat line: 26-46, 211 yards, 1 TD, 0 interceptions

Highlight: Within 24 hours of shocking loss, John Fox out as Broncos coach

THE 2015 SEASON

Score: Broncos 19, Baltimore 13

Date: Sunday, September 13, 2015

Location: Sports Authority Field at Mile High

Denver Post **headline:** DEFENSE'S DAY

The Manning stat line: 24-40, 175 yards, 0 TDs, 1 interception

Highlight: Without a touchdown by the offense, Broncos find a way to win

Score: Broncos 31, Kansas 24

Date: Thursday, September 17, 2015

Location: Sports Authority Field at Mile High

***Denver Post* headline:** GIFT RAPTURE

The Manning stat line: 26-45, 256 yards, 3 TDs, 1 interception

Highlight: Cornerback Bradley Roby returns fumble for winning TD in final minute

Score: Broncos 24, Detroit 12

Date: Sunday, September 27, 2015

Location: Ford Field, Detroit

***Denver Post* headline:** MOTOR GRITTY

The Manning stat line: 31-42, 324 yards, 2 TDs, 1 interception

Highlight: A gutsy 45-yard TD pass on fourth down late in second quarter shocks Lions

Score: Broncos 23, Minnesota 20

Date: Sunday, October 4, 1015

Location: Sports Authority Field at Mile High

***Denver Post* headline:** WHOA, ADRIAN!

The Manning stat line: 17-27, 213 yards, 1 TD, 2 interceptions

Highlight: Unheralded Ronnie Hillman (103 yards) out-rushes Vikings star Adrian Peterson (81 yards)

Score: Broncos 16, Oakland 10

Date: Sunday, October 11, 2015

Location: O.co Coliseum, Oakland, CA

***Denver Post* headline:** A D-PLUS WIN

The Manning stat line: 22-35 yards, 0 TDs, 2 interceptions

Highlight: It takes 74-yard interception return by cornerback Chris Harris Jr. to seal ugly road victory

Score: Broncos 26, Cleveland 23 (OT)

Date: Sunday, October 18, 2015

Location: FirstEnergy Stadium, Cleveland
Denver Post **headline:** IMPERFECT 6-0
The Manning stat line: 26-48, 290 yards, 1 TD, 3 interceptions
Highlight: Defense comes up big in overtime, bails out shaky Manning

Score: Broncos 29, Green Bay 10
Date: Sunday, November 1, 2015
Location: Sports Authority Field at Mile High
Denver Post **headline:** TOTAL PACKAGE
The Manning stat line: 21-29, 340 yards, 0 TDs, 1 interception
Highlight: Hey, Aaron Rodgers! Double-check your seatbelt for a bumpy ride

Score: Indianapolis 27, Broncos 24
Date: Sunday, November 8, 2015
Location: Lucas Oil Stadium, Indianapolis
Denver Post **headline:** FALLING SHORT
The Manning stat line: 21-36, 281 yards, 2 TDs, 2 interceptions
Highlight: Manning loses his final NFL appearance in old stomping grounds

Score: Kansas City 29, Broncos 13
Date: Sunday, November 15, 2015
Location: Sports Authority Field at Mile High
Denver Post **headline:** BENCH MARKS
The Manning stat line: 5-20, 35 yards, 0 TDs, 4 interceptions
Highlight: Injured Manning breaks passing-yardage record, then gets booed and benched

Score: Broncos 17, Chicago 15
Date: Sunday, November 22, 2015
Location: Soldier Field, Chicago
Denver Post **headline:** BROCK PARTY

The Osweiler stat line: 20-27, 250 yards, 2 TDs, 0 interceptions
Highlight: Quarterback Brock Osweiler wins his first game as an
    NFL starter

Score: Broncos 30, New England 24 (OT)
Date: Sunday, December 29, 2015
Location: Sports Authority Field at Mile High
Denver Post **headline:** WIN CHILLING
The Osweiler stat line: 23-37, 270 yards, 1 TD, 1 interception
Highlight: Running back C.J. Anderson's 48-yard TD dash upsets
    previously unbeaten Pats

Score: Broncos 17, San Diego 3
Date: Sunday, December 6, 2015
Location: Qualcomm Stadium, San Diego
Denver Post **headline:** BOLTED SHUT
The Osweiler stat line: 16-26, 166 yards, 1 TD, 1 interception
Highlight: Broncos Country stages friendly takeover, makes sta-
    dium feel like home game

Score: Oakland 15, Broncos 12
Date: Sunday, December 13, 2015
Location: Sports Authority Field at Mile High
Denver Post **headline:** SACK AND BLUE
The Osweiler stat line: 35-51, 308 yards, 0 TDs, 0 interceptions
Highlight: Unable to score TD, Broncos lose to Oakland for first
    time since 2011

Score: Pittsburgh 34, Broncos 27
Date: Sunday, December 20, 2015
Location: Heinz Field, Pittsburgh
Denver Post **headline:** PITTIFUL
The Osweiler stat line: 21-44, 296 yards, 3 TDs, 1 interception

Highlight: Steelers receiver Antonio Brown shreds Denver's vaunted No Fly Zone

Score: Broncos 20, Cincinnati 17 (OT)
Date: Monday, December 28, 2015
Location: Sports Authority Field at Mile High
Denver Post **headline:** PLAYOFF BOUND
The Osweiler stat line: 27-39, 299 yards, 1 TD, 0 interceptions
Highlight: Kicker Brandon McManus makes up for bad miss with clutch field goal in overtime

Score: Broncos 27, San Diego 20
Date: Sunday, January 3, 2016
Location: Sports Authority Field at Mile High
Denver Post **headline:** BACK (UP) ON TOP
The Manning stat line: 5-9, 69 yards, 0 TDs, 0 interceptions
Highlight: Manning comes off bench to help Denver win No. 1 seed in AFC playoffs

Score: Broncos 23, Pittsburgh 16
Date: Sunday, January 17, 2016
Location: Sports Authority Field at Mile High
Denver Post **headline:** STEALWORKERS
The Manning stat line: 21-37, 222 yards, 0 TDs, 0 interceptions
Highlight: Linebacker DeMarcus Ware's fumble recovery fuels dramatic fourth-quarter rally

Score: Broncos 20, New England 18
Date: Sunday, January 24, 2016
Location: Sports Authority Stadium at Mile High
Denver Post **headline:** HI, FIVE-0!
The Manning stat line: 17-32, 176 yards, 2 TDs, 0 interceptions
Highlight: Manning wins for sixth time in 17 meetings against long-time rival Tom Brady

Score: Broncos 24, Carolina 10

Date: Sunday, February 7, 2016

Location: Levi's Stadium, Santa Clara, CA

***Denver Post* headline:** WHAT A RUSH!

The Manning stat line: 13-23, 141 yards, 0 TDs, 1 interception

Highlight: Super Bowl MVP Von Miller rattles Carolina QB Cam Newton with fast and furious pass rush